Low Tech Hacking
Street Smarts for Security Professionals

Jack Wiles

Dr. Terry Gudaitis

Jennifer Jabbusch

Russ Rogers

Sean Lowther

Neil Wyler, Technical Editor

ELSEVIER

AMSTERDAM • BOSTON • HEIDELBERG • LONDON
NEW YORK • OXFORD • PARIS • SAN DIEGO
SAN FRANCISCO • SINGAPORE • SYDNEY • TOKYO
Syngress is an imprint of Elsevier

SYNGRESS.

Acquiring Editor: Chris Katsaropoulos
Development Editor: Mstt Cater
Project Manager: Paul Gottehrer
Designer: Russell Purdy

Syngress is an imprint of Elsevier
225 Wyman Street, Waltham, MA 02451, USA

Notices
Knowledge and best practice in this field are constantly changing. As new research and experience
broaden our understanding, changes in research methods or professional practices, may become
necessary. Practitioners and researchers must always rely on their own experience and knowledge
in evaluating and using any information or methods described herein. In using such information
or methods they should be mindful of their own safety and the safety of others, including parties
for whom they have a professional responsibility.

To the fullest extent of the law, neither the Publisher nor the authors, contributors, or editors, assume
any liability for any injury and/or damage to persons or property as a matter of products liability,
negligence or otherwise, or from any use or operation of any methods, products, instructions,
or ideas contained in the material herein.

Library of Congress Cataloging-in-Publication Data
Application submitted

British Library Cataloguing-in-Publication Data
A catalogue record for this book is available from the British Library.

ISBN: 978-1-59749-665-0

For information on all Syngress publications visit our website at www.syngress.com

Printed and bound by CPI Group (UK) Ltd, Croydon, CR0 4YY

Transferred to digital print 2012

For information on all Syngress publications visit our website at www.syngress.com

Contents

Acknowledgments ix

Foreword xi

About the Authors xiii

Introduction xv

CHAPTER 1 **Social engineering: The ultimate low tech hacking threat** 1

How easy is it? 2

The mind of a social engineer 3

The mind of a victim 3

Tools of the social engineering trade 4

One of my favorite tools of the trade 5

Social engineering would never work against our company 7

What was I able to social engineer out of Mary? 8

The final sting—two weeks later—Friday afternoon 8

Why did this scam work? 9

Let's look at a few more social engineering tools 10

   Keystroke logger—Is there one under your desk? 13

   One of my lunchtime tools 16

Let's look at that telephone butt-in set on my tool belt 18

Meet Mr. Phil Drake 19

Meet Mr. Paul Henry 22

   Traditional AV, IDS, and IPS considerations 25

   Traditional firewall consideration 25

   Flaw remediation 26

Do you have a guest user of your credit card? 26

A few possible countermeasures 27

   Always be slightly suspicious 28

   Start to study the art of social engineering 28

   Start a social engineering book library 28

Summary 29

CHAPTER 2 **Low tech vulnerabilities: Physical security** 31

A mini risk assessment 32

   What did I have at risk? 32

   What were some possible threats while out on the lake? 33

   What were some of the possible vulnerabilities? 33

   And finally, what about my countermeasures? 34

Outsider—Insider threats.. 34
Some things to consider for the security of your buildings? ... 35
    Check all locks for proper operation 35
    Use employee badges 36
    Shredder technology keeps changing as well 36
    Keep an eye on corporate or agency phone books.............. 37
    Unsecured areas are targets for tailgating............................ 38
    Special training for off-shift staff 39
Bomb threats in Chicago.. 40
Check those phone closets.. 42
Remove a few door signs 42
Review video security logs 43
Consider adding motion-sensing lights...................................... 43
Subterranean vulnerabilities 44
Clean out your elephant burial ground 46
Spot check those drop ceilings... 47
Internal auditors are your friends 47
BONUS: Home security tips... 48
Summary 49

CHAPTER 3   **More about locks and ways to low tech hack them............. 51**
A little more about locks and lock picking 52
    What kinds of locks are the most popular? 54
    Purchasing better quality locks will be cost effective 57
    Be aware of lock vulnerabilities 58
Forced entry—and other ways to cheat! 60
    A time-tested low tech method of forced entry................... 61
Let's break into a semi–high security room 63
    Retracting the bolt to open the door 64
    Gaining access to the lock itself 66
Keys and key control.. 70
    Social engineering and key access.. 70
    Who has the keys to your kingdom 70
    Special key control awareness training................................. 71
Bait and switch war story that could happen to you 71
    Padlock shims are not a new threat 73
Some places to go to learn and have some fun 74
    My 110-year-old puzzle 75
More about keys and how to make one if you
don't have one 76
    Five pounds of my favorite keys... 77
Ways to make a key if you didn't bring a key machine 79

One final lock to talk about and then we're done 81

    Rim cylinder locks vs. mortise cylinder locks...................... 83

Summary 85

CHAPTER 4   **Low tech wireless hacking**... **87**

Wireless 101: The electromagnetic spectrum 87

    Why securing wireless is hard 90

802.11 and Bluetooth low tech hacks 91

DoS and availability 91

    Layer 1 DoS attacks 91

    Layer 2 DoS attacks 104

Backdoors and cracks 112

    Crack attack 112

    Tap, tap. Mirror, mirror . . . on the wallplate 115

    Guesssst who got in 116

    Peer-to-peer-to-hack 117

    Ad hoc, ad finem 119

Going rogue 120

    Marveling at the gambit of rogues...................................... 121

    New SSID on the street... 122

    It's a bird . . . it's a plane . . . it's a ROGUE?...................... 124

    Bridge bereavement... 125

Assault by defaults 126

    Open sesame 127

    Default WPA keys.. 127

    More Google hacking 129

Bypassing specific security tools 130

    Going static.. 131

    Counterfeit MACs 132

    MAC switcharoo.. 133

    <html>Free Wi-Fi</html> 134

Summary 134

CHAPTER 5   **Low tech targeting and surveillance: How much could they find out about you?**... **137**

Initial identification 139

Property records, employment, and neighborhood routes...... 142

Disclosure on social networks and social media 144

Financials, investments, and purchase habits 146

Frequented locations and travel patterns............................... 149

Third party disclosures 152

Use of signatures 154

Automated surveillance 155
Target interaction.. 156
Scanners and miniatures.. 158
Summary and recommendations 159
    Recommendations.. 160

CHAPTER 6   **Low tech hacking for the penetration tester ....** **163**
The human condition... 164
    Selective attention 164
    Magic is distraction 165
    Building trust and influencing behavior 166
Technology matters 166
    USB thumb drives 166
    CDs and DVDs 168
Staging the effort 169
    Target organization... 169
Getting things in order.. 170
    Deciding on location 171
    Choosing the strategy 171
    Choosing the technology 172
A useful case study.. 174
    Approaching hotel staff 175
    Approaching conference staff 176
    Conclusion 176
Summary 177

CHAPTER 7   **Low tech hacking and the law: Where can you go for help?** **179**
Meet Mr. Tony Marino... 180
    Low tech hacking interview with Tony Marino,
    U.S. Secret Service (retired)... 180
Meet Special Agent (SA) Gregory K. Baker, FBI.................. 187
    Low tech hacking interview with Special Agent (SA)
    Gregory K. Baker, FBI... 187
Summary 191

CHAPTER 8   **Information security awareness training: Your most**
    valuable countermeasure to employee risk **193**
An introduction to information security awareness................. 194
    The people and personalities of information security
    awareness 194

Data theft and employee awareness.................................. 196
Designing an effective information security awareness
program.. 198
Repetition is the aide to memory...................................... 199
Touch points 199
To team or not to team, that is the question...................... 200
Creating a business plan for your Information Security
Awareness Program... 201
The presentation 202
Components of an awareness program 204
Next steps... 205
The Classification of Data Matrix..................................... 205
Manager's Quick Reference Guide.................................... 206
Finding materials for your program................................... 207
The importance of a good editor....................................... 207
Implementing an information security awareness program ... 207
Who writes the awareness standard? 209
Finding win-win solutions... 210
Building a perpetual awareness program........................... 210
Who should take the training? 211
Getting the program off the ground 211
Making information security accessible 212
A lesson learned 212
The dollars and cents of your program.............................. 213
Above and beyond... 214
Making security part of the company mind-set.................... 216
The importance of communication with other
lines-of-businesses 216
Let's talk more about alliances 217
Keeping your program viable... 220
Other resources 220
Measuring your program's success 221
Identifying key components and cumulative results 222
Summary.. 223

Index... 227

Acknowledgments

It's difficult to write an acknowledgments page for fear of forgetting to thank someone who has been so important in my life. Having spent many decades working and learning in the fields of both physical and technical security, I have been honored to become friends with many of the top professionals in the world who live and work in both areas of expertise.

I always like to start my acknowledgments by letting the world know that I can do nothing without the help of my Lord and Savior, Jesus Christ. I dedicate this book to Him, my wonderful wife Valerie and my son Tyler as he prepares to finish his college career and move on into the business world. My partner Don Withers is like a brother to me in every way. For 12 years now, we have been fortunate to produce our Techno Security, Techno Forensics, and our new Mobile Forensics conferences, which have had attendees from over 48 countries. I want to especially thank all of the other authors and interviewed experts of this book. I know them all well and I know that you will enjoy getting to know them through their impressive chapters. These are some of the most respected and talented security minds in the world and I am honored to have them share this incredible experience with me. I'd also like to thank my good friend Matt Cater, Syngress/Elsevier Editorial Project Manager for his frequent editing help and for being so patient as we worked our way through getting my fourth Syngress/Elsevier book ready to be published. I would not have started on this 6 month-plus project without Matt as my Project Manager.

- **My Contributing Authors:**
  - Dr. Terry Gudaitis
  - Jennifer (Jabbusch) Minella
  - Russ Rogers
  - Sean Lowther
- **My Expert Interviewees:**
  - Phil Drake
  - Paul Henry
  - Special Agent Gregory K. Baker, FBI, InfraGard
  - Special Agent (Retired) Tony Marino, U.S. Secret Service, Electronic Crimes Task Force

I'm going to do my best to include the names of as many of my close friends as I can in this book. I haven't done that with past books, and I wish that I had. Please forgive me if I forget someone. If I do, I'll try to find a way to make it up to you, I promise.

My thanks go out to:

Dr. Greg Miles, Rabbi Sam Nadler (one of the most incredible people that I have ever met), Miriam Nadler, Josef ben Yisrael , Forrest (Pete) Jones, Loretta Jones, Heather Jones, Hilary Jones, Joan Withers, Susan Ballou, Joy Foster, Dean Smith,

Angela Ellis, Sarah Bell, Thelma Allen, Jack Lewis, John Large, Tony Marino, SSA Jim Ramacone, SSA Gregory Baker, Neal Dolan, Laura Hamilton, Chet Hosmer, Kelly Ivey Skinner, Amanda Gulini, Steve Pearson, Amanda Pearson, Tom Eskridge, Sharon Topper, Bob Friel, SAC David Thomas, SA Robbie O'Brien, Christina Fisher, Gary Gardner, SA Doris Gardner, John Sheehan, Jon Gregory, Dan Mares, Sarah Palmer, Norm Burtness, Mark Withers, Dennis Partyka, Jennifer Withers, Majid Hassan, Marjie Britz, Jim Windle, Paul Crowley, Gert Crowley, Derrick Donnelly, Dennis Dowdy, Tracy DeBenedictis, Crystal Edge, Keith Lockhart, Natasha Lockhart, Eric Loermans, Rick Mislan, Eric Thompson, Erika Lee, Erin Uda, Tim Leehealey, Joe Mykytyn, Inno Eroraha, Patrick Murphy, Sharon Coddington, Patty Grogis, Rebecca Waters, Bridget Baldwin, Shauna Gray Waters, Greg Dominguez, Jim Raubach, Laurie Ann O'Leary, Robert O'Leary, SA Robbie O'Brien, Amanda Simmons, SA Earl Burns, Wanda Busbee, Casey Rackley, Richard Rackley, Cathy Drake.

All my best,

—Low Tech Jack

Foreword

Come on, what did we really think was going to happen?

For well over a decade as network defenders we have relied upon the same failed defenses; Signature-based AV, IDP/IPS along with Port Centric Firewalls. We have placed all of our emphasis on "Holy Grail" security products at the network gateway to the public Internet and we have completely disregarded our endpoints. Further, we have neglected two of the most fundamental requirements of network security that historically have always proven to reduce the threat envelope—server hardening and flaw remediation. Lastly, over time we have developed an acceptance of meeting technical security challenges with our written policies without any technical enforcement.

Our adversaries have been paying careful attention, regularly adjusting their attack methodologies to easily take full advantage. Today we find ourselves in a position where our outdated defenses regularly fall prey to the simplest "Low Tech" hacking techniques. It seems that every headline-grabbing intrusion we hear of today first proclaims that it was the result of some new advanced hacking technique but more often than not, it is later revealed that the root cause of the breach was embarrassingly simple:

- Google—spear phishing email provided initial entry
- RSA—spear phishing email provided initial entry
- Sony—social engineering facilitated initial website attacks
- HBGary—a 16 year old girl's social engineering skills provided initial entry
- Stuxnet—malware laden USB sticks handed out for free at a conference provided the initial entry
- Epsilon—spear phishing emails provided initial entry

After nearly every breach we hear the same old excuses:

- We were compliant with all regulatory requirements and therefore not responsible
- We are doing the very same things to protect our information that everyone else is doing and therefore not responsible
- Users did not follow written policy and therefore we are not responsible

Another "trap" we seem to have fallen into: Today we regularly neglect doing our own due diligence and instead choose to pay advisory services to guide us in making the decision on which vendors security products/methodologies we should be using to secure our environments. While at the same time "they" are charging those vendors advisory fees to craft marketing messages that will allow the vendor to gain a greater market share from the advisory services clients. The guidance we seek is actually contained within the various Internet Crime Reports that are freely available on the Internet. They annually report on security incidents and just as importantly on what those organizations were using for defense at the time of the incident. Reading the reports from that perspective can be eye opening:

- If the vast majority of the reports, survey respondents were using Anti-Virus yet the majority still reported issues with malware. Perhaps it is time to reconsider dependence on traditional Anti-Virus products.
- If the vast majority of the reports, survey respondents were using Firewalls yet reported issues with network intrusions. Perhaps it is time to reconsider dependence on traditional Firewall products.
- If the vast majority of the reports, survey respondents were using strong password policies yet reported issues with unauthorized access. Perhaps it is time to reconsider dependence on traditional authentication efforts.

I would advise anyone reading this book to use it as a wakeup call to his or her management. These are not theoretical attack methodologies, they are practical attacks occurring regularly today that have been enabled due to a decade of neglect of our defenses. Every attack noted in this book can be effectively countered with the proper application of user-awareness training, policy, and technical safeguards.

Paul A. Henry
vNet Security LLC

About the Authors

Jack Wiles is a security professional with over 40 years of experience in security-related fields. This includes computer security, disaster recovery, and physical security. He is a professional speaker and has trained federal agents, corporate attorneys, and internal auditors on a number of computer crime-related topics. He is a pioneer in presenting on a number of subjects which are now being labeled "Homeland Security" topics. Well over 10,000 people have attended one or more of his presentations since 1988. Jack is also a co-founder and President of TheTrainingCo., and is in frequent contact with members of many state and local law enforcement agencies as well as Special Agents with the U.S. Secret Service, FBI, IRS-CID, U.S. Customs, Department of Justice, The Department of Defense, and numerous members of high-tech crime units. He was also appointed as the first President of the North Carolina InfraGard chapter which is now one of the largest chapters in the Country. He is also a founding member of the U.S. Secret Service South Carolina Electronic Crimes Task Force.

Jack is also a Vietnam veteran who served with the 101st Airborne Division in Vietnam in 1967 to 1968 where he was awarded two Bronze Stars for his actions in combat. He recently retired from the U.S. Army Reserves as a lieutenant colonel and was assigned directly to the Pentagon for the final 7 years of his career. In his spare time, he is a HAM Radio operator, an NRA Certified Instructor, and enjoys monitoring radiation as his most unique hobby.

Jack wrote Chapters 1, 2, 3 and 7.

Terry Gudaitis, Ph.D., is the Cyber Intelligence Director at Cyveillance. Terry gained a foundation for her expertise as an operations officer and behavioral profiler at the CIA's Counter Terrorist Center. At the CIA, she was responsible for developing terrorist profiles, assessments of informants, and managing targeting teams. In addition to her corporate-related work, Terry has served on the United States Secret Service Advisory Board for Insider Threats, regularly presents at national and international conferences, and has authored publications in numerous security-related journals and books.

Terry wrote Chapter 5.

Jennifer Jabbusch, CISSP, CISO, HP MASE, JNCIA-AC, is a network security engineer and consultant with Carolina Advanced Digital, Inc. Jennifer has more than 15 years of experience working in various areas of the technology industry. Most recently, she has focused in the specialized areas of infrastructure security, including Network Access Control, 802.1X, and Wireless Security technologies.

Ms. Jabbusch has consulted for a variety of government agencies, educational institutions, and Fortune 100 and 500 corporations and has spoken at a variety of conferences including, DeepSec, SecTor, Techno Security, RSA®, InfoSec World, CSI, and many others. In addition to her regular duties, she participates in a variety of courseware and exam writings and reviews, including acting as subject matter expert on the Access Control, Business Continuity, and Telecommunications domains, and lead subject matter expert in the Cryptography domain of the official (ISC)$^{2®}$ CISSP® courseware (v9).

You can find more security topics and musings on her security blog at http://SecurityUncorked.com.

Jennifer wrote Chapter 4 and the Introduction.

Russ Rogers, CISSP, CISM, IAM, IEM, Hon. Sc.D., is the author of the popular *Hacking a Terror Network: The Silent Threat of Covert Channels* (Syngress, ISBN: 978-1-928994-98-5), co-author of multiple books, including the best-selling *Stealing the Network: How to Own a Continent* (Syngress, ISBN 978-1-931836-05-0) and *Network Security Evaluation Using the NSA IEM* (Syngress, ISBN: 978-1-59749-035-1), and former editor-in-chief of *The Security Journal*. He is currently a penetration tester for a federal agency and the co-founder and chief executive officer of Peak Security, Inc., a veteran-owned small business based in Colorado Springs, CO. Russ has been involved in information technology since 1980 and has spent the past 20 years working as both an IT and InfoSec consultant. Russ has worked with the U.S. Air Force (USAF), National Security Agency (NSA), Defense Information Systems Agency (DISA), and other federal agencies. He is a globally renowned security expert, speaker and author who has presented at conferences around the world in Amsterdam, Tokyo, Singapore, São Paulo, Abu Dhabi, and cities all over the United States.

Russ has an honorary doctorate of science in information technology from the University of Advancing Technology, a master's degree in computer systems management from the University of Maryland, a bachelor of science degree in computer information systems from the University of Maryland, and an associate's degree in applied communications technology from the Community College of the Air Force. Russ is currently pursuing a bachelor of science degree in electrical engineering from the University of Colorado at Colorado Springs. He is a member of ISSA and (ISC)$^{2®}$ (CISSP). Russ also teaches at and fills the role of professor of network security for the University of Advancing Technology (www.uat.edu).

Russ wrote Chapter 6.

Sean Lowther is the President and Founder of Stealth Awareness, Inc. (www.stealthawareness.com). Sean is an independent consultant who brings years of experience designing and implementing information security awareness programs at the highest level. He founded Stealth Awareness, Inc. in 2007.

Sean worked at Bank of America for over 7 years, managing the enterprise information security awareness program. The program received the highest rating from its regulators and was consistently rated "world class" by industry peer groups. Sean has worked with BITS, the Financial Services Roundtable Task Force on Privacy, prior to the enactment of the Gramm-Leach-Bliley Act. He produced the video "It's Not If, But When" for the Financial Services Sector Coordinating Council in partnership with the U.S. Treasury Department with the goal to improve critical Infrastructure protection and Homeland Security.

Sean wrote Chapter 8.

Introduction

INFORMATION IN THIS CHAPTER:

- Book Overview and Key Learning Points
- Book Audience
- How this Book is Organized

BOOK OVERVIEW AND KEY LEARNING POINTS

This book arms any reader with the knowledge of how security measures can often be bypassed in situations ranging from physical security to networked enterprise systems—all with minimal technology savvy on the part of the offender. And, although seven of the eight chapters here detail security evasion methods, the true value of the book is realized in the countermeasures provided for each of the attack scenarios detailed.

In a world of content that capitalizes on vulnerability, risk, and fear, this book cuts through the smoke and mirrors of complicated and improbable hi-tech hacks and gets to the heart of the most vulnerable and most-often exploited components of security—human nature, physical containment, and the Internet.

The chapters of this book provide a unique dive into low tech hacking techniques and ways to protect yourself, your business, and your family from them. Although each chapter stands on its own, in combination, the authors have provided an invaluable resource and a holistic approach to increasing security at your home and your office, for critical data, and against rogue Internet records.

BOOK AUDIENCE

The information in this book will prove to be a valuable resource for all types of readers, including individuals, heads of households, small business owners, and even CISOs and directors of international enterprises. There's a little something for everyone in *Low Tech Hacking*, and even the most seasoned security professionals will find new nuggets of data and invaluable resources.

Security professionals will gain insight into areas of physical security and social engineering not previously explored in other books. These readers will benefit from detailed examples of security bypass techniques in the opening chapters and penetration testing coverage, from the more technical wireless discussions, as well as the recommendations for security awareness training from a seasoned professional. The more paranoid infosec professionals will enjoy the tips for finding and removing personal data online. All security-minded readers will appreciate the introduction Jack provides to two agents from the U.S. Secret Service and F.B.I., and the insight they offer in the interview sections.

Individuals, business owners, and those responsible for managing security of themselves, their families, and their businesses will benefit from this insight into the world of low tech hacks, physical intrusion and social engineering, and the measures that can be taken to prevent becoming a victim of such attacks. From understanding which padlocks to use for your kids' lockers, how to shop for secure home locks, to recognizing a false phone technician, the breadth and depth of attacks and countermeasures is enlightening for all audiences.

HOW THIS BOOK IS ORGANIZED

This book is comprised of eight chapters, each addressing a different facet of low tech hacking techniques and the countermeasures that accompany them. The chapters are written and assembled in a way that allows the reader to attain value from reading the book as a whole, or from reading individual chapters in any chosen order.

There is a logical progression, starting with the opening chapter on *Social Engineering: The Ultimate Low Tech Hacking Threat*, followed by *Low Tech Vulnerabilities: Physical Security*, and *More About Locks and Ways to Low Tech Hack Them* in Chapters 2 and 3. Chapters 4 and beyond open into broader topics of low tech hacking, with subject areas that integrate well to give readers a multipart approach to deal with low tech hacks and hackers.

Chapter 1: Social engineering: The ultimate low tech hacking threat

Jack Wiles presents various social engineering topics, from understanding the minds of hackers and victims to methods for protecting personal, household and business information from theft and destruction. Jack shares several examples of true stories to help the reader understand how social engineering attacks happen in homes and businesses, and how to prevent them.

In this chapter, for the first time, Jack reveals the contents of his red team briefcase, never before shared with the public. In all the years of leading a red team to conduct physical penetration tests into corporations and federal facilities, Jack's team went undetected, a perfect record. The first three chapters of this book offer great insight from Jack's personal experience as to how they pulled it off.

The first three chapters, as well as Chapter 7 are authored by Jack Wiles, renowned physical security specialist, professional speaker, inside penetration team leader, author and lead author of *Low Tech Hacking*.

Chapter 2: Low tech vulnerabilities: Physical security

Jack delves into the realm of physical security and provides actionable recommendations for increasing security at home, office, and everywhere in between. In this chapter, you'll find a breadth of advice including signage and lighting recommendations, paper record and electronic drive destruction considerations, securing subterranean entries, identifying drop ceiling vulnerabilities, reviewing security tapes and logs, and even a discussion about being extra mindful of lunch-time discussions.

Chapter 3: More about locks and ways to low tech hack them

As an extension of physical security, locks and lock picking have become their own topic within security. Chapter 3 will prove to be a unique view into bypassing locks. Offering more fresh content in this chapter, Jack divulges, for the first time ever, a variety of ways to bypass or disable locks *without* picking them. Details on creating keys and key copies with, and without, a key machine are addressed, as well as insight into proper key control. Drawing from his years of experience as a bonded locksmith, Jack shares some startling truths about locks and lock mechanisms that everyone should be aware of.

Chapter 4: Low tech wireless hacking

Bringing a slightly more technical approach to low tech hacking, this chapter presents the reader with a variety of attacks and countermeasures for wireless technologies in the home and office. Here, Jennifer (Jabbusch) Minella offers more than 30 unique attacks, organized in five primary categories; denial of service and availability, backdoors and cracks, rogue exploits, default vulnerabilities, and attacks on specific security tools. Wireless ploys bestowed range from disrupting municipal Wi-Fi with an antenna attack to bypassing access control systems with simple spoofing attacks.

Chapter 5: Low tech targeting and surveillance: How much could they find out about you?

This chapter, authored by Terry Gudaitis, Ph.D., a former operations officer and behavioral profiler at the CIA, is a frightening look at the world of targeting and surveillance from a true professional. The information provided, the true stories shared, and the references to resources readily available online are enough to send any security professional or layman running for the no-tech hills. Have you ever wanted to find a deleted tweet, or gather information on an impending corporate merger? If so, this chapter is for you. Even the most tech-savvy readers will find some of Terry's material here poignant.

Chapter 6: Low tech hacking for the penetration tester

Russ Rogers takes several of the low tech hacking components from the other chapters in this book and combines them to orchestrate an assortment of blended-threat attacks. This chapter guides the reader through the nuances of human nature and how to use traits such as selective attention to aide in distraction techniques, and how low tech hackers capitalize on the six basic tendencies of human behavior. In his scenarios, Russ hashes through all the considerations of a planned attack; selecting a target, designating an attack location, factoring corporate culture of the target, and picking the right technology and tools to increase the attack effectiveness. The culmination of this chapter gives the reader an insider's view of a real attack on a company, executed during a corporate event in Las Vegas.

Chapter 7: Low tech hacking and the law: Where can you go for help?

As we near the end of the book, Jack brings the readers a little closer to the world of security and incident response by introducing two agents, one from the United States Secret Service (USSS) and one from the Federal Bureau of Investigation (FBI). The interview-style format gives the reader a unique insight into the thoughts and personalities of the people most able to help in the event of an incident that spans jurisdictions, states, or even countries. In this chapter Jack also incites the readers to investigate public-private collaborative organizations such as the USSS ECTF and the FBI InfraGard.

Chapter 8: Information security awareness training: Your most valuable countermeasure to employee risk

Sean Lowther describes ways to incorporate Security Awareness Training as one of your least expensive and most effective security countermeasures. Jack met Sean about 5 years ago at a security conference and immediately recognized Sean as a world-class leader in the development of security awareness programs for organizations of all sizes. Sean is well known for designing a remarkably effective enterprise-wide awareness program at Bank of America. His program received the highest rating from the bank's regulators, and was consistently rated *world class* by industry peer groups. Sean firmly believes the success of a security plan is achieved by involving each and every employee. This chapter outlines the processes, procedures, and materials needed to build and measure a successful awareness program, as well as tips and tricks to keep employees engaged and make security part of the company mindset.

CONCLUSION

Authoring a book with contributions and content from five people is an interesting undertaking, to say the least. The end result is certainly worth the added effort, and the greatest benefit of involving professionals with such disparate backgrounds is the resulting depth and breadth of insight. This book truly has a little bit of something for everyone. Regardless of how much, or how little, experience each reader has in information security, physical security and hacking techniques, resources like *Low Tech Hacking* serve to reinforce common practices and introduce new nuggets of ideas, tools, and concepts that help us all continue learning and growing.

You can find out more about our authors and the book itself on http://www.LowTechHacking.com as well as by joining our LowTechHacking LinkedIn Group on www.LinkedIn.com.

Stay safe out there!

—**Jennifer (Jabbusch) Minella, CISSP**
CISO, Infrastructure Security Specialist
Carolina Advanced Digital, Inc.

Social engineering: The ultimate low tech hacking threat

INFORMATION IN THIS CHAPTER

- How Easy Is It?
- The Mind of a Social Engineer
- The Mind of a Victim
- Tools of the Social Engineering Trade
- One of My Favorite Tools of the Trade
- Social Engineering Would Never Work against Our Company
- What Was I Able to Social Engineer out of Mary?
- The Final Sting—Two Weeks Later—Friday Afternoon
- Why Did This Scam Work?
- Let's Look at a Few More Social Engineering Tools
- Let's Look at That Telephone Butt-in Set on My Tool Belt
- Meet Mr. Phil Drake
- Meet Mr. Paul Henry
- Do You Have a Guest User of Your Credit Card?
- A Few Possible Countermeasures

Some of the things I will discuss in this chapter have been on my mind since the mid-1980s. I believe it's time that I put them in writing and share a few of my thoughts on what I believe could be the most effective and dangerous threat to any security plan: social engineering! It has, in my opinion, become the low tech hacker's most valuable and effective tool. This age-old threat has taken on a new meaning as what I collectively call "bad guys" have continued to use the art of the con to gain access to intellectual property and if necessary the buildings that house that property.

This chapter, or the rest of the book for that matter, isn't meant to be read as a complete story from beginning to end. Social engineering and ways to prevent it are subjects with many meanings. This will be more of a potpourri of tips, tricks, vulnerabilities, and lessons learned from my thirty plus years of dealing with these issues. As an inside penetration team leader, I was constantly looking for more innovative ways to conduct a successful inside penetration test. It was during those years of physical and technical penetration testing that I gained most of my social engineering experience. These skills helped me to eventually hang up my dumpster diving penetration team jersey and retire from the tiger team (a term sometimes used for penetration testing) world UNDETECTED! Although I came close several times, I was never stopped or reported to security as a possible burglar or corporate espionage agent, even though that's what I effectively was.

As you read this chapter, if you think that it has a strong risk management flavor, that was intentional. Just about every area of concern with security today involves managing the risks associated with staying safe and secure. This chapter, and most of the other chapters in this book are chock full of what I like to call *techno tidbits* of useful risk management countermeasures. Hopefully, many of them will be topics that you might not have considered in the past as you put together your security plan. External, internal, and information systems auditors will find information on a few new potential vulnerabilities that they can recommend countermeasures for.

I've included discussions about social engineering in each of my former books. I've also used the term *social engineering* as a partial title for many of my presentations over the past 15 years. My most popular presentation to date is titled "Social engineering: Here's how I broke into their buildings." Following these presentations, I frequently have people come up and talk to me about some of the things that I discussed. Many of these people are longtime friends and attend pretty much every session that I give at the yearly events where I present. What has been encouraging to me this past year is the number of people who come to me after the presentation saying that they incorporated some of what they learned and that they are now conducting some of their own corporate penetration tests to help protect their companies from the threat of social engineering. Each of them seemed to have experienced the same things that I have over the years of using social engineering as a training tool and somewhat of a hobby. They find that it is often way too easy to get people to give them access to places where they are not supposed to be able to easily access and to things that they should not see.

HOW EASY IS IT?

Way back in 1988, I was a part of an internal security team for a large corporation. On several occasions, I had the opportunity to hear some of the conversations that went on when a "black hat" (in this case malicious) group targeted victims by calling them on the phone. They were using social engineering skills to gain access to proprietary information including passwords. I'll never forget what I heard one of the experienced black hats say to another black hat in training: "Social engineering is the easiest way to break into a system." He then followed up that comment by saying, "The stupidity of the average system administrator amazes me."

That was almost 25 years ago, and that was the first time I had heard the words *social engineering*. Why do I think of it as a tool that could be used by any bad guy from a black hat hacker to a terrorist? Social engineering is what I believe could be the most effective and dangerous outsider–insider threat to any security plan.

In the first three chapters of this book, I will be talking about social engineering, physical security, and a little bit more about locks. If we look at physical security as the target of an attack and locks as the gatekeeper for the entrance into the target, social engineering is often the way that we are able to gain access to the keys that open those locks and possibly the rest of the building. It is often the people who have those keys who become the victims of social engineering. We'll take a much closer look at that as we progress through the book.

THE MIND OF A SOCIAL ENGINEER

Although I've been using and teaching social engineering for almost two decades now, the true extent of the impact of social engineering really became clear to me about 9 years ago. When I was out in L.A. for a meeting on financial crimes security (what else?), I purchased a very interesting book titled *The Art of Deception: Controlling the Human Element of Security* by Kevin D. Mitnick and William L. Simon.

Just above the title on the cover of the book in red letters are the words *Controlling the Human Element of Security*. I found the book to be very well written and full of a lot of good examples of how social engineering works and how companies can try to defend against its use. I also learned quite a bit about a few approaches to targeting a potential victim than I had ever thought of before. A social engineer will continuously learn more clever ways to take advantage of how our minds work in order to perform the illusion or deception. The more that I used social engineering as one of my tools during my penetration testing days, the bolder I became in its use during those tests. After years of success in pretending to be something or someone that I wasn't, I just *KNEW* that whatever I said to the people that I encountered during the tests would be believed, and it was!

THE MIND OF A VICTIM

Any one of us, at any time, could easily become the victim of some form of social engineering. I personally believe that it is not possible to completely eliminate the risk. There are some things that can and should be done to reduce the risk as much as possible and I'll address some of them in the rest of this chapter. Without some form of training (and practice) in learning how to prevent being a victim of social engineering, you could easily become a victim and not even know it.

Our minds work in very trusting and predictable ways, and that means that exaggerated deviations from the norm might not ever be considered. This is what social engineers count on. Without awareness of the problem and without an understanding of how our minds can be fooled, there is little defense against social engineering. For this awareness training to be of any benefit for an organization, it must include every employee of every organization.

We see things all day long and we don't pay close attention to certain details because they are too familiar to us. That's exactly how the illusions that magicians call magic work and also why so many magic tricks are related to simple everyday things like a deck of cards. I use magic in much of my training and it really adds a lot to the attention span of the people in front of me. They are all so used to seeing those 52 cards that they don't even begin to think about how the different card gimmicks being used in most card tricks work. Most of these illusions are self-working yet almost mind boggling to the unsuspecting mind.

TOOLS OF THE SOCIAL ENGINEERING TRADE

If you would join me in taking a look at Figure 1.1, you will see a picture of the social engineering bag that I used for roughly 10 years. It was a pretty expensive bag to purchase. I spent around $200 for it, but it was money well spent. I often thought of it as something similar to those clown cars that you see in the circus. It is very deceptive how much will fit in that bag. Not only could I put all of my social engineering tools in the bag, but also there was a lot of room left over for the things I was able to take out of the buildings once my penetration test was successful. On the outside it simply looks like a briefcase that pretty much anyone within that organization would be carrying to and from work. On the inside were some slightly different items from what you would normally see someone bringing to work.

I took the time to put the contents of the bag on the table for you to see in Figure 1.2. This is the first time that I've ever done that. Not that what I have in the bag is anything special; it's just that I've never shared the contents with anyone in quite this way, especially in a book.

FIGURE 1.1

My inside penetration team bag

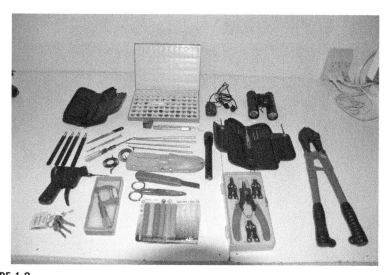

FIGURE 1.2

It's not as innocent as it looks

I wish that I had taken a picture of the bag as I was leaving some of these buildings with everything in it. It even amazed me how much that bag could expand and still look comparatively normal. Some of these things are tools that I have had for more than 40 years. Each has its own purpose and I'll explain some of that as we progress through the book. I know what you're thinking. There's no way that he has a pair of bolt cutters in that bag. Well, they were in there, and I had them with me everywhere I went. On most of our penetration tests the only limitation that was imposed on us by the company hiring us was that we were not allowed to use forced entry. We never used the bolt cutters as a part of our attack, but we did show how easy it would be to bring bolt cutters into the building if someone intended to use them. Most of the items you see were designed to get past various locks we encountered as our team attempted to get into a client's building or to use after we were in there. All right, here's a little quiz just to see if anyone is actually reading this. Anyone who sends me an e-mail listing all of the items that are shown in that picture will be sent a special gift. We will be revisiting some of these tools in Chapter 3.

ONE OF MY FAVORITE TOOLS OF THE TRADE

Most of my social engineering tools come from yard sales, thrift stores, flea markets, pawn shops, and eBay. I highly encourage all of you to take up the hobby of going out to these places and looking for things. As I describe some of these tools, I'll tell you how much I paid for them and where I got them. These are all tools that I used in one way or another for my social engineering exploits. Figure 1.3 is a picture of

FIGURE 1.3

There was a second bag that I took on some of our inside pen tests. Here's a picture of the manual showing my portable key machine: yard sale, $10

the front cover of the manual for a key machine that I purchased a number of years ago at a yard sale for $10.00. What was so nice about this key machine was that it was very small and very accurate, and it had a code micrometer as a part of the machine. This will allow keys to be cut by code if you know the code for that key or the depth of the bitings (sometimes called *cuts* by senior locksmiths). Machines of this size are available new for around $395. I frequently see them for sale on the Internet for anywhere between $95 and $250. If I could borrow a master key for a few minutes and had some of the key blanks that fit the keyway of a given lock, I could duplicate the key (as described in Chapter 3) and get it back to the person that I borrowed it from (typically using a little social engineering) very quickly. I know what you are thinking. How did I know what the correct key blank was for that lock? I knew because I was in that building once before and also managed to borrow the key briefly during my first visit. I learned over the years that social engineering attacks work best (at least they did for me) when they were two-part attacks. During the first visit our team mostly probed the target just to see how trusted we would be if we were able to gain entry. Normally we were never questioned about anything once we were inside. It was just assumed that if we were in the building, we belonged there. That was not a good assumption.

It's time for my first war story. After you read the following description of this social engineering attack, ask yourself if you think you would have fallen for this. This is a perfect example of how a two-part attack can seem so innocent yet be so deadly.

SOCIAL ENGINEERING WOULD NEVER WORK AGAINST OUR COMPANY

That's what a close friend of mine said one afternoon when we were talking about overall security and the threat of social engineering. This was 14 years ago, but social engineering was already a hot topic that most people were at least a little bit aware of. "We have good security and our employees wouldn't fall for anyone calling on the phone trying to get information from them," he said. I said, "Give me 90 days so that you won't know when I'm going to call, and I'll test your theory about your employees' awareness of this problem."

I made the call a few weeks later. "Good afternoon," a friendly voice answered. "Medical Group, this is Mary, can I help you?" I immediately put on my doctor hat, "Yes, this is Doctor Wiles," I began. (It's fun saying that even if it is totally fake). "I'm calling to ask a favor," I continued. "We have a practice similar to yours in Richmond and we're considering purchasing a new medical billing system. Do you use a fully automated system for your accounting, and if so, do you like it?" My friendly voice and simple question didn't raise any suspicion on her part. It was a simple and apparently innocent question.

"Yes we do," she said. "It's called Doctors Database and I believe that they are located in Denver, Colorado."

So far, so good. She seemed willing to talk a little more, so I started asking a few more questions. "Do they offer support when you have problems? We've heard some nightmares from friends who purchased medical billing systems and couldn't get support once they paid for it."

"Yes, we've been very happy with their support," she answered.

I asked a couple more quick questions. "How about upgrades and things that need to be fixed? Do they have someone locally they send to work on the billing system?"

"No, they do everything over a modem attached to the system. We've never had a problem with their needing to be here," she said.

I needed a bit more information, so I pressed on. "Before we make such a big decision, I'd like to speak with someone from Doctors Database to be sure that this would be the right billing system for us. Could you give me the name and number of the tech support person that you work with when you call them for support? I always feel more comfortable after I've had a chance to speak with the people that our administrator will be working with when problems develop. Some of those technical people are very hard to understand."

She apparently had a good working relationship with Doctors Database because she seemed happy to give me a name. "Yes, we work with Jerry Johnson and he's really easy to talk to. He should be in the office this afternoon if you call before 6 PM east coast time. Their phone number is XXX-555-1234 and they have someone available for support by phone 24 hours a day."

Little did she know that I now had almost everything I needed. Just one more question, and I could politely say thanks and goodbye. "I really appreciate your taking the time to help me with this, Mary. Would you mind if someone from my office called your database administrator if our administrator has any user questions after we get the new billing system? It's always easier to ask someone who actually uses the system rather than trying to get the Doctors Database technical people to answer simple questions. I promise that we won't be a pest."

She said that she was the administrator of the database and that she would be happy to answer a few questions for us. (It's wonderful living in the friendly sunny south.) "Thanks so much for helping me with this, Mary," I politely said. "I'll be sure to only have our administrator call you if he really gets stuck. Have a great week and thanks again."

WHAT WAS I ABLE TO SOCIAL ENGINEER OUT OF MARY?

This apparently innocent phone call gave me everything that I needed for my final attack. Here's what I got:

- Her name was Mary, and she was the database administrator for the medical office.
- They used a medical billing system from a company called Doctors Database that was located in Denver, Colorado.
- The tech support person that they worked with in Denver was named Jerry Johnson.
- Jerry accesses their computer over a modem to work on it.

To the casual observer, that's not a lot of dangerous information. Most of it seems to be pretty common knowledge that most people would have been willing to share. I didn't ask much about her computer, and I certainly didn't ask anything about login IDs or passwords.

THE FINAL STING—TWO WEEKS LATER—FRIDAY AFTERNOON

It was 4:40 PM when the phone rang at the Medical Group. John reluctantly answered, knowing that someone calling in that late with a problem could cause him to delay some of his plans for the 3-day weekend. On the third ring, he picked up the phone, "Good afternoon, the Medical Group, John speaking, may I help you."

I immediately assumed my best social engineering voice and started my attack. "Hello John. This is Bill Jenkins from Doctors Database in Denver. We're calling all of our customers about a serious problem with our medical billing system. It seems that our last update had a virus we were unaware of until this afternoon. It's causing all of the accounts receivable records to be corrupted. Our entire tech support team is calling our clients as quickly as possible to let them know about the problem. I know that Mary normally works with Jerry Johnson, but he is currently working with another client and has asked me to handle the fix for your system. Can I speak with Mary?"

There was a brief silence as I could feel John thinking about his 3-day weekend slipping away as we approached 5 PM. He finally answered. "With the holiday weekend coming up, Mary is off today. I act as her backup on the database work when she's off, and I'll try to help if I can."

Things were looking up as I began to spring the trap. "John, I'm going to need to log in to your system to fix this and I don't have Jerry's information in front of me with your modem dial-in number, login ID, and password. If that's something we're going to need to get from Mary, I think that we may have a problem if she's not there." I wanted him to feel a little of the panic that I was trying to convey.

Fortunately, it worked. I could hear him flipping through some papers as we talked. He quickly came back on the line. "I found it here in her notebook. The phone number is (555-867-5309), the login ID is doctor, and the password is also doctor."

I then went into my *good job* routine to make him feel completely at ease. "John, you've been a great help, and I can take it from here. It's been taking about 4 hours to clean this up and I know that it's Friday afternoon. I don't see any need for you to hang around. I'll install the fix, and things will be back to normal when you get back on Tuesday. Thanks again for your help and enjoy the weekend."

WHY DID THIS SCAM WORK?

I have tried to put into words (changing the names and phone numbers to protect the innocent) a two-part attack that I conducted about 14 years ago at the request of a friend. My friend knew that when the attack happened, it would be recorded on audio tape and given to her as a training aid for her to share with her employees. Without a little bit of awareness training, and a little bit of ongoing suspicion when speaking with strangers on the phone, ANYONE could fall for this kind of an attack.

Many of the hundreds (perhaps thousands) of people who have heard the audio version of this two-part attack have told me that they would have fallen for it as well. That first innocent phone call set the stage for a very believable second phone call where the keys to the kingdom were given away. A lot could have happened to that computer from Friday afternoon until Tuesday morning. Did the real Doctors Database (again, name changed—this is not their real name) know anything about this incident? Absolutely not! They would have had no idea that this was going on. Was Jerry Johnson a real person who worked tech support for Doctors Database? Absolutely, that's who Mary worked with on a regular basis. But Bill Jenkins was a figment of my imagination, carefully placed into the believable tale I had spun.

On top of the social engineering attack vector, the Medical Group's passwords were also extremely insecure. I'm not a big fan of static passwords, but that is a topic for another chapter in another book.

LET'S LOOK AT A FEW MORE SOCIAL ENGINEERING TOOLS

You will probably hear me say this many times throughout this book, but I continued to be amazed at how many great social engineering tools are available at your yard sales, flea markets, pawnshops, and thrift stores. This ranges from hats (like the one in Figure 1.4), jackets with corporate logos, tool belts, tools, listening devices, briefcases (like the one in Figure 1.1), spyware, and locks that can be used quite effectively for social engineering. I think it's a great idea to spend some time looking for these kinds of tools. For one thing you learn a whole lot more about social engineering while you are out there thinking about new ways to use it. I also think it's a very good idea for any company to do their own assessment of their vulnerabilities to social engineering attacks. If the company or organization is big enough to have a security team, that team can begin the process of seeing just how vulnerable their personnel are to this threat and others.

Why is the hard hat shown in Figure 1.4 so effective? The main reason that common everyday objects like that are so effective is that we're used to seeing them, and when we do we automatically assume that the person wearing it is really who they seem to be. The real con men of the world know how to take advantage of that.

I have never worked as an installer or a phone company repairman at a telephone company. I have seen many phone company employees around town, and at my home as I have had my phones worked on, and I certainly do remember what they

FIGURE 1.4

My favorite social engineering hat: eBay, $15

look like. There are many other people we see every day in our offices and homes that social engineers often imitate while using social engineering to gain access or information. Some of these are delivery people for various firms. Others are people that wear the same types of uniforms or other clothing items that allow them to look and act like they belong wherever they are.

TIP

For some excellent examples of how uniforms and clothing can be used by pen testers, check out Chapter 6 written by one of the best pen testers that I personally know, Russ Rogers. He provides several interesting and educational ways to look the part during your pen testing missions.

Figure 1.5 is a picture of me wearing a few of the tools that I picked up along the way from many of my favorite hunting grounds. I suspect that you already have many of these tools in your possession just from things that you have around the house.

FIGURE 1.5

My favorite social engineering tool belt: flea market, $3

In addition to the cool tool belt that I picked up for three bucks at a local flea market, there were a few other interesting finds on that tool belt:

- That telephone-looking gadget is a butt-in set worth about $250. I bought it at another flea market for $20.
- Those pliers next to the tape measure along with a nice knife for cutting cable cost $5 at a local yard sale.
- The tape measure was $2 at a thrift store.
- The scissors in my pouch are quite unique. They are capable of cutting a quarter in half (I've never actually tried that—no sense in wasting a quarter these days). $1 at a yard sale.
- The screw driver in the upper right of my tool pouch has become one of my favorites. It has 4 tips and is a very good quality for the $2 that I paid for it at a thrift store.
- The plastic ties were another $1 at a flea market.

If you're keeping track, I have about $40 in this entire social engineering outfit, and much of it is very usable around the house as well. All that I would need to do is wear a different hat, and I could be most any type of repairman or contractor. I think all of us have watched something on TV or in the movies that shows someone masquerading as someone else trying to get into a building. This is a very well-known threat, but it is still one that can be difficult to prevent. This seems to be especially true down here in the sunny South where I live. It seems that everyone is so friendly and helpful that some people really don't stop to think that the person that they are facing is someone who's trying to gain information, entry into a place where they shouldn't be allowed to go, or possibly do someone harm. Throughout the book I will mention various countermeasures. The only countermeasure for threats like social engineering is always being just a little bit more suspicious. You will hear me say that several more times as I mention more countermeasures. Believe it or not, this is something that people can be trained to do in security awareness training classes. As an absolute minimum, it is very important for every employee to have some sort of chain of command for reporting potential security threats. My decades of dealing with people regarding security and awareness have taught me that people really do care, and do want to do something to help protect their work environment.

> **TIP**
>
> While writing this book, I became aware of a new book that is scheduled to be published around the same time as this one. The book is titled *Human Compromise: The Art of Social Engineering* (ISBN: 978-1-59749-576-9, Syngress), and it was written by Mike Murr. I contacted Mike and spoke with him on the phone for about an hour asking some questions about his book. Throughout my years of using social engineering skills, I didn't really realize why they worked. I just knew that I was pretty good at it and seemed to be able to always get things that I wanted from people when conducting penetration tests. I'm absolutely convinced that it was my social engineering skills that allow me to make the statement that "I retired from penetration testing days UNDETECTED!"

The current description of Mike's book (the actual wording is subject to change as the book approaches publication) includes a hands-on approach to teaching you everything from the field-tested methods for reading body language, to the practical techniques for manipulating human perception, plus a whole lot more.

Keystroke logger: Is there one under your desk?

Some of our penetration team's favorite tools were the software and the newer hardware versions of keystroke loggers. These can make a good social engineer's job a lot easier. If we wanted to find out what a certain individual in a client's company who hired us to conduct the pen test was doing on their computer over a certain time frame, we would install a keystroke reader on their workstation on one visit and retrieve the results on a second visit.

By far, the most effective keystroke loggers that we have used are the KeyGhost hardware loggers being sold as security devices (http://www.keyghost.com). When these are installed between the keyboard of a workstation and the keyboard socket on the back of the computer, they look like they belong there to the casual observer. The logger that we used looked like the induction coils that we used to see on some of the older parallel printer cables. It just doesn't look like anything that you need to worry about. If you didn't put it there, you'd better worry! It's logging every single keystroke that you type in.

The version that I used for several tests would hold about 500,000 characters or a half of a megabyte. That might not sound like much, but that's a lot of data when you consider that the key logger is only logging keystrokes. By the way, backspace keys would show up as ASCII characters (control H for you techies) as would any other nonprinting character that was entered as a part of a password, for example. We have left our key loggers connected to target computers for up to 3 weeks and still only filled about 80% of their capacity.

Here's something else to consider if you feel safer entering information into your web browser over a secure socket connection (https). The encryption happens between your browser and the server that is receiving your sensitive information over the Internet. That's a good thing if you're entering your credit card number or bank account access information. The keystroke logger, however, is reading your keystrokes before they get to your browser. Everything will be in the clear when someone (hopefully only you) looks at the data that your keystroke logger collected.

How do you know if you have a key logger connected to your workstation or home computer? You don't unless you physically look back in the rat's nest that lives behind most computers to see if anything looks like it doesn't belong there. Unless you have been made aware of what a keystroke logger looks like, it probably won't look strange to you even if you do see one. I pass one around for people to see at every one of my security training classes. Statistically, I've read that people are 27 times more likely to remember something if they are able to see it and hold it in their hand.

I usually ask my attendees for a show of hands by anyone who hasn't ever seen one of these. Almost every time, more than half of the hands go up. How can you defend yourself against something that you don't even know exists? (Another subtle hint for more awareness training.)

Here's a quick awareness training class using one of my workstations as the target computer. Figure 1.6 shows a workstation in a minimum configuration with only a monitor, mouse, power cord, and keyboard connected to the motherboard. Take a look at that little bulge about 3 inches from the end of the cable that goes to the monitor, the one with the larger connector on the lower left-hand side of the computer. That's the only cable in Figure 1.6 that has an additional piece within the cable. That piece is an induction coil, and you may see one or more on cables found behind most workstations.

Let's take a look at this same workstation in Figure 1.7 after I have installed my keystroke reader between the keyboard and the motherboard socket where the keyboard was connected. Of the two cables in the center next to each other, the keyboard cable is the one on the right.

Now what do we see when we look back there? The keystroke reader looks like a second induction coil and would be very hard to detect if you didn't know what it looked like. I didn't try very hard to hide it, and normally, there are more wires back there than this. There is no way that the computer would know that it is there. It uses virtually no power, and doesn't require that any software be installed to make it work. When I finally remove it and take it back to check out the internal log, the target computer (or you) would never know that it was gone again.

This device can be used as an excellent security device if you suspect that someone is using your computer when you are not there. It is sold primarily for that

FIGURE 1.6

My computer WITHOUT KeyGhost installed

FIGURE 1.7

My computer WITH KeyGhost installed

purpose. That's a good thing as long as you know that it's there. Obviously it can be used for less than ethical purposes as well. When it becomes a threat, it can be a very, very difficult threat to detect. The only countermeasure I'm aware of is to physically check behind the computer to see if anything looks like it doesn't belong there.

> **WARNING**
>
> Unless you are involved with a well-documented rules of engagement penetration test, be sure that you thoroughly understand the laws associated with capturing someone's keystrokes on a computer that you do not personally own. In most cases I suspect that software application versions of keystroke readers would be considered malware. There could be some tampering issues and possibly trespass issues associated with installing hardware versions of keystroke readers. Also be cautious of the many opinions that you could get with a Google query regarding the legality of using keystroke readers. There are dozens and perhaps hundreds of opinions out there about this, and most of them seemed to be just that, opinions. You need to know and understand the law regarding keystroke reading.

If you conduct your own in-house social engineering tests, I'd suggest that you use one of these key loggers just to see if anyone detects it. I suspect that they won't. For your training purposes I believe you will find the log that it generates to be quite interesting. Keep in mind that the key logger is only detecting keystrokes. It doesn't detect anything that was pointed to and clicked on with the mouse. Quite often keystrokes are what you're really after. To me this would be a good example of low tech social engineering using a fairly high tech device. Obviously the learning curve to use this device is very, very short. All that you need to do is to have a way to gain access to a target computer for a few minutes to install the device. When you come back a week later to remove the device, there will normally be no indication that you've ever been there. Maybe I'm just a little extra paranoid from years of doing this stuff, but whenever I'm out somewhere at a hotel or public location using one of their computers to check things like mail, I'll always look behind the workstation if I can. Obviously there are other concerns with network monitoring beyond just key loggers.

One of my lunchtime tools

This little problem remains high on my list of things that we should all be considering every time we go out for a meal in a public place. Many office buildings have public restaurants either in the building itself or within walking distance. Here's what I think happens all too often. We're at work discussing something important, and someone realizes that it's time for lunch. Out we go to the local fast food restaurant of choice that day. There's no reason to let lunch slow down our train-of-thought for the project that we are working on. The in-depth conversation about that new marketing scheme or great new product that we are about to announce continues as if we were still back at the office.

You would be shocked at how many of these kinds of conversations I've heard over the years in public places, things that were discussed in the open, among total strangers, that should not have left the corporate boardroom. It seems like we are all too busy to stop and think about security and controlling who has access to our proprietary information. I occasionally get a chuckle from my friends when I remind them of a time when the national security message was "loose lips sink ships." Judging by the conversations that I have had with some of the people who were alive during that time, pretty much everybody took security seriously. Why has that changed so drastically in this high tech world just 6 decades later? We certainly don't have less at risk than they did then. If anything, we have much more at risk, especially in the world of technology. People were careful and concerned that there could be spies anywhere. Has that threat gone away? I don't think so.

There couldn't be any better example of low tech hacking than simply sitting in a crowded restaurant on a typical day, in a typical city, and listening. The technology that exists today for helping people hear things a little better didn't even exist in the "loose lips sink ships" days. These are very legitimate devices that can help anyone who has a hearing problem be able to hear MUCH better. I'm not talking about hearing aids; I'm talking about amplified listening devices that are available just about anywhere. Let's take a look at a couple of them.

This is the smallest sound amplification device that I found (Figure 1.8), and I'm sure that they come much smaller. This one is about an inch wide, 2 inches tall, and 1/2 inch thick. It's really compact and innocent looking. The sound amplification is amazing considering that this device only cost around $10 new (my $4 yard sale find was another good deal with this one). Figure 1.9 shows a higher end version of the same kind of device.

FIGURE 1.8

Low tech listening device: $4, yard sale

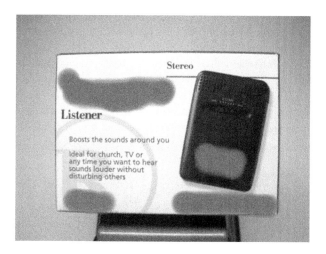

FIGURE 1.9

A slightly better listening device

The listening device shown in Figure 1.9 is a little more expensive and uses a single AAA battery that is easily replaced. The quality seemed to be a little better than the smaller, less expensive model shown in Figure 1.8. The model in Figure 1.9 cost about $25. With so many people today using MP3 players and other small devices with earphones, you need to be aware that these devices might not be noticed in a crowded public or private meeting space if someone were using one of these for other than their intended use. My purpose in describing these kinds of devices is to make you aware of how available they have become at a very low cost.

Just like any other small electronic gadget, I began to see these regularly at yard sales and flea markets. I picked up a few more just to give to friends and to demonstrate while I'm out at conferences. I've not spent more than $5 for any of them that I've purchased at these yard sales and flea markets. Most were $3 or less.

They have plenty of valuable and legal uses. You just need to be aware that some people could use them for other purposes. Have a nice lunch . . . .

LET'S LOOK AT THAT TELEPHONE BUTT-IN SET ON MY TOOL BELT

The interesting little gadget shown in Figure 1.10 has been on my want-to-find list for over 20 years. I finally found one at a local flea market where they only wanted $25 for it. Using my "I want to pay less for everything" skills, I was able to get it for a mere $20. This $250 tool has many uses in the social engineering world. One of its primary uses, which you probably saw in Figure 1.5, is to help me look like a telephone dude. Even if it were never used for anything but letting me look like a telephone dude it is an invaluable social engineering tool for making someone look like someone that they aren't.

For some of its more technical uses, I'm going to introduce you to our first expert interview. One of my long-time friends, Phil Drake, is a telecommunications expert. You may have seen some of his disaster recovery chapters in my former books. He has a tremendous amount of experience in many fields that impact the security world as well as the disaster recovery world. Let's ask him a few questions about this nifty tool.

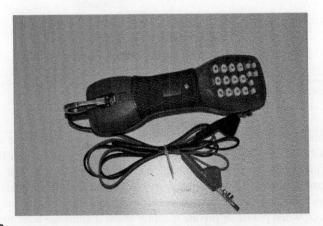

FIGURE 1.10

Telephone butt-in set: flea market, $20

MEET MR. PHIL DRAKE

I wanted to start something a little different with this book. Throughout my decades of working and living in the worlds of physical security, computer security, and disaster recovery, I have met and become friends with many true experts. The first of these that I introduce in this book is a long-time friend named Phil Drake. Many of you may recognize Phil as being a contributing author in two of our other books. In each of them I had him author a chapter that we titled *Personal, Workforce, and Family Preparedness*. Phil is one of the best in the world at helping people deal with those issues. I felt that these topics were so important that I wanted them included in both our first book, *Techno Security's Guide to Managing Risks for IT Managers, Auditors, and Investigators* (ISBN: 978-1-59749-138-9, Syngress), and our fourth book, *Techno Security's Guide to Securing SCADA: A Comprehensive Handbook on Protecting the Critical Infrastructure* (ISBN: 978-1-59749-282-9, Syngress).

In addition to being an expert in the fields of disaster preparedness and recovery, Phil is an expert in the field of telecommunications. It's that area of expertise that I want to ask him a few things about in this interview with the experts. Let's get on with our first interview:

Jack: Tell me a little about how a low tech hacker could use the butt-in set (Figure 1.10) that I purchased at a flea market.

Phil: My first concern about the butt-in set is not technology related at all. It's a social engineering concern as you have already mentioned. Just having the butt-in set (or butt-set) hanging on a tool belt or in your hand and wearing a hard hat make you the "telephone technician," and in most workplaces, that makes you practically invisible. We are so dependent on telecommunications today that service technicians carrying tools and replacement equipment are as common as express delivery drivers. We are conditioned not to challenge these people especially if they are in a rush. We don't want to slow down the "repair" process and cost the company extra money or downtime.

If we see technicians working in or around telecommunications equipment outside a facility (manholes or those light green or tan boxes), we assume they belong there and if they need to check inside the building for a problem, human nature is to help out.

It's looking the part. Of course a fake ID, work clothes, and tool belt are all important to the ruse, but the butt-set is the icing on the cake. It's like a stethoscope: you would never challenge someone with a stethoscope around their neck as you assume they are legitimate medical practitioners, especially if you need one in a hurry.

> **NOTE**
> Let me jump in to the middle of Phil's interview and share a quick story along the lines of what Phil was talking about regarding a phone technician. This one happened at my home on two separate occasions. We had experienced a number of severe lightning storms in our neighborhood, and the cable service for some of our homes seemed to stop working. My home

Continued

NOTE—cont'd

was not one of the homes that was affected by this. On the first occasion that I want to share I simply looked out in my yard and saw two men standing over the service boxes where my cable and phone wires are located. (You do know where yours are located at your home, don't you?) I hadn't called anyone, and my phone service and cable service were working perfectly. Whenever I see things like this that are somewhat unexpected, my antisocial engineering mindset comes to play. My countermeasure for this potential threat was to call the phone company and ask if they had sent someone. In this case they had sent these men to look at all of the phone service in our neighborhood. It wasn't until after I knew that they were supposed to be there that I approached them to see how things were going. It's usually not a good idea to approach strangers first before knowing what they are up to. Figure 1.11 is a picture of the exact boxes that they came to inspect out in my yard.

A second similar situation had happened about a year earlier when someone came to our front door stating that he was from the local telephone company and needed to check our outside service boxes. His appearance was very similar to the picture of me with all of my social engineering gear as shown in Figure 1.5. My call to the phone company immediately following my conversation with him also revealed that he was a legitimate phone company technician. What if he hadn't been sent by the phone company? If that were the case, my next call would have been to my local police department. If he was a bad guy, he may have intended to insert a telephone listening device connected to a small tape recorder. These are readily available and I have had several of them for many years. I don't want to throw a warning into the middle of my tip, but always remember most of what the bad guys do is usually a crime. Installing a device like that with criminal intent would violate some sort of wiretap laws for sure. I like to consider these situations where someone is apparently legitimate and doing things outside your home is one of those trust-but-verify situations. It's always good to take the time to make that phone call just to be sure.

FIGURE 1.11

Telephone and cable service boxes

Technically speaking, the butt-set can use phone lines to make or receive calls without the legitimate subscriber's knowledge. Need to call an uncle in Korea? Find an unlocked access point (those green or tan boxes) in the neighborhood, hunt for dial tone, and make that call for absolutely free—for you. The legitimate subscriber will have a surprise when the bill comes.

These sets also have a "monitor" setting that allows someone to listen to all calls on the line with no interference whatsoever. This is probably the easiest form of low tech phone tapping.

The majority of the butt-sets found in yard sales and flea markets are older analog technology. The race is on to VoIP and the majority of telephone service to large businesses is digital, but there are still many millions of analog lines in use in business and residential locations for someone to play with.

Jack: Do you have any good social engineering stories of how people have used it to gain information about public branch exchanges (PBXs)?

Phil: There have been a number of incidents where "phone technicians" have appeared to try to gain unauthorized access at business locations. This ruse usually takes the form of "we have alarms from your phone equipment" or "we need to replace some of our equipment in your telephone equipment room." Sometimes these "technicians" are challenged; sometimes after hours when the security team is busy, they are not.

Once these people have access to the PBX equipment room they own you. I've seen many logins and passwords written on the administration terminals in equipment rooms. After all, it's a secure area, right? If the information isn't written on the admin terminal, it's more than likely under the keyboard or in a drawer close by.

Once individuals have access to the PBX they can easily allow calls from the outside to access long distance lines for "free" long distance. More importantly, these calls made from a company's PBX are traceable back to the PBX and in many cases not to the outside phone line that originated the call. It's a perfect way for criminals to cover their tracks.

A really interesting case a number of years ago involved a supposed phone company technician showing up to replace a bad circuit pack. The individual was allowed access and shortly thereafter telephone extensions around the building stopped working. Thinking this was just part of the "repair" process, security wasn't overly concerned. An hour later a security guard was dispatched to ask when the repairs would be completed. It was then discovered that a number of expensive PBX circuit packs and related equipment had been stolen.

It took several days and thousands of dollars to put the system back together and restore service. Missed customer calls and lost employee productivity added to the loss.

Of course these individuals may not be interested in phone equipment at all. They may be trying to gain access to the facility to gather information on someone or steal money, property, or confidential information.

Jack: Do these individuals need to be on site or can they do harm from the outside?

Phil: In a recent incident, a large company with a small regional office had a very large surprise. The regional office has a small "key" phone system. This is a simple five-line system and each phone has a button for each of the five outside lines.

The surprise came in the form of an $8,000+ phone bill with long distance calls to North Korea, Yemen, and Somalia. Of course the calls were not made by the office personnel. They were made remotely with the criminals billing phone calls to the regional office with two long distance companies. (They didn't even need to use the butt-in set we were just talking about.)

After a few dozen suspicious calls, one long distance carrier called the regional office to inquire if the calls were authorized. The individual answering the call took the message but took no action; they didn't alert anyone or raise the alarm that something might be wrong.

There was no unauthorized access or system penetration, just criminals knowing what to do and that many companies are too busy to catch them. Complacency scored a win for the bad guys in this example. The company had to pay since they were alerted but took no action. Based on the known criminal activities from some of the countries involved, you can bet that the individuals making the calls weren't making vacation plans or checking the weather forecast.

In addition to having some help on the inside, as in the example above, almost all large PBX systems can be remotely administered. This remote administration can be done through a modem (yes, they are still in use) or more likely via VPN access more recently.

The modems are the problem. They are often forgotten but, if still connected, can be used. Yes, someone needs the phone number, login, and password (hopefully) but that information can be obtained with some investigation and time.

Jack: How about lists of default maintenance passwords for systems like PBX's? Are these lists which make excellent social engineering tools still readily available?

Phil: Yes, there are lists of default passwords and user names delivered with new PBX and VoIP phone systems on a number of hacker sites. Many customers never change these defaults even though every manufacturer strongly recommends an immediate change.

Jack: You mentioned IP phone systems. Are they better secured than their older PBX cousins?

Phil: Of course they are much harder to access remotely for administration and most are being located in data centers instead of an out-of-the-way room in the basement. However, security can still be circumvented by social engineering. That individual posing as a phone technician can now have access to the phone system and the highly secured corporate data center as well. In addition, I wonder how many companies actually check the equipment being carried by contractors and service technicians entering company facilities.

The use of VoIP systems is growing; however, the majority of phone systems in use today rely on technology basically unchanged over the past 20 years.

MEET MR. PAUL HENRY

My second expert interview for this chapter will be with another of my long-time friends and colleagues, Mr. Paul Henry. Paul has spent decades on the cutting edge of technology with a specialty in technical security issues. When I need to know the absolute latest information available regarding security threats Paul is always the first person I call. He provides some interesting answers to my questions as shown below:

Jack: When I last met with you, you were explaining a low tech hacking way of masking the actual cell phone number that you were calling from. To me that's an excellent example of low tech social engineering using a high tech application that anyone can easily use. Can you explain that application to our readers?

Mr. Henry: There are a number of Internet-based services that provide free or low cost caller ID spoofing services. You know something is popular when a web-site dedicated to it arrives—and yes there is one now dedicated to caller ID spoofing— http://www.calleridspoofing.info/. The subject has been a hot topic in the press lately as a large media organization has been accused of hacking in to people's voice mail accounts using caller ID spoofing. Many people don't realize it but still today if some-one calls your cell phone number and can cause your caller ID to be sent to the provider's server using one of the many caller ID spoofing services, they are granted unobstructed access to your voice mail. It is important to note that here in the United States a bill has been passed that makes the spoofing of caller ID ille-gal—the U.S. House of Representatives passed HR 1258, also known as the infamous Truth In Caller ID Act. The FCC has now adopted rules implementing the Truth In Caller ID Act—http://www.dwt.com/LearningCenter/Advisories?find=424483.

With that being said those that offer these caller ID spoofing services simply offer the services from outside the United States to literally get around the law. It is another example of how legislation can perhaps convince a good person not to do bad things but does nothing to prevent a malicious person from doing bad things.

Jack: Do you think that the bad guys such as foreign spies and possible terrorists use many low tech social engineering tools for gaining access to critical information or locations? Please explain a few that you have come across that you found partic-ularly threatening.

Mr. Henry: The mining of data from social web sites like Facebook has become the number one tool in the arsenal of the bad guys. We place way too much work-related information on our social media pages and a simple search of Facebook or LinkedIn can reveal very useful information for a would-be bad guy. Just do a search using Google for Facebook SCADA or LinkedIn SCADA. You might be surprised by the results.

Many SCADA systems are foolishly connected to the Internet and a quick search with Google for some fairly easy-to-guess search terms could have a potential bad guy controlling a SCADA system in minutes — turning pumps on and off or turning off circuit breakers.

Jack: You are considered by many to be one of the top security minds in the world. What is your feeling about how much social engineering is being used to gain physical access to critical information? Can you give us a few examples of some of the things that you have seen?

Mr. Henry: Social engineering has played a major role in every headline-grabbing hack that we hear about today. Simply put, it has become an all too common and in most cases easy path into the very core of an otherwise protected network environment. Why take the time to directly penetrate a network's fortified gateway when you can easily bypass an organization's perimeter defense with a little social engineering trickery?

- HBGary fell prey to the social engineering skills of a 16-year-old girl. She successfully spoofed an email from a senior executive to an IT department employee in an effort drop security defenses and allow inbound connections that facilitated the hack that exposed over 60,000 HBGary and HBGary Federal emails on the public Internet, some of which contained sensitive/confidential company information.
- RSA fell prey to a socially engineered email sent to an internal employee that started the entry into their network that resulted in the compromise of the security of their Token product. RSA will be replacing an estimated 40,000,000 tokens for customers as a result of the intrusion into their network.
- The government of Iran's nuclear fuel centrifuges controlled by Seimens SCADA products fell prey to free USB sticks given away at a security conference (allegedly targeted). As expected, employees returned to work after the conference and plugged the USB sticks into PCs on the company's network and opened the door for Stuxnet to pillage their SCADA systems.
- Multiple energy companies fell prey to social engineering spear phishing attacks on mobile devices. VPN-connected workers were used to gain additional internal access that facilitated the Night Dragon malware infections in the Americas, Europe, and Asia as well as countries in the Middle East and North Africa.
- Social engineering was behind the Operation Aurora attacks in the form of phishing emails to key personnel that directed employees to websites with specially crafted malware the took advantage of a Day Zero vulnerability in Internet Explorer. Successful attacks were carried out against search giant Google and at least 20 other firms, including Adobe, Juniper Networks, Rackspace, Yahoo!, and Symantec.
- A disgruntled ex-Gucci network engineer allegedly went on an IT rampage after leaving the company and using social engineering to trick Gucci IT department employees into activating a token he had taken a month prior to leaving the company. He used it to gain remote access to the company's network where he allegedly deleted virtual servers, shut down the company's storage area network, and deleted a disk containing corporate mailboxes from an email server.
- The Rupert Murdoch News Corp Media empire is still reeling from the *News of the World* tabloid cell phone hacking scandal that all began with social engineering and loopholes in voice mail security (users not changing default passwords) to hack into voice mailboxes. It is far from over and has already resulted in the U.K.-based *News of the World* tabloid being shut down.

Jack: I always like to ask security professionals about their thoughts on an countermeasures that companies can employ to help prevent becoming a victim of social engineering. Can we get your opinion of countermeasures that you have recommended?

Mr. Henry: We have fallen in to the crowd mentality trap in network security. What I mean by that is we as a community know very well that our current defenses such as traditional antivirus, signature-based IDS/IPS, portcentric firewalls, and flaw remediation programs such as Microsoft's WSUS are easily penetrated/bypassed and rendered useless against a relatively low skilled adversary. Yet we continue to use them simply because they are what everyone else is using. After all, if that is what everyone else is doing it must be right . . . .

Traditional AV, IDS, and IPS considerations

First we need to reset our focus. Simply put, it is misdirected today; actually it has been wrong for more than a decade. All of our efforts are at the gateway and seem to involve preventing malware from being delivered in to our environments. We will never break out of the arms race we seem to be locked in to with malicious hackers if we keep playing the game their way. Effectively playing the game their way puts the bad guys in the same position as the casinos in Vegas—the house always wins. We need a game changer and I believe that the most viable game changer is to quit worrying about the delivery mechanisms of malware and apply or focus on not allowing any untrusted code to ever, under any circumstances, execute within our environments.

It is imperative to recognize that the end game for our adversary today is not to trick an internal employee surfing the web into clicking on a specially crafted link that the user cannot resist that leads to a malware-laden website, opening a malicious email attachment with embedded malware, or causing a user to plug in a free USB stick that they picked up at a network security conference that contains targeted malware. The end game is to use these various delivery methods to cause malware to enter the enterprise environment and to execute on internal network resources such as desktops and servers. It almost seems too simple but the reality of our situation is that if we simply prevent unauthorized code that is not explicitly permitted by policy and is not known to be trusted from executing within our network environments, the seemingly unlimited delivery mechanisms available to the bad guys quickly become a non-factor. Who cares how they deliver their malicious code? If it cannot execute it simply no longer matters.

The bottom line with respect to our failed AV, IDS, and IPS solutions that today still continue to expose us to unnecessary risk is to complement them sooner than later with current generation application control/white listing solutions that will allow us to change our focus from malware delivery to the only viable defense in our current threat environment: preventing untrusted and unauthorized applications from executing in the first place.

Traditional firewall consideration

Next we must end on our misplaced trust and reliance on traditional port-centric firewalls—hackers beat us on that effort many years ago. As defenders we always play by the rules and filter applications based on the RFC mandated/recommended service ports:

- WEB Traffic   TCP 80
- FTP Traffic   TCP 21

- Encrypted Web Traffic   TCP 443
- SSH Traffic   TCP 22
- Email SMTP   TCP 25
- Telnet Traffic   TCP 23
- Web Traffic Alternate   TCP 8080
- RTP Traffic   TCP 3389
- DNS   TCP 53
- Multiple MS Uses   TCP 135

By way of our defined security policy, we close all possible ports but typically have to leave those above (and some others) still open in order to conduct our business. Well here is a news flash for defenders: the bad guys know that we must leave some specific ports open and they have no intention of abiding by our policies. They simply created malware and bad-ware that can operate literally across any port or service (no policy restrictions for the bad guys) that we happen to leave open. The bottom line is that if your firewall today does not have the ability to identify applications operating over any port or service, you are destined to be compromised (if you're not already).

Ports are no longer relevant. Simply put, if your firewall cannot identify any traffic operating over any port or service, then you will never be able to control your network traffic. If you cannot control known good traffic you stand no chance at all of controlling any bad/malicious traffic.

Flaw remediation

We foolishly focus the majority of attention on Microsoft issues, and to be blunt, Microsoft is not the issue today. The vast majority of attacks today targets third-party software and browser add-ons. So many organizations rely solely on Microsoft WSUS that only handles flaws specific to Microsoft products. We are clearly missing the target and the bad guys know. What has been the most hacked software for more than the past year? Well, it has not been Microsoft; it has been a third-party product vendor Adobe. Is it any wonder we find ourselves in the mess we are in today?

The solution to our flaw remediation issue is to apply a little common sense — don't rely solely on solutions such as WSUS that are unable to remediate issues with the third-party applications and add-ons that are operating in your environment.

DO YOU HAVE A GUEST USER OF YOUR CREDIT CARD?

Here's another flea market treasure that I found really interesting. The credit card reader shown in Figure 1.12 is capable of storing up to 300 credit card numbers. It's roughly the size of a telephone handset. Finding things like this at flea markets, yard sales, thrift stores, and pawn shops is to me a perfect example of how much expensive high end technology is out there for the taking for a determined social

FIGURE 1.12

Credit card reader: flea market, $5

engineer or potential bad guy. This one was most likely replaced by something just a little more modern. It wound up out there in the surplus world and eventually at a flea market. A device of this size wouldn't work well as a concealed skimmer, but it certainly would be small enough to keep concealed somewhere where the bad guy could get to it and quickly swipe your card when given the opportunity. If you think about your last meal at any restaurant, how did you pay for it? You most likely enjoyed the great meal and then handed your credit card to someone to pay for it. Probably 999 times out of 1000 everything is fine. If that one time the person that you handed your card to was looking to steal credit card numbers, there could be an opportunity to scan your card into a reader similar to this before scanning it a second time into the restaurant's credit card reader to pay the bill. Your credit card number stored in the illegal scanner might not be used any time in the immediate future. It may also be quickly sold to people who want to commit credit card fraud. At the time of the theft of your credit card number in this scenario, neither you nor the restaurant would know that it happened. The restaurant would probably never know it, and you wouldn't know it until the card was eventually used to charge things to your account.

Regarding the use of these fairly technical electronic devices, all that using them requires is very low tech hacking and a little social engineering. This seems to be the trend with fairly complex technical pieces of equipment. It seems that the more high tech a piece of equipment is, the more the developers tried to make it easy to use.

A FEW POSSIBLE COUNTERMEASURES

When we consider the risks, threats, vulnerabilities, and countermeasures associated with social engineering, the countermeasures are things that need to be considered by all employees. The overall sneakiness of the threats associated with social engineering make it very easy for social engineers to catch anyone off guard. We just don't like to think that what appear to be kind and caring people are possibly people who are looking to do things to cause harm. Our human nature just doesn't like to consider these things.

Always be slightly suspicious

The number one countermeasure for the threat of social engineering is to be just a little more suspicious than we normally are as good, friendly, trusting citizens. This holds true for social engineering attempts that come by way of a phone call, or a visit from a friendly salesman. The same principle will help all of us to be more aware of possible terrorist planning activates as well. We all need to be just a little bit more aware of what is going on around us and people who are possibly trying to pretend to be other than who they really are as they try to use the age-old skill of social engineering to breach our security.

Unfortunately, this is a difficult countermeasure to continue to implement. We usually stop being concerned about things that happened even a few years ago. I suspect that this has something to do with our wonderful freedom from most of the bad things that people live with every day in other parts of the world. We can never afford to become complacent again. If we do, it will make life much easier for future bad guys, social engineers, and even terrorists.

Start to study the art of social engineering

There are several new groups on the Internet that now address social engineering topics as their main subject. One of those is located at http://www.social — engineering.org. This group and their website have more information on the subject of social engineering than I have seen on any Internet website.

Start a social engineering book library

I've always enjoyed having a lot of different reference books in my library. Sometimes I'll have three or four open at one time when researching a specific subject. I am one of those people who still really likes to hold the book in my hand and not read it from the screen on some handheld or desk resident device. I do understand the convenience of being able to have so many books on one small handheld device; I just don't think that that will ever be me. Here's another book that I would like to recommend that you consider for your library.

- *Social Engineering: The Art of Human Hacking* by Christopher Hadnagy, (ISBN: 978-0-470-63953-5, Wiley)

This is one of the newer books in my collection. None of these "here's why it works" books existed when I first started using social engineering as a tool for pen testing. It is truly amazing how our minds work and sometimes don't work the way that they should. Christopher is also the lead developer of the website www.social–engineering.org that I mentioned earlier.

TIP

You can have some more fun using social engineering in some innovative ways. Time seems to pass so quickly during the summer that I frequently forget my wife's birthday. Several years ago I decided to do something that I thought would help me to remember it. On my Facebook page I changed my birth date to her birth date. Now each year starting a day or so before her birthday I receive birthday wishes from about 50 or 60 of my friends. Some of these wishes are so kind and heartfelt that I really didn't want them to know that this wasn't really my birthday. I guess they'll all know it now! Hopefully they will forgive me. It was absolutely perfect as a way for me to remember with 50 or 60 reminders to wish my wife happy birthday (and not get into trouble again for forgetting it). Now that I've shared my little secret in print, I have changed my Facebook page once again just to keep everybody guessing. Please feel free to use my little social engineering birthday tip if you like. Happy birthday!

SUMMARY

—Low Tech Jack

The threat of the bad guys of the world using social engineering is most likely here to stay. Hopefully some of my experiences with social engineering will raise your interest level and have you dive a little more into learning how it works and why it works. If you are a penetration team leader, social engineering will become one of your primary tools if it isn't already. If you're a security manager you will want to know how social engineering can be used against your employees and how vulnerable they are to these kinds of attacks. If you're a risk manager or an internal auditor, you will want to know a little more about the potential threat of social engineering and how these kinds of threats can be mitigated through countermeasures and employee awareness training. The con that we call social engineering is an age-old behind-the-scenes threat that we all need to continue to learn about as the bad guys of the world find more and more ways to use it.

Low tech vulnerabilities: Physical security

INFORMATION IN THIS CHAPTER

- A Mini Risk Assessment
- Outsider–Insider Threats
- Some Things to Consider for the Security of Your Buildings
- Bomb Threats in Chicago
- Check Those Phone Closets
- Remove a Few Door Signs
- Review Video Security Logs
- Consider Adding Motion-Sensing Lights
- Subterranean Vulnerabilities
- Clean out Your Elephant Burial Ground
- Spot Check Those Drop Ceilings
- Internal Auditors Are Your Friends
- BONUS: Home Security Tips

Physical security has been a subject I have been very interested in ever since becoming a bonded locksmith in 1971. My full-time job was very technical and began to lead me into the world of computer security. It was the ability to experience both worlds at the same time that taught me how critical physical security is. It seemed to me, while working as a locksmith, that a lot of people really never gave the vulnerabilities of physical security much thought until there was some problem. I don't think things have changed much in the past 40 years, but it is encouraging to see people now begin to really look closely at the risks, threats, vulnerabilities, and countermeasures associated with physical security.

There was something else I noticed while staying closely associated with both the physical and technical worlds of security. While things are constantly changing in the technical security world, in the physical security world, things don't seem to change quite as quickly. As I said in Chapter 1, where we address social engineering, these first three chapters will closely relate in many ways. For the past 20 years, I have thoroughly enjoyed presenting on the subjects of physical security, computer security, and social engineering. More than 10,000 people have seen one or more of my presentations. The reason that I mentioned these presentations is that I get the opportunity to speak with people before, during, and after the sessions. It gives me an opportunity to see what they are doing about security and to hear about the things that concern them. In most cases, I can quickly tell whether or not someone has been a victim. Unfortunately, many of the people with whom I speak have been a victim of some form of physical or technical security threats.

While this is not a book about risk management, in many ways it really is. I heard a senior security director make a statement many years ago at a conference. He stated that their company had now come to the conclusion that all security issues really are risk management issues. Organizations (and homeowners) need to determine what they have at risk, what are the threats possibly targeting what they have at risk, how vulnerable are they to those threats, and what are the countermeasures (what can they do about the threats). Without some form of risk management, there really isn't any way to know what you have at risk or what you can do to help reduce the risk. Current threats are frequently in the news, and vulnerabilities to these threats are also frequently discussed. Understanding risk management is especially critical for small to midsize businesses that may not have a dedicated risk manager.

While I was working on my first book, *Techno Security's Guide to Managing Risks for IT Managers, Auditors, and Investigators* (ISBN: 978-1-59749-138-9, Syngress), I was spending a fair amount of time working from my boat out on the nearby lake. Even though this lake is technically a flowing river, it is still designated as a lake in name and on maps. As a part of a chapter in that book, I gave an example of a risk assessment by looking at my floating office on the boat. Realizing that most of you who will read this book probably did not read that one, I think it's worthwhile to share that risk assessment again.

A MINI RISK ASSESSMENT

I had recently purchased my first boat. It wasn't huge, but it was just big enough for me to use as a floating office a couple of days a week when the weather is nice. Just for fun, I conducted a mini risk assessment of some of the risks, threats, vulnerabilities, and countermeasures associated with my floating office. The risk assessment wasn't intended to be extensive, but it will give you a simple example of the things to consider when conducting any risk assessment.

What did I have at risk?

The first and most important thing at risk while working on a floating office is my life. I also had the boat itself at risk even though I had passed some of the financial risk along to an insurance company, which is what we do with a lot of risks where it makes sense. There was also equipment on the boat that was at risk of not only sinking but of possibly being dropped overboard or being splashed with water from the wake from a passing boat. A sudden thunderstorm could cause problems as well. Depending on lake conditions, too many other boats could cause a problem.

The battery in the boat could die, causing me to lose all power and even strand me on the lake. As you can see, whenever you consider what you have a risk, you will immediately start to consider some of the threats that could increase your risks. What I had at risk out there on the boat was everything that I could lose if something really bad happened. Let's call all the bad things that could happen *possible threats*.

> **NOTE**
>
> Risk management, and especially security risk management, needs to be much more than a listing of best practices for managing risks. Throughout my years of security training and penetration testing, I always ensured that the client corporation's risk managers were a part of our evaluation process. The best book on this subject that I have seen to date is a book published in 2011 titled *Security Risk Management: Building an Information Security Risk Management Program from the Ground Up* by Evan Wheeler (ISBN: 978-1-59749-615-5, Syngress).

What were some possible threats while out on the lake?

I've already mentioned a few as I discussed some of the risks. The possible threats were a little different than they would be if I did a risk assessment of my home office. Weather could certainly be a threat, and so could simply hitting something as I was moving from one place to another on the lake. There was always the threat of a sudden thunderstorm as well as the threat of being hit by another boat. I wouldn't have had much of a threat of being hit by a car (hopefully) or suffering from a commercial power outage while I was out there. The possible threat of theft was small as long as I kept an eye on my equipment while I was launching the boat. Overall, the threats that could hinder my ability to conduct business from the boat would be lower than those from most places.

What were some of the possible vulnerabilities?

I would have been much more vulnerable to severe or any weather changes out there on the lake than I would be in my home office. This is a large lake about 20 miles long. For a few days following a heavy rain, there are hundreds of semi-submerged items floating downstream (remember, this lake was actually a river). If I didn't know the depth of the water that I was in, I would have been vulnerable to running aground or hitting something in water that was shallower than I thought it was. It would most likely just be inconvenient, but just like in any vehicle, I would be vulnerable to running out of fuel. I mentioned not being vulnerable to commercial power failures, but I could easily have been vulnerable to quickly running my only battery down to a point where I couldn't start the engine to get back to the marina. Although I am very careful, I would certainly have been vulnerable to falling overboard. That could be a difficult problem when you're on the water alone.

And finally, what about my countermeasures?

I really enjoy talking about countermeasures. The word even sounds cool. I had a lot of valuable equipment with me that would be at risk while I was out there on the boat. The countermeasures are the things that help me lower my vulnerability to any of the threats that I might encounter that could cause me to lose what I have.

I've learned a lot during the couple of years that I had my floating mini-office. Some of the countermeasures that made me feel comfortable out there were as follows:

- I tried to be on the lake only when I know that most other boaters weren't out there.
- I checked the weather forecast every time before I headed to the lake.
- I always wore a self-inflating life jacket in case I fell overboard.
- I used special waterproof cases for my computer and cell phone.
- A small inverter was onboard to provide me with 110 volts AC from the boat battery.
- The marina and my family were always notified of where I planned to be and when I expected to return.
- A small marina radio was always on board.
- The boat was constantly maintained.
- My weather radio warned me of any pending storms.

I'm sure there are many more issues that could be addressed in this mini-assessment. We all need to at least be familiar with and understand our risks at home and at work.

Just about every area of concern with security today is a risk management issue. This chapter, and most of the other chapters in this book, are chock full of what I like to call *techno tidbits* of useful risk management countermeasures. Many of them will be topics you might not have considered in the past as you put together your security plan. I hope this will help external, internal, and information system auditors to recognize several gaps in their audit processes.

OUTSIDER–INSIDER THREATS

For my definition here, let's consider the outside threats as those coming at you from the Internet or dial-up modem (you do know where all of your dial-up modems are, don't you?) or a simple phone call from a total stranger. The reason that I mentioned dial-up modems is that there are still a lot of them out there. Many maintenance ports on older PBXs, building environmental controls, air handling systems, and access control systems still use modems for maintenance access from off-site, and probably will continue to rely on them well into the future.

I'm not considering insider (current employee) activity in this chapter. For this discussion, let's consider outsider–insider threats as people who never were employees and didn't belong in your building.

This would be the category that my inside penetration team would fit into. When we roamed through the clients' buildings unchallenged, our team definitely didn't belong there (other than being hired to try to get there). A bad guy checking out your building for espionage or future terrorist activities would also fit in this category. In theory, some employee inside the building should eventually figure out that there is a Trojan Horse in the camp. Here's why I keep preaching about the subject of physical security and the subject of knowing who is in your buildings at all times. For more than three decades now, I have observed what I believe is a lack of awareness of this concern. Over the years, I have seen comparatively few articles that address this silent but formidable threat. Remember, when I spent those years doing this for a living, our penetration teams entered the clients' buildings expecting to get caught in an inside penetration attack that was designed to become more bold the longer I had the team in a building. Toward the end of just about every inside pen test, we were openly walking around like we worked in the target building, almost hoping to get caught by someone. We never did!

We were good, but I suspect that there are many bad guys out there who are much better at it than we were, and they won't try to get caught in the end like we did. We were also working under a few self-imposed rules that the real bad guys could care less about. Using forced entry, like a crowbar to get through doors or windows, was a no-no for us. Our main tools were a cool head and our social engineering skills whenever it made sense to use them.

SOME THINGS TO CONSIDER FOR THE SECURITY OF YOUR BUILDINGS

Having worked for decades in the worlds of both physical and technical security, I find frequently that the people who manage these groups don't communicate with each other as well as they should. What we have at risk in the information security world can be considerably different from the things that we have at risk with pure physical security. What I mean by that is that certain locations should be looked at more closely when the risks of compromised or stolen intellectual property need to be more strongly protected against. It's always a good idea for the management team responsible for computer and information security to work closely with the management team responsible for overall building security. Following are a few of the areas where special emphasis is recommended.

Check all locks for proper operation

On every one of my team's penetration tests, we found at least one lock (either interior or exterior) in the building that wasn't functioning properly. This provided us with easy access to buildings and rooms that we shouldn't have been able to get into so easily. If employees are trained for just a few minutes on how to check to see if the locks on the doors that they use every day are working properly, this vulnerability can be all but eliminated. Building maintenance teams should also take a close look at all locks at least twice each year. Slightly misaligned strikes on the doorframes are the most common problem that we find. This is a serious problem, in that it defeats the purpose of the dead bolt feature of the lock. It takes me less than a second with my trusty fingernail file to see if a particular lock (bolt) has this problem. If it does, I'll know (and have the door opened) in a few seconds.

Use employee badges

I know these can be faked, but I still think that it is much better to have some form of visible identification worn by every employee at all times. Most of the companies that hired us did not have a policy requiring employees to wear their corporate ID badges all of the time. This made our social engineering attempts much easier. Once we were inside the buildings, it was as if everyone just took it for granted that we belonged there. Not only were we inside their buildings, but were also inside their firewalls and intrusion detection systems.

Employees can be somewhat trained to even detect fake ID badges. I was working for a large company that did require employees to always wear their ID badges when they were on company property. This was back in the days when color printers were just starting to show up in homes and offices. I created a fake ID that was intentionally made without any thought of quality control. The first time I wore it into the building instead of my real ID, I suspected that I would be stopped immediately and questioned about it. This was a security project, so I was prepared to explain myself. To my amazement, I never had to explain anything because it was never questioned. For the next three months, I wore it everywhere and not one person noticed it. During one of our security meetings, I told everyone in our group about my little experiment and most people were quite surprised that it was never detected.

Part two of my experiment had the most interesting results. I created a picture showing my two personal employee badges side by side. The fake one was quite obvious when seen next to the real one. We began to teach people how to take a slightly closer look at the badges that people were wearing as they walked through our buildings. From that time forward, I only wore my fake ID when I was conducting security awareness training for a group of employees. I was amazed at the number of my friends who had been through a version of the training and would spot the fake ID as I was walking past them on the way to another training class. Some would spot it from 10 feet away. These are the same people who didn't even notice it when they sat in my office just 3 feet away prior to being made aware of the threat. AWARENESS TRAINING WORKS!

Shredder technology keeps changing as well

As with everything else, these past few high tech years, shredder technology has changed considerably. Our team had gotten really good at putting strip-cut papers back together again years ago. We used to take bags of strip-cut documents that we found at the clients site back to our office during the test. Frequently, the bags of shredded documents were sitting outside in or near a dumpster where we simply picked them up and put them in our vehicle. Most of the time, documents that were strip-cut shredded all fell neatly into place in the bag or box where they were stored waiting to be disposed of. Our team was able to reassemble many of these documents within a few minutes. We would even take a document and paste the strips on a piece of cardboard in the shape of a Christmas tree, spreading the strips out as they were glued to the cardboard. Even with up to an inch between strips, the documents were easily readable once reassembled. We never even attempted to reconstruct a document that had been sent through a cross-cut shredder.

TIP

Today's small cross-cut shredders are very inexpensive and durable if you keep them oiled with the special oil available for shredders. I have a small one at home that cost only $39 and it creates a very small particle that would be next to impossible to reassemble. I have tried to wear it out for about 6 months and it just keeps on working. I'd also recommend encouraging all employees to get one for home use. I believe that it is a good policy to shred everything that comes to your home with any family member's name on it. Once you start doing this, it will become second nature and you will never need to wonder who might see your personal information once it leaves your home. Identity theft is on the rise.

Outdated but still sensitive documents should also be disposed of securely. When I worked at the Pentagon for the final 7 years of my military career, we were required to place certain sensitive (not classified, simply sensitive) documents into a safe containing a burn bag. To this day, I still use a burn bag at home for documents that I need to destroy that are too bulky for my shredder. It's a great way to clean out the barbeque grill on a cold sunny day. I feel good every time that I destroy sensitive personal documents rather than simply throwing them in a trashcan.

Keep an eye on corporate or agency phone books

When conducting a physical penetration test, the company's phone books were the first things that we went for. Once we got our hands on a corporate directory, the social engineering began. Most corporate phone books are laid out in a way that conveniently shows the entire corporate structure as well as chain of command, building addresses, and department titles. That kind of information also let us know the order in which to try entering the various buildings if there were several. Wherever the human resources department was located was usually where we went last. Here's why. As we tried to enter all of the other buildings by simply walking in the door like we belonged there, we were frequently challenged by a receptionist and asked where we were going. Our social engineering answer was always the same: "We were told that this is where human resources is located and we're here to fill out a job application." In every case, the receptionist simply sent us in the right direction. We thanked her or him and walked out the door and directly into the building next door to try the same con. The phone book even gave us the human resources manager's name to drop if we needed to be a little more convincing that we belonged there but were simply lost. It also gave us the rest of the important people in the organization whose names and titles we could drop if we needed to when challenged.

In addition to the names in the directories, most contained the physical location and chain-of-command ranking for the most important person in each department. It was often their offices, file cabinets, and trashcans that we spent the most time in during our nightly visits.

Employee awareness of the importance of a corporate directory will help ensure employees know how to safeguard this valuable corporate property. Old directories are still quite accurate, especially regarding buildings and department locations. They should be burned or shredded rather than simply thrown into the dumpster (we might even get hit if you throw them in while we're in there looking for goodies).

If paper directories can be eliminated altogether that would make our job a little tougher. Everything that you do to make it a little harder for the bad guys will make you a less likely target—they're looking for an easy mark. Online directories are better only if you don't let the social engineers get into your building. Once we were inside, we began looking for a monitor with the infamous sticky pad note on the side with the person's login id and password written on it. Once we logged onto the network as them, we could usually get to an online company directory if there was one.

Let me address one additional countermeasure while I'm on the subject of the login ID and password being written down and attached to the monitor or under your keyboard. Maybe that doesn't happen where you work, but we found at least one person who had done this on every job that we were hired to do. There is another reason we like to use someone else's login ID and password to get onto their networks. If we are able to do that, not only are we on their network on the inside of any firewall, but everything that we do will show up in some log as being done by the person who let us log in as them. Many larger companies now use at least some form of two-part authentication using either biometrics or a handheld authenticating device of some type to attain two-part authentication. Fortunately, some forms of biometric access control are getting to be very reasonable in price. Everything you do in the way of authentication will greatly reduce your vulnerability in this form of instant identity theft.

Unsecured areas are targets for tailgating

This was one of our most successful entry techniques regardless of the security procedures at the building. For some reason, people in the outside smoking areas didn't ever question our being there, and we were able to eventually walk in right behind them as they went back to work. We found that many corporations had good security at their main entrance points but were lacking at other entry and exit points. Members of our pen testing team were able to gain access on several occasions through parking deck or garage entry points that required card access. We would simply follow someone who was headed to the door and walk in behind him or her as we were pretending to search for our access cards that didn't exist.

> **WARNING**
>
> *Tailgating*, frequently called *piggybacking*, is simply following someone into a building after they open the door with an access card or by entering a door code. The bad guy will often pretend to be searching for his or her access card while waiting for someone to enter with a legitimate card. If there is no guard at the entrance, the bad guy will probably go unchallenged and unnoticed. You really need to think about this one before you decide how you want to solve it. You can't place the legitimate employee in the position of having to challenge the bad guy to ask for identification.
>
> The legitimate employee probably didn't come to work for you to be a security guard. On the other hand, you don't want bad guys just walking into your building. This problem is as old as dirt, but the solutions just keep getting more complex and expensive. Some companies employ cameras that photograph everyone who enters the building. Others are now employing biometrics scanners and other high tech devices. As with everything else in the security field, you need to get a system that is appropriate in cost for what you are trying to protect.
>
> At a minimum, you can make your employees aware of this threat and have them notify their immediate superior that someone followed them in and note the time and date of the incident. This same employee awareness session should instruct all employees to display an ID so that fellow employees, who may not know them, don't think that they are tailgating as they walk in behind them.

I have found it very interesting to learn things about people, in general, from the very people I have trained over the past three decades. I think about this often as I write about, or present on, topics relating to security. One very encouraging aspect I notice is that employees really do want to do whatever they can to help with overall security. It's amazing to watch their awareness level rise as I describe certain scenarios. There is something else that I have been saying for decades: "By far, the least expensive and most effective countermeasure for the overall security of any organization is the employees of that organization." If the employees of an organization are trained and taught to be aware of anyone not wearing proper identification where identification badges are used, the corporate security posture can be greatly increased.

> **WARNING**
>
> The countermeasures for this vulnerability really aren't as simple as we might think. Most employees who work at and are entering a building aren't security people. They are simply trying to get back to work. Even though someone trying to enter a building using the tailgating or piggybacking method should be challenged, challenging them is an uncomfortable situation for most people. Unless there is a strong corporate policy requiring all employees to challenge anyone they can't identify, this is a difficult problem to deal with. As an absolute minimum, employees should be trained on when and how to notify security if they suspect an unauthorized person has followed them in.

Special training for off-shift staff

I can't emphasize enough the need to train all of your second and third shift employees, and especially your janitorial services people, about the threats of social engineering. Obviously, pre-employment screening and possibly bonding are essential for any outside firm that you allow inside your buildings at any time. This is especially true for building access outside the normal 8 to 5 Monday through Friday standard work schedule. Frequently, these people have access to the master keys for a large section of the building and sometimes the entire building. They need awareness training to better prevent them from becoming victims of bad-guy social engineers who would like to borrow their keys for a minute or who get them to open a certain room.

This team should also immediately know whom to contact should they see anything suspicious that should be reported. If there is no immediate supervisor on duty during the evening or night shifts, everyone on that shift should know how to quickly contact the security forces. It can be very dangerous for them to approach a stranger themselves in an attempt to get them to leave.

This suggestion may not seem to fit in the context of this book, but let me mention it anyway. There is another very good reason to train your janitorial team (at least the team supervisors) to be extra watchful during the evening and night shift work hours. I have been teaching bomb recognition classes for the past 20 years. These same social engineering skills and physical building penetration methods could apply in any situation where the collective bad guys are trying to get into your building. The eyes and ears of the people who work in your building every day are critical when it comes to detecting anything or anyone unusual in the vicinity of the building. Bomb recognition training for key individuals and having an effective bomb incident plan are countermeasures that can be employed with considerable effect.

BOMB THREATS IN CHICAGO

This is a good time for a little side story that will let you see how the many risks, threats, vulnerabilities, and countermeasures overlap in the worlds of physical and technical security.

Several years ago, I received a call from a friend from the Chicago area asking for some help. He said his company has office locations in several cities throughout the country and one office out of the country. A series of bomb threats called into their corporate headquarters were causing them to lose a little sleep. They just wanted our team's suggestions for what they should do about it. This meant a trip to Chicago for us in February. (For the warm-blooded person from the sunny south that I am, that was a bit like a trip to Greenland in mid-winter.) We went anyway.

Prior to going, I decided to look on the Internet to see if I could find anything out about this company. This could also provide a hint as to why someone would call in these bomb threats that fortunately were only threats, so far!

The company flew in their senior managers from around the country and we suggested that their corporate attorneys and risk managers attend the training as well. They were going to learn everything they wanted to know but were afraid to ask about bombs and bomb threats.

We arrived a day early, and we asked if they would like for us to take a look around their corporate headquarters building to see if we saw any glaring physical vulnerabilities that could allow someone to easily place a bomb in or close to the outside of their building. The outside perimeter was about as close to perfect as I had ever seen in a building of that size. As we were looking at the various locations from the inside, my eyes kept being drawn to their newly installed access control system. Each employee had been issued an ID card that would allow him or her to enter certain doors at specific times of the day. The system also kept track of the times that they entered and left the building.

My fellow team member gave me a strange "you've done it now" kind of look when I said that a simple metal coat hanger might be able to compromise the entire system. I was about to be put to the test as we approached the next set of outside access doors in that part of the building. The person who had hired us was standing there with a metal coat hanger and he handed it to me.

Keep in mind that we were walking around inside the nicely heated building without our coats. I was asked to go outside and attempt to open the doors with the coat hanger. On the other side of those doors it was still Greenland in February. I politely said I would go outside (without my coat) and try for a few minutes. All that I asked is if I started to turn blue, please "open the door from the inside and let me back in."

That was never necessary. I was back inside in less than 30 seconds and everyone was standing there with a deer in the headlights look as I calmly walked through the quarter-of-a-million-dollar security system with no indication that I had ever been there. This was not the first time I had seen this issue with an improperly adjusted access control system. The system detected motion from the inside that automatically unlocked the door when someone was moving toward the door. I noticed that it detected us walking past the door from a considerable distance away. It was just too sensitive. I also noticed that the locking mechanism opened only one of a pair of double doors and that the motion sensor was mounted dead center between the double doors. The only thing protecting the opening between the double doors was a thin piece of weather-stripping. While I was standing outside briefly freezing to death, it was a simple matter of taking my thin metal coat hanger and sliding it between the two doors while rapidly moving it up and down. Within seconds, I heard the familiar click that I was hoping to hear. The security system thought I was inside because that's where it saw the motion of my coat hanger.

All of the senior managers, attorneys, risk managers and security team members were in a training room the following morning for their day of bomb threat training. I opened the meeting by letting them know that this was most likely a low probability threat but that they were smart to decide ahead of time to learn as much as they could about what they should do about these threats. We were going to spend the rest of the day learning about bombs, bomb threats, bombs in buildings, bombs outside of buildings, and all kinds of other scary things. It was going to be a fun day.

As I was finishing up my introduction, I walked around the room and placed a small packet of one to three pages in front of four of their most important people. As the four targeted people started to look through the papers placed in front of them, I simply stated that this is your high probability threat and something you need to address immediately in our opinion. The papers contained just about everything we would ever need to know about these people. Where they lived, how they most likely traveled to work, in some cases, where they went to college, where their children went to school, and much more. All of it was gained from a few social engineering phone calls and about an hour searching the Internet for information about them. Much of the information about these people (and possibly about you) was out on the Internet. It's not easy, but these people-finding search engines all have an opt-out option to have your name and contact information removed from their databases. Just type the words "people search engines" into www.google.com for the most recent list of these services. You should put your name in some of them to see what information is out there about you. You will most likely be surprised at how many places your name pops up.

CHECK THOSE PHONE CLOSETS

If your building is in rented space, or in a multi-tenant building, it's a good idea to have someone perform a thorough check of your hard wiring for the phone lines. You don't know who was in there before you were, and old wiring is sometimes not removed when new tenants move in. On more than one occasion, our teams found old phone cable wiring still in place and being used in an inappropriate manner by inside employees. While we are on the subject, the need for physical security also comes into play when considering the corporate PBX (Private Branch Exchange), which is the internal phone company for larger corporations. The PBX may still have a modem for remote maintenance needs, and the phone number for that modem may be written on the wall right near the modem. Our pen testing teams frequently found access to many of the rooms where PBXs were located by using our social engineering skills to get someone to open the door for us.

REMOVE A FEW DOOR SIGNS

It always amazed us to see rooms that had a sign over them saying *Computer Room* or *Phone Closet*. Obviously, the people who work there know where it is, and there is no reason for anyone else to know what's in there. It's all right for the room to have a number on the door that building maintenance would understand, but there is little reason to make it so easy for the bad guys to find their best target. This may sound like I am getting a little too picky, but I'm not. The more difficult you make it for people who don't have a need to know about these critical rooms, the more secure you will be.

TIP

If you are going to have high security locks on any doors in your building, then dedicated computer rooms and phone closets would be first on my list of rooms needing the most secure locking mechanisms.

REVIEW VIDEO SECURITY LOGS

Normally, after we have completed our mission and have taken all of the evidence that we have been there out to our vehicle, we would re-enter the building and try to be seen by the building security cameras that we knew were there. Hopefully, there were some we didn't know about. We would even jump up and down waving our arms just to see if anyone would eventually report us. As far as we know, we were never reported as being seen on the tapes recorded by those cameras. One of three things must have happened: the cameras weren't working (unlikely), the people looking at the playback of the video missed seeing us on the tape (probably unlikely), or they were never looked at (most likely). I'd recommend that someone in the company periodically test this process. If there were internal auditors in the company, this would be a good audit step. That entire expensive surveillance system is worthless if whatever is captured on tape isn't ever seen by a human who can do something about it.

This is another area where I believe that the people responsible for the techno security of the systems need to talk to the people responsible for physical security. Cameras and lights have always been countermeasures I like to see in and around buildings and personal homes. They can scream "go find an easier target" to the bad guys of the world. There may be areas where additional cameras could be recommended to help improve the security of critical areas or rooms. The team responsible for overall physical security might not know about these areas unless you tell them. They may already be monitoring areas that you aren't aware of, which could help you if you have an incident.

The reason I mentioned personal homes several times throughout this chapter is that your home can be another area of vulnerability for physical penetrations or social engineering attempts to gain specific information. Many people now do much of their work from home on workstations connected to the Internet at high speed. I employ as much physical security at my home office as I have at every other office where I have worked. The technology associated with home security products has increased significantly while the prices for that security have dropped along with the cost of the latest computers.

I recently installed a number of digitally controlled security cameras around the perimeter of my home as well as motion-activated security lights in all approach areas. This may sound a little paranoid, but I know I am much more protected than most of my neighbors and my family feels very safe knowing it would be difficult to attempt anything around our home without someone knowing about it. The security cameras are also motion activated, so the only thing I see is recorded activity when there is movement detected by the camera monitoring software. With the rapid advances in technology, these kinds of sophisticated security systems are very affordable and powerful.

CONSIDER ADDING MOTION-SENSING LIGHTS

Most of our social engineering-based inside penetration tests would have been much less successful if the companies that hired us had motion-sensing light controls installed in every office throughout their buildings. These are not the same kinds of light controls that I installed around my home. Those would help on the outside of any building. What I am talking about here are the motion sensors that turn on the lights inside an office or room when someone walks in. These same sensors turn the lights off after a preset time once the final person leaves the room.

Every penetration test we were hired to conduct had several buildings of opportunity for us to attempt to enter, and every one of them had at least a few lights on all night long. While we were conducting our initial surveillance of the buildings, that was one of the first things that we noted. Are there lights left on at night, and if so, are they the same lights every night? In most cases with a building having about 15 floors there would be six or eight lights left on. Our assumption was that whoever was assigned to that office was either still there or forgot to turn the light off when they left. Either way, it created a good situation for us. If a random number of lights were left on each night, the security forces would not have any easy way to decide if everything was normal at any given time.

As they patrolled from the outside (we were watching them do this from the outside and from the inside once we got into the building), they really had no reference for what would be a normal building profile. As we became bolder toward the end of a penetration test, we would even turn certain lights on just to see if security would become suspicious of this activity. No one ever did.

Several of the buildings we penetrated didn't have anyone working in them at night. If motion-sensing lights had been used throughout these buildings, we would have looked for softer targets. If we had entered a room in a completely dark building, the light coming on would have been very abnormal for any security team member who saw it.

There is another good reason to install these sensors. Over time, the energy saved by having the lights automatically turn off when there was no human around needing light could eventually pay for the additional cost of the sensor.

SUBTERRANEAN VULNERABILITIES

This is certainly not a new topic, but it is one that I suspect that most people don't ever think about. Those of us who work in major cities, and even in small cities, walk over manholes every day. That's certainly nothing to be concerned about, but do we ever consider what's under those small circles of metal? While most companies don't own the manhole covers (and what's under them) surrounding their building, it's still a good idea to check on their security. The extent of the infrastructure that exists below the streets of most cities is incredible. Figure 2.1 a boring picture of a boring manhole on a boring street. Pretty neat huh?

If you enter the words "manhole security" in Google, you will find a few interesting articles about how manholes can be protected as well as a few stories that discuss the problem with manhole cover theft in some cities.

One of my fondest memories of a manhole in the movies was seeing Mother (Dan Aykroyd) working away in a nearby manhole at the beginning of the movie *Sneakers* in 1992. His penetration team was hired to test the security of a bank. The story was

FIGURE 2.1

Boring manhole cover

pure fiction, but the vulnerability of what could be accessed from within certain manholes was real. Here's a manhole cable vault that Mother would have been proud to work in. The picture in Figure 2.2 was taken on the other side of a typical manhole cover that you would see as you walked over it.

Most manholes like this have long since been secured, especially since 9/11. That doesn't mean that you shouldn't become aware of any manhole that could be used to access your building. This is even truer for multi-tenant (that's most of them) buildings in large cities.

FIGURE 2.2

More interesting stuff on the other side of the manhole

CLEAN OUT YOUR ELEPHANT BURIAL GROUND

What happens when that computer (and elephant in this analogy) that you purchased a few years ago finally dies or becomes too old to do any work for you? I'll bet that it gets moved to your elephant burial ground with the rest of the electronic equipment that still looks new and valuable but isn't fast enough to keep up anymore. You can't simply put it out for the trash collectors to pick up, so there it sits, sometimes for years.

This burial ground was a prime target for our penetration teams as we conducted our vulnerability tests from inside our clients' buildings. We frequently used our social engineering skills to find out where the old computers were stored. If it was in a locked room, we would find a way to either get someone to open the door for us, or we would use our lock picks or pick gun to open the door.

TIP

Old disk drives will be an area of concern for years to come. Terabyte drives are now readily available (and cheap) at stores like Office Depot for anyone to purchase. Less than 15 years ago, I was thrilled to be able to purchase a 200-megabyte disk drive for $200. I was the first person that I'm aware of in my circle of friends to own a drive of this size for a mere $1 per megabyte. Now I'm seeing 500-gigabyte disk drives on sale for around $50 after rebates. This growth in technology is now happening so fast that most of us just take it for granted. The bad guys don't!

The tip here is to be careful with those old disk drives. This applies to the computers at home as well as at the office. There is much valuable data on them, and the risk is climbing as the storage capacity of every drive climbs rapidly each year. Be certain to remove all disk drives from computers that you plan to donate, give away, or simply throw away. I smash mine up with a hammer before disposing of the drives at my local electronic recycling center.

Old habits die hard, and this one will probably be no exception. As a country, we have been throwing away just about everything since the end of World War II. During the war, security was on everybody's mind, and each person encouraged friends and neighbors to be careful what they said and what they threw away. (I wasn't around during World War II, but I was the product of a happy homecoming after the war.) As individuals and companies, we need to bring back just a little bit of that way of thinking. We need to become aware of this problem and encourage each other to be more careful with assets by being more careful with our trash.

TIP

Many of the topics presented for thought in this chapter and throughout the entire book are just as appropriate in our homes as they are in our offices. This is especially true of our home office computers, networks, and trash!

Most of us are inundated with snail mail at home as well as at work. I have a policy in our home that nothing leaves in our trash can that clearly has any family member's name on it. This requires a little extra effort to destroy a single page of a credit card offer each time I receive one. If it has a name and address on it (obviously everything that arrives at my home does), I destroy that part of the document. Every small thing that I can do to protect my family from things like identity theft or credit card fraud helps me to sleep better each night.

SPOT CHECK THOSE DROP CEILINGS

On several occasions, we used our social engineering skills to get into buildings and then install a sniffer in the telecommunications hub for that floor. I recommend that all companies have their building maintenance teams perform a spot check above all suspended ceilings at least twice each year. We have been amazed at some of the things that we found up there while we were conducting the penetration test. You may even stumble into a security vulnerability you weren't even aware of.

There is one thing we learned about telecommunications and wiring throughout buildings. Wires just never seem to go away! This was especially true in multi-tenant buildings. In many cases, the office space was in use by another company or organization that had different needs from the current company occupying the same space. There was only one occasion where I can remember finding something in the drop ceiling that we believed was placed there for covert reasons. On another occasion, we found undocumented phone line extensions that were apparently used by a former tenant. They were not disconnected, and one of those lines was connected to a phone in a secure conference room. The people who had hired us to conduct this test were very surprised to learn that. It was our opinion at the conclusion of our penetration test that these extension lines were not added maliciously. They were simply left over from when the office was used by the prior tenant. I also suspect that our team was the first to have looked into the space above the drop ceiling in that building. There is simply no way to know what is up there unless someone looks!

This suggestion of checking out the space above the ceiling tiles would also be a suggestion I would make if considering places to hide things like bombs. We walk under drop ceilings day after day and normally have no reason to think about what might be up there. Usually, there is a least a foot of clearance between the grid work holding the drop ceiling in place and the ceiling itself. I have seen as much as 3 feet of clearance. You may be amazed at what you find hidden up there (hopefully it's not ticking).

INTERNAL AUDITORS ARE YOUR FRIENDS

I have a lot of personal friends who were internal auditors for a variety of different sized companies. I suspect most of them would be very happy to hear me say that they are friends of the people who work in their respective companies. For most people, it isn't any fun being audited.

Just about everything I have mentioned in this chapter would make a good spot check audit point for an internal auditor. Someone on the good-guy side of the fence needs to check for these possible vulnerabilities and insure that the proper countermeasures are employed before they are exploited and become security incidents.

My experience with auditors over the years has been that things usually happen once they have made a suggestion for improving in a certain area of concern. Many of the larger corporations have information system auditors who have a primary responsibility for looking after the technical world within a corporation. That's a lot to keep up with. Most mid-sized corporations have internal auditors who have the information system responsibility in addition to the audit responsibility for every-thing else that needs to be audited. I believe that much of what I talk about in the following chapter regarding locks should also be something that is audited from time to time. This is especially true knowing that much of what I discuss in Chapter 3 has been well known to the good guys as well as the bad guys for years now (thanks to YouTube and security-related websites).

BONUS: HOME SECURITY TIPS

I probably spend more time considering home security than any other topic. Maybe it's because I now spend most of my time there. I also like the feeling of having a well-defended home for my family any time that I'm away. I watch the local news and keep up with the current threats in the vicinity of our city. If there ever was a place that needed security in depth, it's your home. Your job as the owner of a home or the head of your family is to make your home a tougher target than the rest of the homes in your neighborhood. You certainly don't want anything to happen to any of your neighbors, but if the bad guys are cruising the neighborhood looking for a place to hit, you want that place to be any place but yours.

In preparation for writing this chapter I looked up a number of different web links but I decided not to use those. By the time any book goes to print, things change on the Internet. What I had decided to do is to give you a list of topics to enter in the search field for http://www.YouTube.com. For several years now, I have been mak-ing a statement while speaking at security meetings that "if it's on YouTube, you had better know about it". I can't think of a single thing that I have tried to find more information about where I haven't found that information with a quick YouTube search. It's absolutely amazing! So many of the things in the physical security world, and especially the things that deal with locks and bypass methods, used to be known only to a select number of people. Now they have become common knowledge for everyone in the world.

TIP

I have used several of the digital security cameras sold at stores like Sam's and Costco, and for the money they are excellent. The quality of the cameras that are available in a system costing about $1500 is pretty amazing. I spent another $1500 having someone wire mine, and I'm very happy I did. It's very comforting to know that when my driveway motion sensor activates with a mild beep, I can go to my security camera logs and see what caused the driveway alarm to activate. The current systems that come with the standalone computer and a good size hard drive can record for about 4 weeks before overwriting the logs. Even though my cameras have infrared sensors for nighttime use, the motion-sensing lights around our home are what really bring the camera's lens to life. Light is paint for video and still photography. The more light, the better. Most systems even have the ability to produce a file with any given camera in the system and create a runtime version of the viewer that could be given to police if necessary.

The combined system with motion-sensing cameras, motion-sensing driveway devices, and motion-sensing lights provide a peace of mind for my family that I really can't put a value on.

SUMMARY

—Low Tech Jack

I've thrown a lot at you in this combination of risks, threats, vulnerabilities, and countermeasures associated with improving your physical security posture. What I have tried to address in this chapter is what I consider the low-hanging fruit that the bad guys of the world are very aware of. Most of the vulnerabilities mentioned are fairly easy to fix once you know about them. Many of you who read this book won't even be responsible for correcting your corporate vulnerabilities, but you might be able to get this book to someone in your organization who can correct them.

Security will always be a long-term team effort. This is true for every size company as well as every size family at home. If you have a computer in your home and you access the Internet to pay your bills or check your bank statement, you need to consider security every time you do. Even though we are in a very technical world that will do nothing but get technically more complex, we can't ever forget about physical security at home and at work. If you become a victim of identity theft, you will spend about 2 years getting your financial life back in order. Prevention is your absolute best countermeasure for most, if not all, of these possible threats.

Stay safe out there!

More about locks and ways to low tech hack them

INFORMATION IN THIS CHAPTER

* A Little More about Locks and Lock Picking
* Forced Entry—And Other Ways to Cheat!
* Let's Break into a Semi–High Security Room
* Keys and Key Control
* Bait and Switch War Story That Could Happen to You
* Some Places to Go to Learn and Have Some Fun
* More about Keys and How to Make One If You Don't Have One
* Ways to Make a Key If You Didn't Bring a Key Machine
* One Final Lock to Talk about and Then We're Done

As I was preparing to write this chapter, I found myself thinking back over the past 45 years of my life. I consider myself one of the most blessed people on the planet when I think about all the things that I've been able to do and learn. I became somewhat of a techno geek while attending vocational-technical high school back in the mid-sixties. I've found electronics to be absolutely fascinating. In my senior year I was able to design a variable-speed (computerized) control for a synchronous motor using a handful of transistors. It was considered by the school to be their first computerized control of an AC synchronous motor. When I visited the school about 10 years later, I was pleasantly surprised to see that they were still using the training manual that I had written describing how to construct this computerized control. It had taken me weeks to figure out how to do this. Using the manual, a new student could learn how to do it in less than an hour. In a sense, all of my time spent on experimenting, designing, and working with these transistors was pretty high tech, but it became a low tech process for the people who had the manual in front of them describing how to do it. This is exactly what happens with just about everything that starts off high tech it becomes fairly low tech to implement or exploit once you know how.

A LITTLE MORE ABOUT LOCKS AND LOCK PICKING

"What in the world does this have to do with locks?" you might be asking yourself. As I reminisced a little more, I remembered my return from Vietnam in the late 1960's (not 1860s like some of my friends think - I know - I'm old!). I had always enjoyed the physical security world, but I'd still had a tremendous interest in the worlds of technology and technical security. Shortly after returning from Vietnam in the early 70s, I decided to become a locksmith. After completing about 6 months of training I had an opportunity to purchase half ownership of a locksmith shop in Baltimore. I learned a lot during the few years that I worked as a locksmith part-time. One of the things that I learned that greatly impacts some of what I'll be discussing in this chapter is that locks don't change very much. Most of the types of locks that I worked on 45 years ago are still in use today. Many of them had been used for decades before I became a locksmith. The difference between locks used in the physical security world and the current world of technology fascinated me. I've been saying this during presentations for years, "regarding technology, if you can buy it, it's obsolete". Over the years I have continuously said "The biggest potential problem with technical security is a lack of proper physical security." Throughout this chapter I'm going to be talking about a few things concerning a few types of locks that have existed for over 100 years, as well as some suggestions for ways to improve our knowledge of what makes a good lock versus a not-so-good lock. I hope you will learn a few things along the way.

> **WARNING**
>
> Please keep in mind that conducting any of the activities mentioned in this chapter on locks you do not personally own could very well be illegal. If you are a paid penetration tester, conducting an inside penetration test, you need to be sure that you have permission from the company that hired you to use this form of attack. My main reasoning for even discussing any of this is to make people aware of the possibilities of things that the bad guys can do, should you let them into your building. This is why for 20+ years, I've been preaching about the need for increased physical security to prevent access to these critical resources in the first place. I personally would not suspect that most inside penetration tests would go to this level of testing. You wouldn't be testing the ability to do this to a lock as much as you would be testing your social engineering ability to have someone open that door to let you into the room to be able to conduct this attack. As I've mentioned several times throughout this book, once we were inside the buildings it was assumed by everyone that we came in contact with that we belonged there.

As with many of the things I write, this chapter will have an interesting flavor of risk management. Just what are the risks, threats, vulnerabilities, and counter-measures that we should consider when looking at the locks in our homes as well as at work? Another statement that I have been making for years regarding security in general is that if there's a discussion of a certain situation on YouTube, you had better know about it. If it's on YouTube, you can bet that all of the people that want to exploit it have probably already seen it.

FIGURE 3.1

My 110-year-old lock: eBay, $3

Figure 3.1 is a picture of the oldest pin tumbler lock that I own. On the bottom of the lock, there is a patent date of 1901. This is a pin tumbler lock very much like the locks in most of our homes. I tried for quite some time (unsuccessfully) to open it. As you will see a little later in the chapter, it can be picked open. I have had some fairly sophisticated lock picks for decades. As with anything else in life, practice, practice, practice is the only way to stay good at just about anything. Unfortunately, I don't practice very much with my lock toys any more because of other time commitments. I still have several hundred locks in my collection and find each one to be a very interesting puzzle. I'll also be recommending a few places to go and a few books to learn a little more about these cool mechanical devices. It is very encouraging to me to see more and more (mostly young) people begin to take up lock picking and lock knowledge as a fun hobby. Even mentioning lock picking as a hobby is a fairly new thing for me. For years the inner workings of locks were considered the secret things of locksmiths and lock manufacturers. I've always been one to not necessarily agree with that need for secrecy. My feelings have always been if the bad guys of the world are aware of certain things including vulnerabilities, the good guys need to be aware of them as well. I want to say this once again, because I think it's critically important. If there is a vulnerability that's explained in detail on YouTube and other places on the Internet, you and whoever is in charge of security for your organization had better know about.

WARNING

Possessing lock-picking equipment is not legal in some states. If you intend to pursue lock picking as a hobby, or as a part of conducting your own "official" penetration test, you still need to be sure that you are not breaking the law in any way by making or using these tools. Laws and restrictions about owning and using lock-picking equipment vary greatly between states, counties, and cities. In some locations, it is a crime to use your lock picks to open your neighbors' home, even upon their request, if they lock their keys inside and ask you to help.

Continued

WARNING—cont'd

As with almost any subject today, there is a wealth of information regarding the legal issues associated with lock picking available on www.google.com by entering "are lock picking tools legal to own" or something similar. Another link showing information on this subject is http://www.lockwiki.com/index.php/Legal_issues, which shows the current requirements in all fifty states as well as a few other countries. Another website with a little more detail regarding the laws of each state is http://www.lockpickguide.com/legalityoflockpicks.html.

The bad guys' that I collectively refer to throughout this chapter most likely won't care if they are legal or not, but you need to care!

What kinds of locks are the most popular?

In many ways, locks are the hardware versions of the passwords and authentication devices that we use to gain access to our computers. They are also what I like to call the low-hanging fruit of your perimeter security. Unfortunately, many times, they are the devices on which we spend the least amount of money (including in our homes). I'm going to try to convince you to spend a little more money for a whole lot more protection when selecting locks for your office or home.

In preparation for this part of my chapter, I wanted to see what kinds of locks people typically purchased for their personal use. I do a lot of people watching while I'm out and about. It's fascinating. Last fall, as I was looking around at the locks available in different stores, I watched as several people came over to the area where the locks were displayed and quickly picked up a lock or two for school. Most of them chose an inexpensive brand of combination lock that has been a standard for decades. That didn't surprise me, and in most cases, it is the required lock for the lockers in many schools. I also watched as several people purchased padlocks with keys. What every one of them did wasn't a surprise either—most of them purchased the CHEAPEST lock that they could find. I watched this over and over again. Little do they realize that they got what they paid for.

For those people who didn't purchase a combination lock, most of them picked up either a cheap pin tumbler padlock as shown in Figure 3.2, or a warded padlock as shown in Figure 3.3, none of which costs more than $5. The keys for these two types of locks are shown in Figure 3.4. The key on the right is the warded padlock key, and the key on the left is the pin tumbler key. These locks looked as strong as the better locks on the outside. Anyone who knows even a little bit about locks knows that these less expensive locks are just going to keep the honest people honest. They are not high security locks. How about a quick lock awareness war story to give you an example of how easily the wrong type of lock can be bypassed:

NOTE

Our penetration team had been inside the building of a customer who had hired us for about 4 hours when we came across a row of file cabinets that must have contained some important documents. There were about ten tall file cabinets in a row, and each of them had a vertical bar attached to the cabinet with a padlock securing the bar to the cabinet. This was more security than we frequently saw on these kinds of cabinets.

When we were working on the inside of a building (after social engineering our way in), we tried to look at everything that we thought could be a vulnerability. I took the time to quickly examine every lock on these file cabinets. It wasn't surprising to me to find one that looked the same as the others on the outside, but was drastically different on the inside. Someone had replaced one of the pin tumbler padlocks (Figure 3.2) with a warded padlock (Figure 3.3). In less than 10 seconds, I opened the warded lock, taped my business card on the INSIDE of the file cabinet to prove that we were there, and closed the lock again. The bad guys could have gotten to the entire content of that file cabinet just as quickly. Warded padlocks are among the oldest lock designs in existence. A skeleton key capable of opening many hundreds of locks can be created by filing down some of the bittings on any key for one of these locks.

Why was this one lock different from the rest of them? I suspect that someone either lost the key to the original (slightly more secure) lock or lost the lock itself. If that happened, they could have simply gone to the hardware section of their local store and purchased a lock that looked like the rest of the locks on those file cabinets. If they went with the mindset of most people that I watched purchase locks, they would have purchased the least expensive lock that they could get as long as it looked as strong as the original lock.

Let's take a look at a few types of locks to help you learn which ones are more secure than others: Figure 3.2 shows a pin tumbler padlock. It's the exact kind of lock that we saw on most of the file cabinet where padlocks were used in buildings that we were pen testing. Pin tumbler locks are also the most common type of lock that we see in homes and office buildings on doors. These locks can be picked with a little practice.

The warded padlock that we found on a file cabinet during one of our pen tests looked about the same as the more secure pin tumbler padlocks, but it had a different keyway, as seen in the lock shown in Figure 3.3.

FIGURE 3.2

Pin tumbler padlock

FIGURE 3.3

Warded padlock

I was able to open this one (Figure 3.3) in less than 10 seconds, and you could too. Opening locks like this one isn't even lock picking in my opinion. The pick sets for these are more like master keys. A simple pick for warded padlocks like this one can be made by simply filing down all of the bittings as shown by the arrows in Figure 3.4.

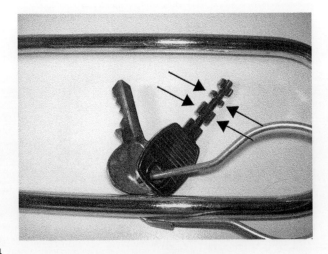

FIGURE 3.4

Pin tumbler and warded keys

Purchasing better quality locks will be cost effective

So, are there any padlocks that are reasonably secure and not terribly expensive? My favorite has always been a lock that looks a little different but has a lot of leave-me-alone features. One of my favorites is a lock made in Germany and it's quite secure for its price of about $25. It's the pin tumbler lock shown in Figure 3.5 with all five of its pins being mushroom-type driver pins. Mushroom pins are shaped somewhat like an hourglass. This shape can cause the pins to bind as someone attempts to pick them.

While I don't consider this lock to be maximum security, it is considerably better than most of the inexpensive locks that I see out there. This is the type of lock that you will see on about 90% of the storage facilities that allow you to use your own lock. It is a pin tumbler lock and does offer a few additional security features. First, it would be more difficult to attack with bolt cutters or even a hacksaw. You can't see it by looking at this lock, but this lock also offers something that I really like called *key retention*. What that means is that while the lock is unlocked, you cannot remove the key from the lock. The key is retained in the lock until it is secured again. When I remove the lock from my storage location, I immediately place the lock in my pocket with the keys still in the lock. That same keychain also contains the keys to just about every other lock that I need access to. With a huge lock in my pocket I am very unlikely to attempt to start the car as I leave the storage area without seeing this monster hanging on the key ring. With the key retained in the lock whenever it is unlocked, I always know that, if the key is in my pocket with no lock attached to it, the lock is locked somewhere, hopefully back on my locker at the storage facility. I can't tell you the number of times that I returned to a storage facility that didn't use this key retention process to double check that I had really locked the door. I've always liked key retention type locks for that very reason.

FIGURE 3.5

Disk-type pin tumbler lock: eBay, $15

Let's consider a couple of other features of this lock. In addition to being difficult to remove by pure force, it contains pins that are mushroom shaped. These are much more difficult to pick than standard pins. There is something else that I've watched develop as more and more locks are manufactured. I've begun to see a number of locks that look very much like this one but aren't designed with anywhere near its quality. This lock retails for around $25. There are versions of this out there that retail for as little as $5. As we've all heard many times throughout life, you will definitely get what you pay for.

Be aware of lock vulnerabilities

There is one vulnerability for this type of lock that is all too common. I have incorporated my own countermeasure in an attempt to prevent this from happening to me. As I look through the complex of this storage location I see every one of the locks like this placed on the HASP (the device on the door where the lock is placed) the same way that I had placed the one in the photograph. The keyway where you would insert your key is open for easy access. In my mind, a lock placed in this position would be most vulnerable to drilling. This is an old/new threat that is now much easier to use with the advent of battery-powered drills. In the 70s when I started as a locksmith we didn't have battery-powered drills. If we couldn't get to a location where power tools were needed, we would have to come up with a generator or some sort of auxiliary power from our locksmith van. Things have changed! Very powerful battery-operated drills are now available everywhere. If I can get to that keyway and begin to drill out those pins, thereby creating what's known as a *shear line*, I will be able to retract that bolt and remove the lock. The lock would certainly be destroyed, and there would be evidence of forced entry, but the contents of the storage shed (or whatever else was being secured by the lock) would most likely be gone. I'll be discussing drilling again later as we talk about a few other issues with locks. For now, let me show you what I did to slightly change this vulnerability for my lock on my storage facility. Let's take a look at Figure 3.6.

At first glance, this looks like the same picture as the photo in Figure 3.5. It is but with the exception that the keyway is no longer in the same vulnerable position. Doing this doesn't completely remove the threat of someone coming along with the battery-powered drill and drilling out the keyway. What it does do is make it much more difficult for someone to be able to do that. The space between the keyway and the side of the building frame is now only a couple of inches. For me, that makes it just a little bit more difficult to get my key into the lock. It also makes it much more difficult, even with a fairly small battery-powered drill and short bit, to be able to easily drill out that lock. The bottom line is that my lock is now a slightly tougher target than most of the rest of them in that complex. As a fun exercise, one afternoon I drove through the complex looking at locks that people used. I didn't find any of them that have made the changes that I did to make it more difficult to drill. What I did find really didn't surprise me either. I saw countless locks that I'm sure cost no

FIGURE 3.6

Lock turned 180 degrees

more than $3 to $4 that people would put on their storage containers obviously full of valuable material to them. It just continues to amaze me after 40+ years of dealing with this that so few people really understand the vulnerability of these very inexpensive locks. I have always tried to use the best available security for whatever I was trying to protect. In some cases that required a very expensive lock or vault or safe. In other cases, like the entrance to my home crawlspace where there is little of value, it might not be necessary to have an incredibly expensive lock. I see this time and time again in homes as well as in industry where we were conducting penetration tests, that these devices were just misunderstood. In many cases people could spend not even twice as much as they currently spend on locks and get something considerably better and more secure.

TIP

We're going to dive a little deeper into some of my thoughts on locks as we go through this chapter. I do want to encourage you to consider purchasing Deviant Ollam's excellent book titled *Practical Lock Picking: A Physical Penetration Tester's Training Guide* (ISBN: 978-1-59749-611-7, Syngress). It's an excellent book, and Deviant is well known in the industry as a person actively pursuing the hobby of lock picking. I own the book and I find it excellent for a number of reasons. Deviant has a unique knack for explaining with drawings exactly how certain types of locks work. Some of the things that I will be covering in this chapter and the rest of the book will be my thoughts, experiences, and opinions concerning locks and bypass methods. These fascinating mechanical devices will play an important part at our homes and at work well into the foreseeable future. The lack of knowledge, or even a basic understanding of locks and the way that they work, has surprised me throughout my career in security.

FORCED ENTRY—AND OTHER WAYS TO CHEAT!

Unfortunately, getting past whatever is keeping a certain door cabinet or window locked often causes damage. Even picking a lock with spring steel picks rubbing against brass pins can cause some damage. Sometimes the good guys, and most of the time the bad guys, could care less about this potential damage. I want to talk a little bit about the vulnerability of forced entry. As with most things concerning locks, these vulnerabilities are not new. If we look at any door as an example, and want to simply get it to open, there are a number of ways to do that. In emergency situations, the good guys will do whatever they have to do to get through that door. Let me show you a picture of a typical rim cylinder lock that would control the dead bolt lock on a typical door (Figure 3.7). This could be a door at an office or at your home.

For a rim cylinder lock, this one is very high quality. The weight of the lock is not always an indication of quality, but usually a very lightweight lock will not be as strong as a stainless steel or an all-brass high quality lock. The serrated copper-looking piece sticking out the back of the lock is the tailpiece. When the key is inserted, and all of the pins are at the proper shear line, the plug will turn, which will turn the tailpiece and retract the bolt. This sounds like a simple process, and it is. That tailpiece is inserted through a mechanism that turns the bolt and retracts it from the strike in the door frame. When I'm asked the simple question, "What allows the door to be opened?," I answer by saying, "The retraction of the bolt is what allows the door to open." We'll take a look at the bolt in a few minutes. The important point here is that the bolt itself is retracted by the movement of the tailpiece. If the lock cylinder and the tailpiece were not there, a simple screwdriver would easily act as a tailpiece to turn the mechanism to retract the bolt.

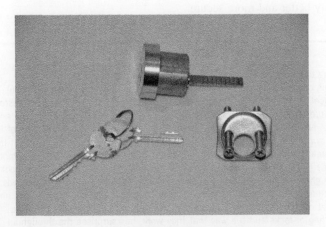

FIGURE 3.7

Rim cylinder lock with keys and mounting plate: eBay, $4

In Figure 3.7, there is also a silver piece of metal with two screws sticking through it. This is the mounting plate. It would be located on the inside of the door and the screws would be fastened to the back of a lock through the holes in the mounting plate and into the threaded holes in the lock body. This is the way that most rim cylinder locks are installed in our homes. The potential weak point in this construction is the two holes in the mounting plate. Most of the mounting plates for the locks in my collection are made of fairly soft sheet metal.

A time-tested low tech method of forced entry

At first glance, this is going to sound like cheating. I have on occasion had the need to get into a house very quickly without a key. This was when I was a practicing locksmith years ago. This low tech way of entry was often used in emergency situations where someone's life was in danger. If a bad guy was exploiting this form of entry, it would certainly be considered forced entry. (There are YouTube examples of this vulnerability as well.) I am sharing it to let you know that anyone with access to the Internet could now know how to do this. As I will continue to say, if it's out there on the Internet, you had better know about it. Just enter this into your favorite search engine: "How to use a dent puller to remove an auto ignition lock." The dent puller that you will see described in a number of places on the Internet is what we refer to as a *slide hammer*. The one that I have weighs about 3 pounds and has a drill chuck on the end of it (Figure 3.8). This has one of those case-hardened screws in the drill chuck. This method of forced entry could be used to remove a lock cylinder in an automobile or in a home or business. With the rim tumbler lock such as shown in Figure 3.7, it would be a simple matter of twisting the screw directly into the

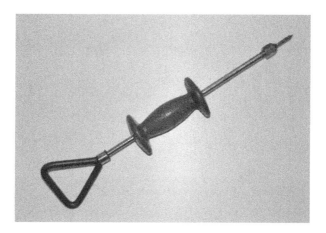

FIGURE 3.8

Slide hammer: flea market, $10

keyway of the lock and sliding the weight on the slide hammer back heavily several times. The entire cylinder and tailpiece came out every time that our locksmith team needed to use this forced method entry over 40 years ago. This is not a new vulnerability. With the tailpiece removed, it would be a simple matter to place a screwdriver into the lock and retract the bolt. As I said earlier, what allows the door to open is the retraction of the bolt. It really doesn't matter to the door how that happened. In this case it happened with forced entry.

There are a couple of countermeasures that can make this exploit a lot more difficult. In my locks at home, I installed a small steel washer between the head of the screw and the mounting plate. Doing this would require a lot more force to remove the cylinder. I'm not going to say that this would prevent the cylinder from being removed, but it would make it a lot more difficult.

Another countermeasure would be to construct or purchase a steel mounting plate. If the mounting plate were considerably stronger, the physical strength of the screws would then be the weak point.

If our concern is the wrong people getting into our homes or buildings, we really do need to understand the strengths and weaknesses of the devices that we used to prevent that. This is also why I like to see a number of books on the subject of locks, lock picking, high security locks, and bypass methods. We just can't defend ourselves against things that we don't understand. I always enjoy removing the mystery.

TIP

I'd like to mention a few of the books that I personally have in my library on the subject of locks and lock picking.

- *Practical Lock Picking: A Physical Penetration Tester's Training Guide*, Deviant Ollam, ISBN: 978-1-59749-611-7, Syngress

I really like Deviant's book. I wish I had his talent for creating those excellent drawings. He explains exactly what's going on inside the lock predominantly for picking. This is what most people are interested in as a hobby and I think that's excellent. I've been saying this for years: the more that people know about locks, the more likely they are to choose a good one for the things that they are trying to secure. If you are going to buy your first book on lock picking, get Deviant's book.

- *The Complete Book of Locks and Locksmithing*, Sixth Edition, Bill Phillips, ISBN-13: 978-0-07-144829-1, McGraw Hill

This 588-page book is a classic in the world of locksmithing. This book covers the history of locks, the tools of the trade, types of locks and keys, and a number of other interesting topics should you decide to get into the field of locksmithing. It's a fascinating field that I have been dabbling in for over 40 years.

- *High-Security Mechanical Locks: An Encyclopedic Reference*, Graham W. Pulford, ISBN: 978-0-7506-8437-8, Butterworth-Heinemann

This is one of the most detailed books by Elsevier that I have ever seen on locks. At just over 600 pages, it goes into great detail about the subject of high security locks. I enjoyed his discussion of warded locks all based on the type of lock that I show in Figure 3.3. Some of the warded locks that he describes are over 700 years old.

- *Open in Thirty Seconds: Cracking One of the Most Secure Locks in America*, Mark Weber Tobias, ISBN: 978-0975947920, Pine Hill Press

I've known Mark for several years, and he is one of the most respected high security lock specialists in the world. This is an excellent book on the history of conventional as well as high tech locks to include some of their vulnerabilities. There's not another book out there quite like it, and I highly recommend it.

- *How to Open Locks with Improvised Tools: Practical, Non-destructive Ways of Getting Back into Just about Everything When You Lose Your Keys*, Hans Conkel, ISBN: 978-0966608717, Level Four Publications

This is an interesting book that I picked up a couple of years ago. It addresses interesting low tech ways to get into just about everything you can think of. I've not tried all of these myself, but it does look like most of these bypass methods would work. The one that I find the most interesting is the discussion of a bypass method for a very common knob set like you would find in your home. I do know that the procedure described in the book works, because I used it myself as a working locksmith. The interesting part about this bypass method is that it is completely nondestructive and just about as fast as using your key.

LET'S BREAK INTO A SEMI–HIGH SECURITY ROOM

The scenario that I'm about to describe is one that I used many years ago to gain easy access to a room over a several-week timeframe. The target room of interest was secured by a high security lock. My goal was to find a way into the room the first time and then establish a means to get back into the room fairly quickly on additional visits during our penetration tests for clients. The process that we used involved a little bit of social engineering, a little bit of locksmithing, and a little bit of ingenuity knowing how this particular lock worked.

This combined process is why I like to see people learn more about locks. It can be challenging to come up with countermeasures for some of these exploits. You'll see what I mean as we go a little deeper into the process of gaining control of this lock.

The lock shown in Figure 3.9 was rather expensive considering many of my other purchases. It was originally a display model for a very high security lock. Buying a lock like that gave me an opportunity to see exactly how locks of this type work and how they were installed. Most of the new lock enthusiasts that I've met buy as many things on eBay as I do. As I've said several times throughout these chapters I highly encourage people to begin to learn more about locks and how they can be compromised. This lock is a dead bolt type of lock similar to what you probably have on your doors at home. Those doors at home have two locks. One of the locks is typically a key-in-knob lock where you place your key into the doorknob and rotate the plug to retract the bolt. This bolt will be spring-loaded, which will allow you to open and close the door by simply turning the doorknob. The bolt on the lock in Figure 3.9

FIGURE 3.9

High quality high security lock: eBay, $45

is a dead bolt that needs to be manually retracted with the key from the outside or with a thumb latch from the inside to retract the bolt. If you had the opportunity to hold this lock in your hand, you would be amazed at the quality of the craftsmanship and the physical weight of the lock. It is an expensive lock, but you are definitely going to get what you pay for. Most of the locks in your home will not be of this quality. That doesn't mean that they're not good locks; it's just that most people do not put locks that cost hundreds of dollars each in their homes.

Retracting the bolt to open the door

Let's talk about how a bolt actually retracts. Remember what I had said earlier: the door is allowed to open when the bolt retracts. To open this very high security lock shown in Figure 3.9, you need the correct high security key if the lock is working properly. There may be other ways to open it by retracting the bolt. This is where a little bit of social engineering came into play during one of our pen tests as we needed to get into the room being secured by a lock similar to this. Who in the building would have the keys to that room? As our pen testing team found time and time again, the people whose job it was to keep the building neat and tidy frequently had the keys to everything. In almost every case it was simply a matter of looking like we were supposed to be there and needing a favor. In a few sentences, I'm trying to describe something that may have taken several days and multiple visits: which was to gain the trust of the right people who had these keys. This was always the case with social engineering and inside penetration tests. Once we were inside the buildings, almost everyone that we came in contact with eventually believed we should be there. Their guard was down. Over the years, the thought of how easy it was to get into most buildings has bothered me. There have been many studies about how intellectual property becomes compromised. Unless someone was caught inside your building, you may not know they were ever there. To the best of my knowledge, very few people who saw us during the penetration test even remember that we were there.

I'm not going to describe the social engineering story that we used to convince them that we needed to get into that room. Once they opened the room and gave us a little bit of time, we were able to determine exactly which locks were used on those doors. The lock shown in Figure 3.9 is similar to the locks that we found on the doors in these buildings. It is an excellent lock for me to show you the mindset of penetration testing using a multi-entry attack. I found it very interesting over the years that for some reason multifaceted attacks seem to really throw people off guard as to your intent. I believe that most people would have fallen for the attack I described in the social engineering chapter where I made two phone calls to that medical group. Both calls seem so innocent, and yet when you combine them they lead to a devastating effect. This seemed to be the case with dealing with locks and entry through doors in most of the buildings that we were targeting during our pen tests. If we could determine the keyway of the lock being used, we could normally obtain key blanks for that exact keyway. The portable key machine that I purchased at a yard sale many years ago was very accurate. I used it on several penetration tests to reproduce the building master keys after we were able to use our social engineering skills to borrow the keys from someone in the building who had access to them.

After figuring out how the lock in Figure 3.9 works by spending a few minutes studying it, I was able to devise a low tech hacking means of defeating the bolt mechanism. Since this was a dead bolt, I didn't have any springs or deadlocking plungers to worry about. Notice that I said defeating the *bolt* mechanism, not the *lock* mechanism. Figure 3.10 shows what I came up with as one way to low tech hack the bolt.

I had to borrow our dining room table to take a picture of this because it was almost invisible on my standard white background. I needed to make something fairly

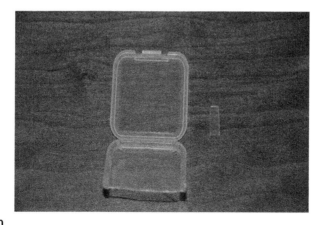

FIGURE 3.10

Jack's low tech bolt hacking tool: free

stiff and about a 1/32 of an inch thick. I began cutting up a plastic flash drive case that looked to be about the right thickness. The only piece that I wound up using was that small clear piece to the right of the picture. In seeing how the bolt operated in the lock in Figure 3.9, I noticed that if I stop the bolt from traveling that final 1/8 of an inch, the bolt would appear to be deadlock, but it wasn't. If I allow the bolt to go into full deadlock by completing that final 1/8 of an inch travel, the lock could only easily be opened with the key on one side or the thumb latch on the other. Obviously with the door closed, I wouldn't have access to the key on the outside of the door or the thumb latch on the inside of the door. With the dead bolt not properly engaged because of my improvised small piece of plastic, and depending on the tolerance of the door in the doorjamb, I might be able to get a very thin fingernail file or something smaller into the opening to begin retracting the bolt. This would be much easier to show you than it is to explain. If you look at your locks at home from the inside of your home you will see what I mean. Most homes are constructed with a fair amount of an opening between the door and the door frame. I have found deadbolts on doors that had no protection against using a thin knife or a fingernail file slipped between the door and the door frame to retract the bolt. I know I've said it before, but I'll say it again. What allows the door to open is the retraction of the bolt.

Gaining access to the lock itself

Please keep in mind that this is just an example of one quick way to defeat the lock. In order to be able to get this small piece of plastic into the lock mechanism, it would be necessary to temporarily remove the lock from the door. This can be done from the inside, especially considering the inside faceplate of the lock is only secured to the door with several screws that are accessible from the inside of the door. This brings up another good point about the things that we experienced during our inside penetration tests. Every time we started the test, especially when we were in the process of getting into the building, we always felt like we would immediately be caught. Once we were in the building, that feeling of possibly getting caught continued for a while. It didn't take very long for our penetration team to realize that we could pretty much do anything once we were inside the building because people just felt like we belonged there. I'm still amazed at that. I'm convinced that in most places, if someone walked by while we were doing just about anything inside the building, we would go unchallenged. On one occasion we saw two people trying to move some equipment, and we stopped what we were doing and offered to help. They were most thankful and didn't even ask us our names, much less what we were doing there. Scheduled security awareness training would go a long way in helping to keep employees more aware of who should be challenged or at least reported if they are not recognized. Keep in mind that this company had already been a victim of theft, which is why we were hired to see where the vulnerability might exist in their operational security.

Figure 3.11 shows the lock with my little piece of plastic added to the top of the bolt. I didn't take the time to securely fasten it to the top of the bolt, but I did hold it

FIGURE 3.11

Jack's low tech bolt hacking tool placed in the bolt: free

there while I was experimenting with the bolt and saw that the piece of plastic did prevent the bolt from completely locking in place. If a device like this were installed in the lock permanently, the bolt could possibly be retracted with the small fingernail file or knife blade at a later time.

In Figure 3.11, you will recognize that little piece of plastic (indicated by the arrow pointing to it) sitting on top of the bolt on the left-hand side near the cut-out. That small piece of plastic prevented the final 1/16 of an inch of travel in the bolt that prevented the bolt from opening fully. I held the little piece of plastic in place and operated the lock with the key as well as with the thumb turn. In both cases it felt like the lock was locked. It even looked like the bolt was fully extended. Figure 3.11 shows it in the compromised position. That bolt is not securely locked open. With enough room between the end of the bolt plate and the strike in the door frame to get a small thin knife or fingernail file into the opening, the bolt can easily be retracted.

TIP

I'll say it again: the real vulnerability here isn't the keyway, and it isn't the quality of the lock or the solid stainless steel bolt. The real vulnerability in my opinion would be the ability to get to that lock and borrow the key to get into that room and then compromise it. Security is a very difficult ongoing task that every employee of every company needs to be a part of. Frequently when I'm out presenting at a conference, I'll ask the question, "How many of you are a part of your company's security team?" Considering that I'm usually speaking at a security conference, quite a few of the hands go up. I then say, "If you see me present again, and I asked that question, I would really like to see every hand go up." It takes all of us to create true security in our homes and in our workplace.

This quick scenario is really designed just to show that locks are in some ways like puzzles. That's pretty much how most of the lock enthusiasts that now pick locks as a hobby look at it. I think that's wonderful! The more that employees, and especially the security teams, know about locks, the more they can insure that the proper locks are used for given situation. They will also know quite a bit about ways to defeat these locks and possible ways to prevent that.

Here's one more quick example of things that we don't typically think of but that the bad guys just might. This example is going to use our same high tech lock shown in Figure 3.9. I've used this in several training classes just to describe a little bit about pin tumbler locks and ways to defeat them. After letting people in the class who wanted to examine and operate the lock, I asked if they noticed anything unique about it. So far, of all the people that have looked at that lock, no one has. This is another low tech hack that we would normally not think about when dealing with pin tumbler locks. This lock is designed in a very interesting way that allows it to pretty much feel the same if there are pins in the lock or if there aren't. In this case there are no pins in the lock. If you think about it, removing even a few of the pins from any pin tumbler lock makes it really easy to pick. If even one pin were left in a pin tumbler lock, that lock may well appear normal to anyone using their key to open the lock. I suspect the lock could exist like that for years until it was worked on by a locksmith or a building mechanic for some reason. What that would do is allow virtually anyone with even a little bit of lock-picking experience to pick that single- or even two-pin lock. Maybe I just think a little differently from some people, but I just don't think too many people ever think of these kinds of low tech vulnerabilities.

Over the years I've trained a lot of internal auditors on auditing physical and technical issues associated with security. I think it would be a good idea to occasionally audit the status of the locks within the building. This was something else that we found every time we conducted an inside penetration test. There always seemed to be at least one door that was no longer functioning properly. It was normally a key-in-knob-type lock or a pushbutton combination lock where the bolt would stick partially open. This would frequently be a problem with doors that were exposed to outdoor elements. Let me show you what I mean. Take a look at Figure 3.12.

I've been keeping an eye on this door for about 3 months now. I guess I've been looking at locks and doors for so many decades that I just can't help but do it pretty much everywhere. This is one of about 20 doors that secure entrances to a multi-tenant office complex. This is a perfect example of what our inside penetration team typically found at least once on every job that we did. These locks are mechanical devices, and in this case all of them are exposed to the outside elements. I found this lock in this condition on about a half-dozen occasions throughout the past 3 months. If the weather was extremely cold, or if we were experiencing a lot of rain, the lock (bolt) seem to fail and not close all the way. This is one of those maintenance issues that needs to be audited. Aside from this glaring problem, this is a pretty substantial door. It contains security glass and a pretty expensive pushbutton lock. Seeing that exposed bolt

FIGURE 3.12

Door to a secured office complex

that was supposed to retract into the lock and then spring back open once the door was closed is a very open sign that security has failed. You can't see it in this picture, but stenciled onto that door in fairly large letters is a sign that reads "Please be sure that door is closed behind you." I'm not saying anyone was at fault here for going out the door without making sure that it was locked. That's just not something that the typical person would do. They expect it to close and automatically lock like it does every other time. It's also possible that the person who went through the door is still on the inside, not knowing that the lock did not lock behind them.

This office complex is fairly large and is used by hundreds of people. On several occasions I have seen the doors to inside secured areas such as this one propped open. This was the case when someone obviously had a number of things to take into or out of the facility and just decided that it was too much trouble to continue to unlock the door. On at least one occasion, I saw one of the doors that was propped open on successive visits spanning several hours. In this case I suspect that whoever propped the door open just left and went about their business, and when they were finished, they didn't bother removing the board that they used to prop the door open.

None of these security issues is rocket science. It's just that we seem to have become a nation that isn't as careful as we should be about simple matters of security. Many of the inside penetration tests that our teams conducted were contracted because the organizations were suffering serious loss of intellectual property. The situation with locks in large buildings is one of the areas where I like to see all employees become involved. They don't have to know a lot about locks, but they can be trained to immediately report any locks that they feel are not working properly.

KEYS AND KEY CONTROL

The types of keys used in most buildings have remained virtually unchanged since Linus Yale invented them in 1861. Just about all of our homes and most businesses still use his pin tumbler locks for their primary perimeter defense. I have no way of knowing how often the master, grand master, and possibly great-grand-master key systems in buildings are changed. I do suspect that it's not very often because it can be an expensive process.

Social engineering and key access

While using our social engineering skills during each penetration test, our team always tried to make friends with the janitorial team. Sooner or later, we would need to ask a favor, and borrow their keys for a few minutes. Typically, their keys would open all of the doors on that floor and sometimes the entire building. A few minutes was all that it took for us to make a copy with the portable key machine that we brought with us in a small bag. Very few people have any idea of how the internal details of locks and keys work. Common knowledge of how locks work is another area of physical security that has changed greatly during the past few decades. When I became a bonded locksmith in the 1970s I found learning about the "secret things" about locks to be fascinating. Back then, I couldn't even purchase lock picks or key blanks until I graduated from a credited locksmithing school and had proper identification. Now, about 40 years later, we have much more at risk, and anyone can purchase lock picks at several local hardware stores or from the Internet without any questions asked about why they wants them.

Regarding the use of lock picks to get into buildings and rooms, I don't suspect that many pen testers use them. Lock picking does require a lot of practice, practice, and more practice, which is required for any pen testing skill. The easy availability of these devices is something that corporate security specialists need to consider as they plan their countermeasures.

Who has the keys to your kingdom

I'll be mentioning a few things about key control throughout this chapter. It is absolutely critical that you know who has the keys to your kingdom. This is another situation where the risks are very similar at home and at work. When I train senior executives and even law enforcement agents, I always encourage them to change the locks on their homes if they suspect anyone has compromised one of the keys. When you first move into your home, even a newly constructed home, you have no idea who has copies of those keys. Keys are the hardware equivalent of passwords, except that they are normally much more difficult to change. If you aren't absolutely certain that no one has been able to duplicate your keys, you should consider purchasing new locks, or having the combinations (pins) changed on your current locks.

TIP

Attempt to set up some form of key control if you don't already have a system in place. It is very important to know who has the keys to your kingdom as well as how many doors can be opened by each key. It is very seldom a good idea to have one key that opens everything in the building. That may be more convenient for certain things, but it does open the security concern of controlling who has those keys and how easily they can be duplicated.

Master keys are an additional concern if you rent space in a large building or office park. You might have a very strict policy of your own for your company, but if the management company that handles the building rentals isn't as careful with their master keys, the entire building could be at risk. Unless the keys are of a high security design like the Medeco line, they can be duplicated anywhere. Even if the disgruntled building maintenance person turns in his or her keys upon being fired, there is no way to be sure that copies weren't made. You should ask the building manager about the corporate policy regarding issue and security of the master keys.

For certain high value (to you or your organization) areas, it might be wise to install special locks on critical doors. Highly pick-resistant Medeco locks are some of the most effective. In addition to providing additional security, they add another level of due diligence should you need to document your attempts to prevent intrusions.

Special key control awareness training

Conduct special employee awareness training for everyone who works on the evening and night shift. That's when I took our team into the pen testing clients' buildings most of the time. We used our social engineering skills to befriend these people, and to the best of my knowledge, our being there was never reported by any of them.

Another prime target during our evening and night visits was the janitorial team. The main reason we always tried to befriend the people on the janitorial team is that they usually had those important keys that we were trying to get our hands on. These are some of the most important people in your company when it comes to protecting your buildings when most people are gone. They spend some time in just about every room in the building each week. If you don't train anyone else in your company, these people need to be well trained in how they can help. They should be made aware of your security policies and what they should do if they see anything suspicious. This would include strangers asking to have any doors opened, suspicious packages, doors that are opened that should be locked, etc. The members of the out-of-hours janitorial team are some of your most valuable resources. Tell them that, and teach them how they can help.

BAIT AND SWITCH WAR STORY THAT COULD HAPPEN TO YOU

I'd like to share a war story with you that happened to a friend of mine and it involves one of his locks. This friend was exercising at his local gym when this happened. He completed his exercise routine went to the locker room to take a shower. When he returned from taking a shower, he seemed to have a problem.

The combination lock that he had been using for years no longer opened. He tried it many times and it just wouldn't open. Consider the situation: he's standing there in front of his locker wearing a towel. Everything else that's important to him is inside the locker. If this happened to you, what would you do? Obviously, you can only try the combination so many times before you finally give in to the fact that it's not going to open. This has never happened to him before. Perhaps the lock was broken.

He and his towel obviously had to get some help in getting the lock opened. The manager of the gym wanted to be sure that this was really his locker before cutting the lock off. Without identification, the manager wasn't sure of what to believe. This was truly a Catch-22. If you think about it, the manager was confronted with an interesting situation. He has someone standing there asking to have a lock cut from a locker that the manager doesn't even know whether or not he has the right to open. In this case, the manager did finally go and get some bolt cutters and cut the lock off. To my friend's dismay, when they opened his locker, it was empty. Everything that he had in that locker had been stolen: his wallet, car keys, and some other very important items. As far as I know, law enforcement was immediately involved and the incident is still ongoing. Let's consider how the bad guy could have possibly used some low tech hacking to get into that locker. The bad guy also wound up using a little bit of low tech social engineering to place another lock on the locker that looked like the original lock. All of this bought the bad guy time to get away.

Figure 3.13 shows a lock that is virtually identical to the lock that belonged to my friend. There are several brands available of these combination locks, and they have remained unchanged for decades. This is perhaps the most common lock in the world. That doesn't make it a bad lock, but it does mean that more and more people are now beginning to realize ways to bypass the locking mechanism and cause it to open. I don't know how the lock was opened in the incident involving my friend, but I

FIGURE 3.13

Combination lock and a commercial shim

do know of several low tech hacking ways that these locks can be easily removed. Probably the most common way with a pair of bolt cutters. It's possible that this happened to my friend, but usually people walking around with bolt cutters might look a little more suspicious than others.

The little V-shaped item to the left of the lock in Figure 3.13 is a commercial padlock lock shim. This is one area where I differ slightly with the descriptions that you see on YouTube or even in Deviant's book as well as the *No Tech Hacking* (ISBN: 978-1-59749-215-7, Syngress) book that Johnny Long wrote (I wrote the Social Engineering chapter in *No Tech Hacking*). There are many excellent hacking descriptions of building these shims with empty soda cans, or better still, beer cans. My concern with spending a lot of time doing that would be cut fingers. I also know the amount of pressure that is needed to shim open padlocks similar to this one even with a spring steel commercial shim like the one shown in Figure 3.13. My other reason for not wanting to spend the time to make a shim out of a soda can is that the commercial versions, which work very well, cost only about $1.50 each including shipping. For me, it's just not worth the time and aggravation and possibly bloody fingers to build my own.

Padlock shims are not a new threat

Something else that I found interesting about using these padlock shims is the information among the lock enthusiasts about a vulnerability that's been known in the locksmithing world for over 40 years. While this is another vulnerability well documented on YouTube that you certainly need to know about, I don't think most non lock enthusiasts know about it. For the past several years I have taken padlocks with me as I present at various security conferences. I always let people experience the use of the shims on several of my personal padlocks to show them how they work and how easy it is. Among the hundreds of people who were in the various audiences, I don't think that many of them knew about that vulnerability before I mentioned it during the presentation. Most seemed very surprised as well as very interested in the fact that a lock that they had been familiar with since childhood could be opened so easily with a small piece of metal. All of this helps enforce my feeling that more and more people need to know and understand how locks work as well as ways that they can become compromised.

The vulnerability described here, and the impact that it had on my friend, standing there with nothing left but a towel, made me think of possible countermeasures. The scenario would have been slightly different if the bad guy had simply removed my friend's lock and left the locker completely open. The reaction of getting management involved could have been much quicker if that had happened. By adding the little social engineering twist of placing another lock in its place, the bad guy immediately created a diversion. If you've ever owned a combination lock with the serial number on the back of it, can you tell me that serial number? Probably not! So unless you can remember the serial number (and I don't plan to try), I usually suggest that people take one of those etching tools and make some mark known to them somewhere on the back of the lock. It can even appear to be an accidental scratch. This won't stop the bad guy from taking your lock. But if you suspect that something like this has happened to you, you could probably quickly find out that the lock now securing your locker is not your lock.

In this scenario, where we're at a gym, there are a number of other things you could do to become a little tougher target. For years, when I was going to a local gym, I would use a key lock that was also a key retention lock similar to the one shown in Figure 3.5 but not as big. I did that for the same reason that I described what I like about the key retention lock earlier in the chapter. If that key was on the little wrist strap on my arm, I knew that the lock was locked somewhere. It could not be taken out of the lock if the lock was still (opened) unlocked. Many times when going to that same gym I would see locks of the type shown in Figure 3.13 on several lockers left unlocked. If you think about it, unless the locker was empty and the person went home and forgot the lock, it should never be on the locker unlocked unless you are standing there. Those people simply walked away and forgot to lock the lock. With the key retention lock, that can't happen. In most cases the key retention lock will also look considerably different from the majority of the locks in the gym. Most will look like the lock in Figure 3.13. If your lock looks different from everybody else's, and functions somewhat differently from everybody else's, you will automatically become a tougher target. It will be very difficult for the bad guy to have the right lock to be able to exchange yours with his.

I don't want to belabor this simple war story, but I do want you to understand that being a tougher target, and being a little bit more difficult to compromise than the next guy, is really the name of the game with security. If you are targeted personally, it will be very difficult for you to prevent certain things. Most situations similar to what happened to my friend are probably random thefts of opportunity. He didn't suspect that he was targeted. He may have been watched by a bad guy to see when he went to the shower, knowing that he would most likely be gone for about 5 minutes or more, and the bad guy could spend that time taking everything that my friend owned out of his locker.

SOME PLACES TO GO TO LEARN AND HAVE SOME FUN

I find it encouraging to learn about more and more local lock pick enthusiasts groups starting up. As I've said many times throughout this book, I believe that the more you know about locks and the ways that they operate, the more likely you are to choose a good one for your security needs. Let me tell you a little bit about the team from FALE (FALE Association of Locksport Enthusiasts) located in Winston-Salem, North Carolina. I had occasion to spend the day at a conference with them in May 2011. The FALE team that day consisted of Matt Block, Adam Sheesley, Jon Welborn, and Evan Booth. Check out their website at http://www.lockfale. com to learn more about them.

The lock collection that they had with them looked very similar to mine as they spread the locks out across three tables. In the exhibit area of the conference, I watched as people gathered around their tables and began the journey of learning what makes locks tick. It seemed like no matter how quiet or busy the exhibit hall was, there were always people gathered around those tables being fascinated with locks, and ways to open them. People can't seem to get enough of these truly interesting puzzles that we also use for some pretty critical security applications. It's a good idea to learn as much as you can about how and why they work.

My 110-year-old puzzle

I brought some of my locks with me, including my antique favorite with the patent date of 1901 stamped on the bottom. Many of the conference attendees who were standing at the FALE tables learning about locks were impressed with it and found it as fascinating as I did. Toward mid-afternoon I handed it to one of the FALE association leaders to see if he could open it. I wanted to be sure that the picking efforts didn't destroy it because lock picks are made of spring steel, and the pins inside the lock were 100+-year-old brass pins. The FALE team members were familiar with how the mechanism worked, and that was impressive to me in itself. This turned out not to be an easy task even for these young experts. I was again impressed with their ingenuity as they showed me a new device that I didn't know existed that allowed them to open the lock. Figure 3.14 is a picture of the newly opened lock.

From what we could see of the lock, this was truly one of the first pin tumbler padlocks. They quickly determined that there were four pins securing the plug. The lock was quite ingenious the way it was constructed. I had never seen anything quite like it. The FALE team knew that this lock required hitting the shear line with all four pins while pushing up on the lock shackle. I left for a while to view some of the rest

FIGURE 3.14

My 1901 padlock picked open by the FALE team

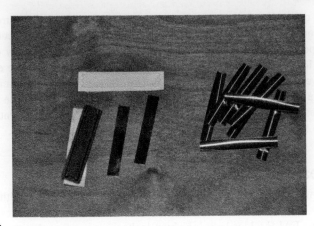

FIGURE 3.15

Low tech hacking shims and commercial shims

of the conference, and when I returned the lock was opened as shown in figure 3.14. They had opened it by using a plug shim in a way that I had never used. They used an improvised plug shim between the lock body and the plug on the side of the plug where the key enters. In addition, they used a shim that I did not recognize (see Figure 3.15). This is such a perfect example of using what I would consider low tech hacking for locks. I had never seen shims that thin. Figure 3.15 shows my standard shims on the right-hand side of the picture. The shims that they used, as shown on the left-hand side of the picture, come from the security devices that are found on most DVD cases. Someone discovered that if you cut the case open, there were two tiny pieces of metal inside that worked perfectly as shims. I don't do nearly as much with locks and keys as I used to, but on the day that I met the FALE team I learned a few new tricks from them. That improvised plug shim shown sticking out of the lock in Figure 3.14 is one of these shims from a DVD security device.

There are several devices that locksmiths use that are referred to as *shims*. The commercial shims, and the low tech hacking shims from the DVD security tags, are used as a shim to turn the plug in a pin tumbler lock. The lock shown in Figure 3.14 is one example of how they can be used. The shims commonly used to open the shackle of padlock are shown in Figure 3.13.

MORE ABOUT KEYS AND HOW TO MAKE ONE IF YOU DON'T HAVE ONE

My fascination with locks, and especially keys, has gotten out of hand a couple of times over the years. It seems like every time I see some neat little gadget or lock-related item, I need to have it. In the class that I was conducting a couple of years ago about penetration methods, I brought close to 100 locks with me for the demonstration. The students had a lot of fun, and obviously this was a very hands-on demonstration. I'm going to spend the next little while talking about keys. For the sake of time, I'll narrow that down to discuss keys for pin tumbler locks. Since these are the most common locks that we see in our homes and offices, they are also the most likely to be attacked or tampered with by the bad guys of the world. For this next discussion, I'm going to assume that you know a little bit about the keys in your pocket. The notches in the key of varying depths are called *bittings* (some of us old guys still call them *cuts*). These need to be very accurate down to a couple thousandths of an inch in order for the pins in the lock to reach the shear line when the key is inserted, thus allowing the plug to turn. Those bittings each appear to be at a random depth. They aren't. Each lock manufacturer has a series of specific depths for the bittings on the keys for their locks, and there are normally between six and nine different depths of bittings for each keyway from that manufacturer.

Five pounds of my favorite keys

Here's an eBay find that has been one of my favorites over the years. Figure 3.16 is a picture of 5 pounds of pin tumbler keys that I spotted one afternoon for sale on eBay. To the untrained eye, it would appear to be a box of random keys from many manufacturers. I saw it as something completely different. You might not be able to see it in the picture of this box of keys, but each of the sets of keys from a respective manufacturer were held together by keychain. If I remember correctly, I was the only one who bid on this apparent 5-pound box of junk keys. I paid $10 for the box of keys, and another $10 to have them shipped to me. When I received them,

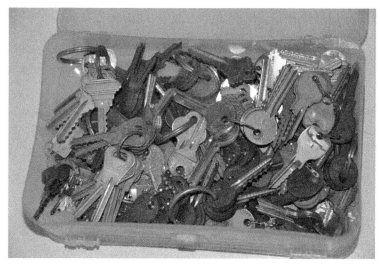

FIGURE 3.16

Five pounds of keys: eBay, $20.00

and opened the box to take a look, I was pleasantly surprised to see that they were exactly what I thought they were. These were 32 sets of depth keys from virtually every lock manufacturer that I was aware of and a few I had never even heard of before. These must have belonged to some retired locksmith. If I were to go out and buy these today as individuals sets, the retail price for what I had in that box would be over $1,000. Not a bad buy for 20 bucks. I love eBay!

Depth keys are quite interesting. Those that have 10 keys in their sequence will have a key with bitting depths starting with zero and ending with the key with all of the bittings cut to a depth of nine. The zero depth is the shallowest, and the nine depth is the deepest. If you begin to dive deeper into the world of locksmithing, you will eventually need to know a little more about key coding. This is another area where there is a lot of information on the Internet about this subject. There is another interesting find in this box of depth keys. Using bump keys is not something that was just discovered. It has been well known for a number of years, but again, with the Internet and new groups coming online to learn about locks, there are few people who have not heard about bump keys and bumping a lock opened. These bump keys are sometimes called *999 keys*. As I look at my sets of depth keys, many of them have a total of 10 keys, starting with key 0 and ending with key 9. Knowing this and seeing all of those sets of keys let me know that I also now had the beginnings of a complete set of bump keys. This was another bonus from my $20 purchase.

So now some of you are wondering, "Why should I care about all these keys?" Here's where a bit of knowledge, and little bit of social engineering, can be used to create a key for a lock that you have no key for. As mentioned earlier, our pen testing teams never failed to be able to use their social engineering skills to encourage someone to open certain doors for them. Keep in mind that locks on doors at work and locks on doors at home are quite easy to remove if you do it from the secured side of the door. If you are standing in front of the door that is locked, and you need a key to open the door, you are standing on the unsecure side of the door. Locks are designed to be difficult to remove from the unsecure side of the door. Take a look at this in your house the next time you examine your locks. You never want it to be any easier than it has to be to open the door from the outside without using a key. From the inside it's a different story. That's how the locks were designed to be removed should they ever need to be replaced or rekeyed. If it is a dead bolt lock, the screws to remove the thumb latch or the inside cylinder lock are on the secured side (inside) of the door. All that you frequently need is the correct screwdriver. Most key-in-knob locks have a small spring-loaded latch somewhere in the vicinity of the doorknob on the secured side of the door. If I can remove that lock, I will be able to shim the lock open (with one of the plug shims shown in Figure 3.15) and remove the plug. Using the proper set of depth keys, it will be easy to determine the necessary bittings (cuts) needed to then go out and have a key made. From that point on you would never need to pick that lock again. You would have your own key.

> **TIP**
>
> I'm intentionally not covering every detail of exactly how to do this. This will be your homework as you look at other books, check out YouTube, and look around the Internet using some of the keywords that you've seen in this chapter to begin your studies. I do want to mention that should you be shimming a lock that has master key pins, you will be able to use your pin tumbler shims (Figure 3.15) to open the lock, but you won't know whether you've hit the shear line that involves a master pin that could either be in the plug or the cylinder if the actual master key were used. The key that you create will open the lock that you're standing in front of, but it most likely would not be a master key that would open any other lock.

WAYS TO MAKE A KEY IF YOU DIDN'T BRING A KEY MACHINE

On several occasions, our penetration team was able to become friendly enough with the right people to have them let us borrow their keys to open a certain door when we didn't have our portable key machine with us. Our team always returned the keys within a few minutes and thanked them. Please keep in mind that this wasn't a situation where we just walked up to a total stranger and said may I borrow your keys? Getting to the point of building that much trust frequently took us several days or longer using social engineering skills. Keep in mind that we were always in buildings where we should not have been allowed such unlimited access. Now that I had their keys for just a few minutes, I was able to use a few more of my tools to find a way to create a copy of their key. Figure 3.17 shows a couple of those

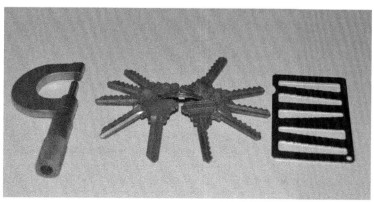

FIGURE 3.17

Micrometer, depth keys, and a key gauge

tools. The tool on the left is a micrometer that reads accurately to 1/1000 of an inch. There are micrometers specifically called *key micrometers*, but that's not what this is. It does function as well as an official key micrometer for my purposes. I bought this one at a yard sale many years ago for a few dollars. In the center of Figure 3.17 is one of the sets of depth keys from the box shown in Figure 3.16. I tried to photograph these keys in such a way that you could see the different depths of cuts on them. The key on the left of the pile pointing straight down is the zero cut key. Clockwise all the way around to the other key pointing straight down we go from 0 to 9. If you look closely you will see that each key seems to have bittings (cuts) that are a little deeper than the one just before it. Typically, the difference between bittings (cuts) is roughly between .015 to .020 of an inch. The device on the right of Figure 3.17 is a key gauge. It is designed for specific brands of keys, and the brand of key for each slot is marked on the gauge.

There are several things that I can do with these devices if I can hold your key for just a few minutes. In order to find the depth of the bittings on your key I could measure it with the key micrometer on the left, or I could use the key gauge on the right. To use the key gauge, I would slide your key into the gauge and read the number from 0 to 9 for each of the bittings on your key. Let's assume that this is the lock in your house, and I borrowed your key for a few minutes. If I determine that the depths of the bittings on your key are say, 35218, I can then take the depth keys using a simple inexpensive key machine or even a pippin file (a special file for use on key blanks, retail about $25) and duplicate your key. These depth keys are very accurate. Even if I don't have the key machine or a pippin file, I know that I can take this to the stand where they cut keys at the local flea market and have them make me a key from this code. Technically, this is not the code to your key but the numbers that equate to the depths of bittings for those respective numbers for that manufacturer. It is amazingly accurate and somewhat easy to do, and there are descriptions of very similar things on YouTube and other places on the Internet. I don't want you to be afraid to use your keys, but I do want you to be aware of a few of the ways that people can duplicate your keys, or even create one of their own from scratch with a few simple tools. ALWAYS BE CAREFUL WHO HAS ACCESS TO YOUR KEYS!

After reading this chapter I would like for you to think about your keys every time that they are out of your sight. This is especially true when you are places other than home. I've watched countless times over the years as people hand their complete set of keys to a parking attendant for valet parking. Think about what you have in your car. Not only would your keys be there, which as we've seen can be fairly easily duplicated, but much of your personal information resides on the registration for that vehicle. It's a little more difficult to duplicate most of the newer car keys. Obviously you need to give the parking attendant your vehicle key in order to have him or her drive your vehicle to the lot where the cars are to be parked, but you don't need to give anyone that much unlimited access to the rest of your keys.

WARNING

This warning will begin with one of my war stories. As I go about my normal day-to-day activities, I can't help but look at things through the eyes of security. Sometimes I see things that I almost can't believe. I was in the downtown area of a major city in a public parking garage that was a part of a major multi-tenant office building, and I had to use the restroom. (Don't panic, I'm not going to get too personal). As I walked over to wash my hands I noticed that there were a set of keys hanging out of the paper towel rack. Remember, this was in a public restroom in the garage of a very large multi-tenant building in the big city. Having spent a number of years in the locksmithing business and having a pretty good idea of what a master, grand master, and great-grand master key might look like, there were at least two of them on that key ring along with the key that opened the paper towel rack. This is pretty bad news. The little key that opens the towel rack to allow people to put in new paper towels is pretty much the tip of the screwdriver. It really isn't there for security at all. The rest of the keys on that key ring very well could have been the keys that open many of the doors in the entire building. Not a good situation. If those keys fell into the wrong hands, I have no idea how much it would cost to rekey a building of that size. Most likely, it would never be done. I turned the keys in to the building security office, and briefly mentioned that I didn't think that it was a good idea for such critical keys to be on the same key ring as the device that opens the towel rack. It was obviously left there by mistake by whoever just cleaned the restroom. I'm sure that wasn't intentional.

Key control is absolutely critical. It just seems to be so easy to become complacent about the things that we have been using all of our lives. Who has the keys to your kingdom?

ONE FINAL LOCK TO TALK ABOUT AND THEN WE'RE DONE

The final lock that I would like to talk about in this chapter is also the most common: locks found in office buildings and places other than homes. This is another pin tumbler lock typically containing either five or six pins. Most of these locks used in industry will also be set to some level of the master key. The additional pins in each stack actually allow for more potential shear lines to be hit when picking or shimming the lock open. Figure 3.18 is one of my photographs of a mortise cylinder lock.

At first glance this lock doesn't look much different from the rim cylinder lock that I showed in Figure 3.7. The main difference isn't the lock itself or even the keys. What makes this lock a little bit more commercial is the way that it installs into the main lock body. If you look closely at the lock you will see threads completely around the main body of the cylinder. This lock literally threads into the main body of the mortise lock in a similar way to threading a bolt into a nut. There are two screws that secure the lock in place by passing through the horizontal notch that you see cut through the threads. Figure 3.19 is a good example of an older but complete mortise lock set.

I have loosened one of the set screws for the outside cylinder and left it hanging so that I can explain it to you. Normally this screw would go horizontally into a threaded unit that lets it enter its respective channel in the mortise cylinder lock.

FIGURE 3.18

Mortise cylinder: eBay, $2

FIGURE 3.19

Mortise cylinder lock: eBay, $2

With that screw in place, the door closed, and the bolt extended as you see it, the lock itself cannot easily be removed with brute force. There are a couple of things that I've added to this picture that I need to explain. One of them is the Teflon plumbers tape that you see in the foreground. There's more of that tape around the cylinder that was screwed back into the mortise lock body. The reason for the tape is the social engineering version of the way that a lock like this could possibly be compromised by a bad guy or by a good guy conducting the penetration test. The tape allows the lock to remain in place securely while anyone using a key to open that lock would think that it's completely normal. Without that set screw being in place, the lock is completely vulnerable. It would be a simple matter to insert a blank key (one with none of the bittings cut) to use as a lever to simply unscrew the lock cylinder from the mortise lock body. A screwdriver could also be used, but that could leave marks. Using a key blank would not leave any indication that the mortise cylinder lock was tampered with. Uncut key blanks are also very strong. Without the bittings being cut into the blade of the key it hasn't lost any of its strength. The final thing in that picture is the little key hood that I've placed over the key. This has become a low tech hacking way of covering the bow of the key so that you can not see that the key had "do not duplicate" stamped into the brass. When having a key duplicated at my local flea market, I have never seen the key machine operator remove the key from a keychain to cut the new key. I suspect that most people never look under those little key hoods to see if this is a key that should not be duplicated.

Rim cylinder locks vs. mortise cylinder locks

Mortise cylinder locks are different from rim cylinder locks in that they cannot be easily removed with a slide hammer (see Figure 3.8) as I described earlier in this chapter. They have other vulnerabilities, but the ease of removing the lock cylinder itself is not one of those vulnerabilities. The keyway is, however, still susceptible to being drilled if forced entry is used. The vulnerability of removing the lock greatly increases if I'm given the opportunity to open the door. Once the door is opened, the door edge as well as the normally secured side of the door are now exposed. The door edge is where the set screw resides that prevents this cylinder from being removed. If someone allows me to go into that room, in a fairly short time frame, I can remove the lock without damaging it, shim it opened so that I can remove the plug without any keys, use my depth keys to determine a shear line that will open that lock, reassemble the lock, and put everything back to normal. This would not take long for a person with some lock knowledge, and thanks to the Internet, many people now have that knowledge. I'll say again, the key that I could produce by doing something like this most likely would not be the master key that opens every door. It would simply be the key that would let me back in that door. (Once again, complete details of how to do something like this will be left to your additional study and practice.)

Let's go through one final social engineering attack scenario where I do have access to that key for a few minutes. To make this more interesting, let's assume that the key that I am able to borrow for a few minutes is one of the building master keys as is frequently the case. Again, our normal mode of attack was to befriend certain individuals over a period of time, gain their trust, and eventually ask for the small favor of being given access to our target room. This sounds like it could never work. Trust me, it worked pretty much every time. Figure 3.20 shows the target key, the key gauge that I showed you in Figure 3.17, and three small key covers (one of them is shown in Figure 3.19). These kinds of key covers can be used for more than just making certain keys on your key ring easy to spot.

FIGURE 3.20

Key covers, target key, and a key gauge

Let me first address the key covers . These are available for less than a dollar each at pretty much any place that cuts keys. Keep in mind, probably 99% of the places that you go to have a key cut are not locksmith shops. I've seen a number of small key cutting shops working out of the back of a truck at a flea market. One of these is a small dealer that I have make all of my keys. Recently I asked him if he has ever been asked to cut a key using depth keys. He said no but that he would be happy to if I showed him how to do it. As you can probably tell by now, I really enjoy watching people while I'm out there practicing some of my favorite hobbies. I've seen a number of keys cut at this particular place where the key had one of those little hoods over it to make it easily identifiable for the owner. When a key like that is on a key ring, there is no need to remove the key from the key ring in order to copy it. There would be no way for the person cutting that key to know whether or not the key under the hood was marked "do not duplicate." Using one of those little hoods is certainly a low tech hack way of hiding the fact that the key should not be duplicated. I've never seen anyone look under the hood to see what the key said.

Now onto the key and the key gauge in Figure 3.20. Let's pretend that that key is the building master key and you were kind enough to loan it to me for just a minute or two to open the door. All that I would need to do is use my micrometer shown in Figure 3.17 to tell me the depth of each of the bittings on that key. This key could then be cut on a key machine that is capable of cutting keys by code. The key machine that I found at a yard sale several years ago for $10 could cut keys by code. If this were a key from a home or from a lock that was not on a master-keyed system, I could take the depth keys shown in Figure 3.17 to my local key-cutting buddy along with the code that I could easily read from the key gauge in Figure 3.17 and have him create an exact copy of that key.

Let's take this same scenario to your home. In most cases when we were doing inside penetration tests we would learn a little bit about some of the senior management in that company. This is totally hypothetical, but if someone were to be able to get hired on to the cleaning service that cleans the executive's home, how hard would it be for them to pick up the executive's keys off of the kitchen counter and measure the cuts with the key gauge? Who doesn't leave their house keys on the counter of their home when they are in the home? If the bad guys can get access to the executive's home, they can quickly get enough information from any key to be able to duplicate it later. The bad guys wouldn't need to take the executive's key out of his home or even have access to it for more than a minute or so.

SUMMARY

—Low Tech Jack

The contents of this chapter could easily become an entire book. I do need to bring it in for a landing somewhere, and this is as good a place as any. My main purpose for including a chapter like this is to give people an idea of some of the ways that low tech hacking can be employed to compromise mechanical locks and gain physical access. As I mentioned several places throughout this book, I have seen enormous changes in the availability of information regarding locks, keys, and bypass methods over the past 40+ years. The existence of sites like YouTube, and the Internet in general, has provided everyone (including the bad guys of the world), with a lot more information about what I like to call lock threats and vulnerabilities than was available just a decade ago. What I don't see much of out there on the Internet are discussions about possible countermeasures for these vulnerabilities. I've said it hundreds of times over the past 40+ years that the number-one countermeasure for most security related issues is employee awareness training. Hopefully, this chapter will help open everyone's eyes regarding the ever-present clear and real threat to the physical security of our most valuable intellectual property and technical assets.

Low tech wireless hacking

INFORMATION IN THIS CHAPTER

- Wireless 101: The Electromagnetic Spectrum
- 802.11 and Bluetooth Low Tech Hacks
- DoS and Availability
- Backdoors and Cracks
- Going Rogue
- Assault by Defaults
- Bypassing Specific Security Tools

We interrupt this *Low Tech Hacking* title to bring you a little slice of slightly higher (but still low tech) hacking technique. Nestled among the physical security and locks, we bring you low tech wireless hacking; a chapter dedicated to thwarting wireless systems of all types, armed with everything from a bobby pin to a yagi antenna.

Although I'm probably better known in the security social circles (if there are such things) for dissecting the more complex protocols and vulnerabilities in wireless, general networking, and 802.1X technologies, I'm excited about the opportunity to contribute low tech material. Every day I see network administrators who have painstakingly figuratively hermetically sealed the windows in their castle, only to leave the doors wide open. As Jack says, "Don't hit your head on the low-hanging fruit!"[1]

Wireless is a pretty broad topic. The term *wireless* was first used to refer to radio transceivers. As homage to this ancient wireless terminology, I'm including a variety of technologies in this chapter, centered around the more traditional 802.11 wireless LANs (Local Area Networks) and similar wireless systems that afflict—I mean, simplify—our lives.

WIRELESS 101: THE ELECTROMAGNETIC SPECTRUM

At a very broad level, the wireless technologies we're covering in this chapter use EMR (electromagnetic radiation). EMR of various wavelengths give us light, colors, AM and FM radio, and electronic devices in the electromagnetic spectrum. In order

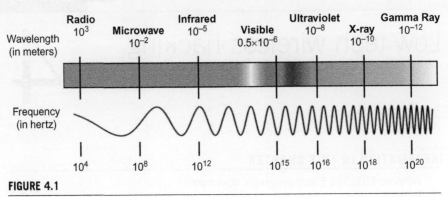

FIGURE 4.1

EMR (electromagnetic radiation) spectrum chart comparing wavelengths and frequencies of common EMR subsets

of longest to shortest wavelengths, we have radio, microwave, infrared, visible light, ultraviolet, X-rays, and gamma rays. Figure 4.1 below is a graphical representation of the EMR space, with wavelengths and frequency noted for key subsets of EMR ranges. As part of my research for this book, I was hoping to construct and analyze attacks for a gamma ray laser, but that was frowned upon by several parties and turned out to be cost-prohibitive. In lieu of that, I narrowed the scope of our happy little wireless chapter to cover more specific types of EMR, such as radio waves and devices in the industrial, scientific, and medical (ISM) band.

The radio spectrum of EMR is used for transmission of data via modulation, meaning it conveys the message by modifying properties of the wave such as frequency, phase, and amplitude. Television, mobile phones, wireless networking, and amateur radio all use radio waves. The use of the radio spectrum is regulated by most governments through frequency allocation. One such designation is the ISM band.

The ISM band is a subset of radio bands reserved internationally for industrial, scientific, and a variety of medical purposes. Many of the technologies that first pop in our head when we hear "wireless" live in this band. The lines of RF are blurry, at best, with quite a bit of exception and overlap, making it difficult to present technologies in order of frequency. Instead, below is a list of some popular ISM applications, in a relatively random order. The units of measure in the ISM band are GHz (gigahertz) and MHz (megahertz). To put those in perspective of one another, 1 MHz = 10^6 (1,000,000) Hz, and 1 GHz = 10^9 (1,000,000,000) Hz. Looking at Figure 4.1, the ISM band would be in the general area of the EMR spectrum where microwaves and long wave radios live.

- **Home and Office**
  - **Microwave Oven**
  2.45 GHz
  - **Car Alarm**
  2.45 GHz (between channels 8 and 9 which interferes with WLAN channels 6 and 11)

- **Cordless Phones**

915 MHz, 2.450 GHz, and 5.800 GHz bands. DECT phones are outside ISM.

- **WiFi/Wireless LAN (IEEE 802.11)**

2.450 GHz and 5.800 GHz bands

- **RFID**

13.56 MHz (used by biometric passports and contactless smart cards)

- **RC Equipment**

2.4 GHz (used by toys, from gas powered cars to miniature aircraft)

- **Video, CCTV, Security Systems**

2.4 GHz and other various

- **Phones and Broadband**
  - **Mobile Broadband Wireless Access (MBWA) (IEEE 802.20)**

1.6 to 2.3 GHz

  - **Wireless Sensor Networks**

868 MHz, 915 MHz, and 2.450 GHz bands (to monitor temperature, sound, vibration, pressure, motion, or pollutants)

  - **Metro Area Network (MAN)/WiMax (IEEE 802.16)**

2 to 11 GHz band

- **Wireless Personal Area Networks (PANs)**
  - **Bluetooth (IEEE 802.15.1)**

2.4 to 2.4835 GHz (used by iPod Touch, PlayStation 3, telephones and headsets, Nintendo Wii)

  - **ZigBee (IEEE 802.15.4)**

2.45 to 2.4835 GHz band (used by wireless light switches with lamps, electrical meters with in-home-displays, consumer electronics equipment)

If we were to collapse some of these more common wireless network technologies into four broad use cases, as in Table 4.1, it becomes apparent that these systems are implemented with very different standards and technologies but that all live in the same general frequency of 6 GHz, plus or minus 4 GHz.

Table 4.1 Chart of Common Wireless Network Uses and Associated Technology and Frequency in the ISM Band

Use	Technology	Frequency
WLAN (Wireless Local Area Network)	Basic enterprise wireless with IEEE 802.11	2.4 to 5 GHz
WPAN (Wireless Personal Area Network)	Bluetooth and Zigbee with IEEE 802.15.1 and 802.15.4	2.4 GHz
WMAN and Broadband (Wireless Metro Area Network)	WiMAX and MBWA with IEEE 802.16 and 802.20	2 to 11 GHz
WWAN (Wireless Wide Area Network)	Cellular technology such as CDMA, GSM, 3G	2 GHz and lower

Why securing wireless is hard

Throughout my years working in various aspects of technology and security, I've come to realize one simple concept; out of sight is out of mind. Organizations habitually overlook security of wireless communications because they can't see it. If they can't see it, then I suppose their logic is that no one else can either, and it's safe. If you come across my Mom, you can ask her about the many times, as a toddler, I glided through the living room, one hand up to my head acting as a blinder. I was told, "I don't want to see you come out of your room." I figured if I couldn't see them, they couldn't see me, and I was following the instructions given perfectly. When you're 4 years old, it seems logical. Apparently a faction of network administrators never outgrew that mindset. It's a little less excusable when you have 5 or 10 years of network management under your belt.

People have been looking for ways to visualize or materialize wireless for many decades, as evidenced by the extensive development and use of frequency monitoring tools from the early 1900s. Figure 4.2 is an example of a WWII-era frequency analyzer used by the U.S. military. We've come a long way since then, with devices like this small enough to fit in the palm of a hand and affordable enough for hobbyists. My goal in this chapter is to let everyone "see" wireless, by explaining how it works, describing types of devices that share common mediums and functionality, and offering plain English explanations of security vulnerabilities using real-world examples. The attacks included are part of the low tech hacking subgenre of wireless assaults. If, in reading these scenarios, you grasp just one new concept or think of one new way to attack (and therefore secure) a system, then I've accomplished my task.

FIGURE 4.2

A frequency monitoring device from WWII used to pick up RF signals in the range of 30 to 1000 MHz, or megacycles as they were called at that time

802.11 AND BLUETOOTH LOW TECH HACKS

When someone hears the word *wireless*, two of the most common initial associations are first with traditional wireless LANS for home and enterprise networks, and second with wireless PANs (personal area networks) such as Bluetooth. This section is dedicated to the variety of low tech hacking techniques for these popular wireless structures.

Since we're dealing with a slightly higher low tech topic than other low tech tricks in this book, I've decided to rate each hack on a scale of one to five, with five being the most technical of the low tech hacks.

DoS AND AVAILABILITY

Attacks on service quality and availability of wireless are probably some of the easiest and least technical and have the most impact. Denial of service (DoS) can result from some of the most cleverly architected technical attacks and, conversely, from some of the most Neanderthal-style physical tampering.

When discussing wireless security, we often talk about layer 1 and layer 2 attacks. Specifically here, we're looking at DoS attacks, broken down by layers.

Layer 1 DoS attacks

Layer 1 in wired networking is the physical connection layer. And so too, in wireless, layer 1 is the physical (albeit unseen) layer of RF. For extra credit, I threw in a couple of extra physical, non-RF attacks here too.

Archetypal antennas

• Removing, replacing, and tampering with antennas

    Low Tech Level 1

The simplest and most fun thing you can do to disrupt a wireless system is muck around with the antennas. This low tech hack earns a respectable Low Tech Level 1. What many network administrators and wireless users don't understand is that the integrity and strength of wireless signals have everything to do with the antenna, the antenna type, direction, and connectivity to the access point (AP). Figure 4.3 shows samples of three different access point types from a common wireless vendor. Note the six external antennas on one model. Other APs shown have integrated or internal antennas. The number of antennas used and the placement of each greatly affect coverage and performance of the wireless network.

To extensively disrupt a wireless system, one needs only to tamper with the antenna system enough to throw off the expected RF pattern. This type of tampering can be easily achieved by simply removing, replacing, or adjusting the angle of the

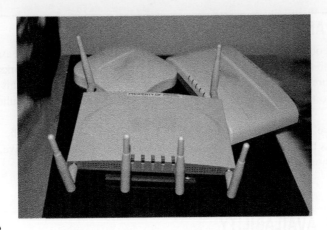

FIGURE 4.3

Examples of various APs from a manufacturer, demonstrating internal and external antennas

antenna(s). As we'll see in other sections, antenna placement and direction are key to maintaining wireless coverage.

Whether an AP has a built-in omnidirectional antenna or an external directional antenna, every antenna has its own unique RF radiation pattern. The proper terms for these patterns are *beamwidth, azimuth*, and *elevation*. Beamwidth is a simple concept: it tells us how broad or directed the overall power is, so we'd use this to describe whether we want to cover a wide localized area or fire a signal down a narrow directed path (e.g., between rows of racks in a manufacturing warehouse). Azimuth (a term borrowed from navigation and astronomy) and elevation give a better picture of the actual coverage area by showing the full propagation pattern. Azimuth is the view you'd get if you could see RF and you were looking down on the antenna from a birds-eye view. The elevation is the view you'd get seeing RF from the side.

As shown in Figure 4.4, external antennas can take on many shapes, sizes, and forms. Antenna manufacturers include specific information in their product datasheets, detailing the beamwidths and coverage patterns, as shown in Table 4.2 and Figure 4.5, but without this information the shape and size of the antenna is a good enough indicator of the antenna type, coverage, and purpose.

Omnidirectional antennas, if you couldn't deduce this from the name, are designed to radiate, for the most part, in all directions in a semi-flat vertical plane. The coverage pattern for these is most often likened to a doughnut. Patch antennas are designed to radiate along two planes, typically in front, behind, or below, which is why they're most often found on sides of buildings or other vertical walls. Yagi antennas, usually long and narrow, have a radiation pattern that mimics their shape, and these are used to provide strong directional signals such as is needed for point-to-point wireless. These are usually found high, on top of buildings, poles, or towers, and will likely have a matching antenna on the other end.

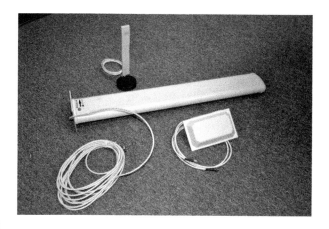

FIGURE 4.4

Assortment of external antennas, including a directional yagi (middle), patch (lower right), and laptop wireless NIC signal extender (top left)

Table 4.2 Sample Beamwidths for Common Antenna Types

Antenna Type	Horizontal Beamwidth	Vertical Beamwidth
Omnidirectional	360 degrees	7–80 degrees
Patch/panel	30–180 degrees	6–90 degrees
Yagi	30–78 degrees	14–64 degrees
Sector	60–180 degrees	7–17 degrees
Parabolic dish	4–25 degrees	4–21 degrees

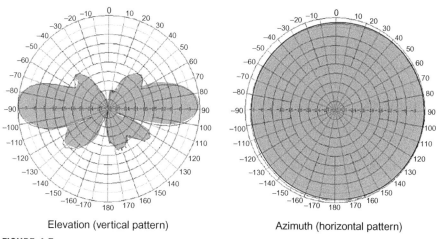

Elevation (vertical pattern)   Azimuth (horizontal pattern)

FIGURE 4.5

Azimuth and elevation radiation charts for a typical omnidirectional antenna

Directional dangers

• Sending wireless bridges off course

Low Tech Level 1

The majority of antennas you'll come across are omnidirectional, servicing a general area around an AP. If you happen to find wireless APs with strong directional antennas, there's a specific purpose for that: to direct the signal to (or away from) a specific area. Directional antennas can be used for signal containment or directional coverage, but often, and more interestingly, they're used in wireless bridges. Even the slightest changes in a directional antenna can wreak havoc on the wireless system. If that AP is serving as a bridge, a malicious person could easily take out an entire building or portion of a network by removing, replacing, or re-aiming a directional antenna. Imagine you're yelling across a field to your friend. No matter how loud you try to be, if you're turned around facing the other direction, he or she may never hear you. The same is true with RF signals traveling to and from wireless APs. The antennas are precisely placed in order to provide the best directional signal to the next hop.

A network administrator would be hard-pressed to troubleshoot this type of attack remotely. If the wireless team has a good monitoring system or WIPS, they're more likely to spot the RF changes picked up if sensors and monitoring APs are in the immediate area. Full remediation would probably involve a visual survey of the APs and antennas, and possibly a physical RF site survey using a laptop and wireless survey application. Since hunting down this issue may be nearly impossible after the fact, the best mitigation is preventing it in the first place. Organizations with external APs or antennas should carefully select their mounting locations and ensure there's appropriate physical security protection for the devices. Mounting on rooftops, maintenance areas, and tall poles or using secured enclosures is strongly recommended. For more on physical security, be sure to read the guidance provided by Jack in Chapters 1 and 2.

> **NOTE**
> Scattered, reflected, and diffracted, please! You may like your hash browns served fancy style, but scattered, smattered, reflected, or in any way distorted is no way to take your RF. Aside from tampering with antennas, forced reflection is probably the simplest and most effective wireless disturbance. As you can probably construe from the word, reflection happens when RF signals bounce off something. Think of it as completely rerouting the path of the RF signal, away from its intended users, and off into some black hole of space (or other unintended users).

Meet evil Doctor Reflecto

• Shielding and deflecting RF signal

Low Tech Level 1

If we don our wireless hacker cap, we'll determine the most effective reflective material would be something with a smooth surface that won't absorb RF. Our material would also need to be larger than the waves that carry the RF signal. Standard IEEE

802.11 wireless radios will emit waves that are approximately 0.8 to 5 inches (2 to 13 centimeters) in size. Eight tenths of an inch corresponds to the 5 GHz bands and 5 inches for the 2.4 GHz bands, in case you were curious. This hack might require something as simple as aluminum foil, so it too gets a Low Tech Level 1.

An evil Doctor Reflecto could easily disrupt wireless availability by positioning a metal sheet, enclosure, or even just some aluminum around the antennas or between the AP and the designated service area. Depending on how much of an evil genius he is, Reflecto may have an extraordinarily good grasp of antenna patterns and may be able to strategically insert a reflecting item outside the immediate area of the AP antenna, but in a spot that will greatly disrupt service to wireless clients. Places where APs may be hard to reach, such as airports and warehouses, would be prime targets for this type of attack.

As with antenna security, preventing direct shielding at an AP can be accomplished with good physical security by way of smart mounting and appropriate locked or hidden enclosures. Enclosures usually run around $50 to $300, depending on requirements for security, power, mounting, and conditioning. Figure 4.6 shows a popular style of ceiling tile enclosures, designed to house an AP out of sight and install easily in standard drop ceiling grids.

There are a variety of enclosures designed to conceal access points and prevent tampering. Products like the ceiling tile enclosure shown in Figure 4.6 will protect APs installed throughout a mid- to large-sized organization with many APs, while lockable racks and cabinets (see Figure 4.7) help prevent physical access to APs and other network equipment that may be more centrally located in smaller offices. Also be sure to refer to Chapter 3, where Jack provides some invaluable information on lock mechanisms and guidance on picking trustworthy locks.

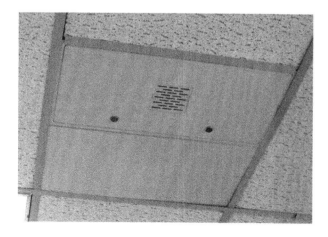

FIGURE 4.6

Example of a locking ceiling tile enclosure for access points

FIGURE 4.7

Example of a lockable rack housing wired and wireless equipment

Foiled!? How effective is Evil Doctor Reflecto's power?

How effective is this low tech hack against modern enterprise APs? That's exactly what I set out to answer. To test this onslaught of RF, we staged the setup in our office labs at Carolina Advanced Digital. We started with a baseline site survey to document the ambient RF and signal strengths and then we piled on the heavy metal. I enlisted the assistance of one of my colleagues.

The first test was simply to place an enterprise 802.11b/g/n dual-radio AP inside a standard metal enclosure. With no visible reduction in RF strength, we layered on a couple of steel doors and shelves taken from some of our equipment racks. I wasn't too happy with the selection, since they were all textured and coated metals. Remember, when we channel our inner hacker, we know our most effective materials will be very smooth and reflective.

Figure 4.8 shows the pretamper setup with a commonly used metal enclosure and one of the more advanced 802.11b/g/n multi-radio access points currently available. It's worth noting that the AP is of the newer variety, since the radios and power options on this unit are far superior to basic 802.11a or b/g radios from several years back.

Convinced the textured steel doors wouldn't do the trick, I moved on to the next metallic test: aluminum foil. I carefully crafted a few sheets with 90 degree angles and placed them strategically to cover most of the enclosure, shown in Figure 4.9. Upon measuring, we found the RF signal took a hit, but not a big enough one for me to put my Low Tech Hack stamp of approval on Doctor Reflecto.

Back to the drawing board. Before our first test, I didn't bother researching the best distances to use in separating the foil to create an RF trap, I was just layering it in thin sheets. For our second attempt, I still didn't get mathematical with it – after all, this is supposed to be a low tech hack, not a get-your-calculator-out-and-properly-space-the-foil attack, right? I decided to rather indiscriminately throw on a few added layers of foil. Luckily, my Dad was in the office. Upon seeing my crazy shenanigans, he suggested we ground the foil just as a final blow. Five minutes and some wire

FIGURE 4.8

Standard enclosure and 802.11b/g/n access point used in our testing

FIGURE 4.9

The tamper tests continue with aluminum foil covering the enclosure

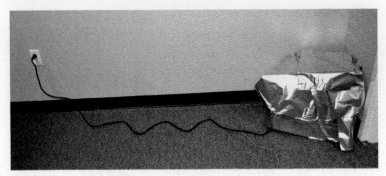

FIGURE 4.10

The tamper tests continued with grounding the foil

strippers later, we were all set with a grounding wire, complete with plug. Figure 4.10 shows the result of our rigging.

If this didn't do it, then I was ready to declare this Low Tech Hack myth BUSTED. With fingers crossed, I foiled a bit more, rigged a hemostat to clip the ground on, and went back to my cohort to see what our RF readings were showing.

The results were promising, we effected more than a 10 dB loss, even at close range (less than 50 feet). The hit in signal quality would certainly be enough to interrupt the operation of latency-sensitive devices like Voice over WiFi phones and specialized medical and manufacturing equipment. In larger buildings with more distance between the AP and clients, we could also affect a sizable RF loss that would hamper connectivity of laptops as well. Our little hack was redeemed!

If you compare Figures 4.11 and 4.12, you'll see the signal degradation affected with the grounded foil. Figure 4.11 shows the normal signal strength. Pay attention to the white dotted line labeled "Bradford" (which happened to be the SSID name used in the lab that day). Now look at Figure 4.12, showing the Bradford SSID signal post-tampering. You'll see the dotted white line there is lower than it was in Figure 4.11. In fact, Figure 4.11 shows a signal at −60 dB, while the signal in Figure 4.12 hits −75 dB, meaning we affected a 15 dB signal loss with our grounded foil, tested from less than 50 feet away.

After the testing, we ended up with quite a pile of aluminum foil. Figure 4.13 shows a shot of the aftermath. Not wanting to waste the foil, I neglected to throw it away. I think pieces of it floated through the office for a few days, some reincarnated as hats, while others were used as creative wall hangings.

The John attack

- Using electrical engineering smarts to short an antenna

    Low Tech Level 0.5

In other low tech hacking news we came up with a simple yet effective way to launch a DoS attack on wireless via electrical tampering. I've dubbed this one "the John attack," so named because my father popped up with this little gem while I was

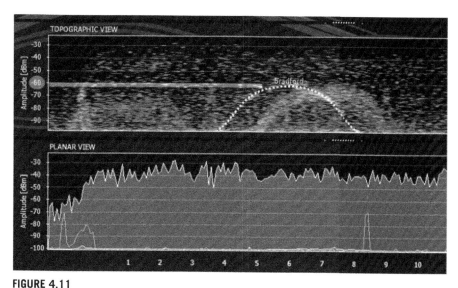

FIGURE 4.11

NORMAL: RF analysis with AP in enclosure, no foil

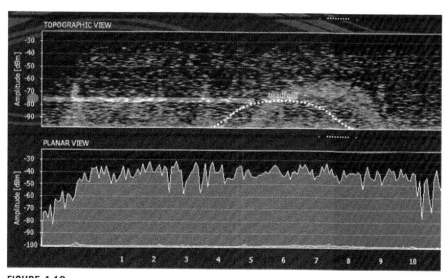

FIGURE 4.12

FOILED: RF analysis shows a 15 dB loss with aluminum foil shielding and grounding

conducting my foil experiments. This attack gets its own section, since we're attacking the electrical properties of the system instead of just an antenna. This hack is worthy of a Low Tech Level 0.5, our lowest tech hack in the chapter!

In true MacGyver style, we're back to hacking with aluminum foil, paperclips, or anything conductive and malleable.

FIGURE 4.13

The aftermath of research

Placing a piece of foil, or anything conductive that you can shape a bit, around the base of the antenna connector (as in Figure 4.14) and reconnecting to the AP will cause an immediate short. This ridiculously simple hack will create a huge impedance mismatch in the connectors and reduce the antenna power to almost nothing. In fact, it's quite possible this little manipulation will cause permanent damage to the antenna.

FIGURE 4.14

Shorting AP antennas through impedance mismatch

Securing the APs and antennas, as suggested earlier, will thwart this attack. If your physical security doesn't hold up, this attack will prove difficult for network staff to troubleshoot remotely. Frankly, it would be difficult for them to pinpoint the problem even with a visual survey of the AP, since the hacker would likely have left the antenna in place after his assault on the system. The AP and antennas will appear normal upon physical inspection, but one or both antennas would be destroyed by the electrical short.

WARNING

One of the worst things an ill-intentioned hacker can do is get someone else in trouble with *The Law*, as they call it here in the South. The most trouble an attacker can cause (short of launching a threat to the White House from a wireless network they're not authorized to use) is to get the FCC involved. The Federal Communications Commission (FCC) regulates interstate and international wireless and wired communications, including radio, television, satellite, wire, and cable.

The wireless communications we mere mortals use are in unlicensed bands set aside for that purpose. We're not radio or television stations. We're just trying to surf the Internet without a wire tether. The FCC takes their job very seriously and once an unlicensed system starts to interfere with a licensed one the RF Cops will surely come a knockin'. Keep reading to see how illegal gain can be used to cause trouble with the FCC.

Your debut on COPS

• Getting ousted with illegal gain

Low-Tech Level 2

Unlicensed wireless will draw attention from the FCC if it's operating in the wrong band or is too high powered. Each combination of AP and antenna will have a set output power based on the AP type, the configuration (power settings), and measured gain of the antenna. If an attacker were really peeved at a neighbor or business, he or she could change out the antenna on a wireless AP with one that would cause the system to operate outside the conditions allowed by the FCC. If you get it just right, not only will the transmission be illegal, but it will interfere with a target signal, the owner of which will surely complain and the RF Cops will be pulling up in their black vans before you can say "shenanigans."

Although this attack requires minimal technology to physically execute (an antenna change), I'm giving this hack a slightly higher Low Tech Level 2 since the attacker will have to be familiar with FCC regulations and procure the illegal antenna to carry out this attack. Instead of providing the specific calculations, I'll just say that there are many online retailers that are more than happy to sell antennas that would be (in almost all circumstances) illegal to use in the United States. Perhaps the antenna is okay in other countries. . . . You see where I'm going with that one.

As with the other antenna attacks, mitigation can be accomplished with good physical security by way of smart mounting and appropriate locked or hidden enclosures. In addition, in an enterprise environment with wireless sensors, monitoring APs and RF management tools would catch sudden spikes in signal or power changes.

> **NOTE**
>
> To discuss these next low tech hacks, we have to have a little bit of background on some of the more fundamental nuances of the technology. Wireless, because of the physical properties of RF, is a half-duplex system. Wireless things are listening and then either sending or receiving, not both simultaneously. Without getting into too much of the boring stuff, 802.11 systems use a combination of detection methods to determine whether it's okay to transmit. When one station wants to talk to an AP or another station, CSMA/CA (Carrier Sense Multiple Access with Collision Avoidance) kicks in to see if the airwaves are clear. If they're not, the station (and any others in range) will hold off until the RF medium isn't busy. The severity and footprint of a collision avoidance attack depend on how it was initiated. We'll look at a couple of specific scenarios, each with different methodologies and effective reaches.

Contraptions of mass disruption
- Jammers, noise makers, and homemade interference

Low Tech Level 2

Homemade, store bought, or by accidental act of idiocy, jammers can destroy wireless service. There are a few ways jammers work their evil magic on wireless systems. One method employed by jammers sends a signal out of the same frequency and strength as the target, thereby canceling the signal. As illustrated in Figure 4.15, if two waves are in opposite phase, the net result would be the horizontal x-axis, with net of 0. This is precisely the technique used by many of these disruptive devices.

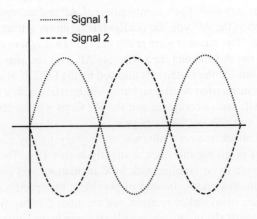

FIGURE 4.15

Two RF waves cancelling each other out

The most popular jammers of this type were all the buzz just a few years ago as techies wrote articles on cell phone jamming. But that takes some calculations and adjustments to be effective. For our low tech hacks, the two easiest ways to jam up wireless are by raising the noise floor of the wireless and by exploiting the collision-avoidance mechanism used by wireless. Here we'll examine the former, which is what most people consider to be jamming, or intentional interference. Even without the frequency-matching requirement, I'm giving this attack a Low Tech Level 2. It does require some electronics, but can be pulled off with unadulterated off-the-shelf products or a small pile of household electronics cobbled together.

Jammers can be easily built from homemade electronic components or by repur-posing another device that's designed to transmit on the frequency you're attacking. At the time of writing, even with the fast adoption of 802.11n, the most prevalent wireless is still 802.11b/g operating in the 2.4 GHz band. With that little piece of info, an attacker could look for transmitters using 2.4 GHz and have quite a bit of fun. I've seen everything from cordless phones to audio-video (AV) wireless transmitters used to demonstrate DoS on 802.11b/g networks. Ah, the possibilities are limitless.

Aside from homemade contraptions of mass disruption, there are a few purpose-built jammers and testing equipment that could be dangerous in the wrong hands. The attack is basically the same, but these devices are likely to be higher-powered than homemade ones and therefore have a much more effective attack range. There are legitimate uses for such devices, such as enforcement of no Wi-Fi zones on private property and by law enforcement and military to block communications or stop remote detonation. It's worth noting these jamming devices are illegal in most countries, including the United States, under the Communications Act of 1934. Remember those RF Cops mentioned earlier? Yeah, they'll find you!

Off with her head!

- The Queensland attack, continuous transmit endpoints

    Low Tech Level 1

Our next low tech hack explains how the half-duplex properties of RF can be exploited to launch a localized DoS attack. The Queensland attack was so named after it was discovered by a group of researchers at Queensland University in Aus-tralia. It's actually an attack on the clear channel assessment (CCA) function of the previously mentioned CSMA/CA feature for collision avoidance. In a nutshell, if something is always transmitting, then all other wireless stations in range think the airwaves are busy and stop transmitting. The actual attack was executed using a rather outdated testing application called Prism Test Utility that shipped with many 802.11b NICs. That software is still available online. With this tool, an attacker can set the station in a continuous transmit mode. With that option enabled, a constant RF signal emanates from the wireless devices. It's not data, just noise, much like a narrowband signal generator.

This is a comparably effortless attack. A hacker only needs this (free) tool and a laptop for a localized attack. If an attacker wanted to scale this to mastermind levels, he might take the tools and launch a distributed DoS (DDoS) by distributing a malicious payload that would execute this attack without the users' interaction. This type of attack could be targeted at a location, an organization, or even the entire Internet.

There's not much that can be done to stop this hack from occurring. The best defense against the Queensland attack for an organization is a WIPS system or an integrated security option built in to the wireless, both of which could contain an unruly endpoint via RF. Without control over the endpoint launching the attack, the best recommendation is mitigation and containment. Since this attack affects 802.11b, another option may be to standardize on 802.11n in the environment. Of course, for every attack you dodge by changing technology, you introduce a new one! Read below for more on why the Queensland attack targets 802.11b.

TIP

The Queensland attack is isolated to 802.11b networks, since 802.11a/g/n standards use orthogonal frequency-division multiplexing (OFDM) to help cope with RF medium issues. It's worth noting here because 802.11b and 802.11b/g systems are affected and in common use as organizations are still transitioning to newer and higher-bandwidth technologies like 802.11n.

Layer 2 DoS attacks

Layer 2 DoS attacks occur when an evil-doer messes around with the 802.11 frames versus the RF as in layer 1. However, akin to the Queensland attack and other exploits at layer 1, most layer 2 strikes are aimed at vulnerabilities within the documented processes required for wireless networking to operate. What that means for wireless network managers is that many attacks can't be completely prevented but can be mitigated, monitored, or secured in other ways.

It's probably fair to generalize that as we move up the stack, our technical difficulty will also increase. So, as we move into our first layer 2 attacks, you may notice the Low Tech Levels hovering around 3 and 4 versus 1 and 2 found in the previous sections. Many of these attacks can be easily launched by someone only vaguely familiar with wireless technologies, using open source applications readily available on the Internet. Even though the underlying processes may be slightly higher tech, the execution is pretty low tech.

Farewell attack

• Forcing deauthentication and disassociation

    Low Tech Level 5

A group of student researchers from the Vietnam National University and the University of Texas at Dallas wrote a document outlining a proprietary lightweight solution they devised to protect wireless systems from unauthenticated disassociation and deauthentication attacks. In that document they refer to these spoofed deauth/dis-association attacks as *farewell attacks*. Although I hadn't seen them referred to as farewell attacks before that document, I found it appropriately short and catchy and am adopting their appellation. The document title is "A lightweight solution for defending against deauthentication/disassociation attacks on 802.11 networks" and is available on the University of Texas site at http://www.utdallas.edu/~neerajm/publications/conferences/attacks.pdf.[2]

Here's the foundation for understanding these farewell attacks. The management messages sent between APs and wireless stations are unencrypted, unauthenticated, and unacknowledged, which means that neither side has to decode them to read them, and neither side can be certain the apparent sender is the actual sender. Also, these frames are notifications, not requests, so the recipient doesn't have the opportunity to give an acknowledgment or say okay. Think of it as the equivalent to a person announcing "I'll be back in ten minutes" and then walking out the door, versus asking "May I be excused?" and waiting for a reply. And so we have the farewell attacks, which allow hackers to leverage this behavior to force other stations to disassociate or deauthenticate from the AP.

I'm assigning this attack a Low Tech Level 5, the highest technical designation of the low tech hacks. As you'll see, the concept is extremely simple, but it does require that the attacker have a more capable wireless NIC (usually an after-market install) and enough know-how to download the right tool or driver.

If you don't spend your free time sniffing wireless packets, you may not be privy to all the goings-on that happen when a station connects to an AP.

Here are the four stages a client may go through while connecting to an AP:

1. Unauthenticated and unassociated
2. Authenticated and unassociated
3. Authenticated and associated
4. Authenticated, associated, and 802.1X authenticated

There are different types of key exchanges and authentication in wireless (WEP, WPA PSK, WPA Enterprise, 802.1X), the succession of which is inserted at different points along this procedure of connection.

Armed with an NIC and driver that support wireless packet injection, an attacker can easily spoof either a station or AP MAC address for a successful attack, and can take aim at a single device by using a unicast or all devices by using a broadcast address. Most hacker types will opt to automate the process with popular tools like Aireplay-ng (part of the Aircrack-ng suite), Nemesis, AirJack, and Winsock Packet Editor.

The order of the connection stages above is important because there are two very similar attacks to discuss: a forged disassociation and a forged deauthentication. The attacker may opt to send either type of spoofed messages. Association depends on authentication as a requisite, so by default, a deauthentication will force a disassociation also. If we pretend this is a board game, the disassociation will knock them back a space or two, while the deauthentication will put them back at the start line.

Besides a few obscure proprietary solutions, there's no standard-based answer for the farewell attacks. But wait: there is hope. In 2009 IEEE approved a standard designed to protect certain types of 802.11 management frames. Aside from this new(er) 802.11w standard, network administrators are best served using WIPS (wireless IPS) and monitoring systems to pinpoint and identify trouble areas in the wireless networks.

TIP

IEEE's new 802.11w standard for management frame protection is coming. The IEEE 802.11w standard aims to mitigate certain types of WLAN DoS attacks. 802.11w extends strong cryptographic protection to specific management frames, thereby mitigating certain classes of DoS attacks on WLANs, such as deauthentication and disassociation attacks. However, there are limitations of 802.11w's ability to thwart certain DoS attacks:

- 802.11w provides protection for certain specific 802.11 management frames only, specifically, deauthentication frames, disassociation frames, and action management frames. Hence, DoS attacks based on management frames not protected by 802.11w are still possible (e.g., association-based attacks, beacon-based attacks).
- DoS attacks based on 802.11 data and control frames are outside the scope of 802.11w.
- RF jamming-based DoS attacks cannot be mitigated via 802.11w.

I know what you're going to ask. "If this standard was passed in 2009, why aren't we using it?" The answer is pretty simple. 802.11w will require a code change/firmware upgrade on both APs and clients and that just takes time to plan and roll out. Manufacturers have to have their firmware tested and certified and organizations have to do extensive testing on clients in controlled environments to verify proper operation.

Rogue on rogue

- Using rogue mitigation from a rogue AP to attack wireless

  Low Tech Level 3

Possibly one of my favorite attacks ever, rogue on rogue, earns a midrange Low Tech Level 3 rating. This oh-so-simple attack yields similar results to a broadcasted farewell attack described above but with one key streamlining difference. Instead of using a laptop with a special NIC and software or drivers, a hacker can launch this attack simply by introducing his own access point and enabling rogue mitigation from his rogue AP. Let me phrase it slightly differently: an attacker can launch a DoS attack from his or her rogue device by telling his AP your legitimate network is in fact the rogue and enabling mitigation.

Rogue detection and *rogue mitigation* are features on many autonomous APs, wireless controllers, and a variety of integrated and overlay wireless IPS (WIPS) systems. *Rogue detection* just tells the network administrator, "Hey we see these other SSIDs and MACs" and may let the administrator manually adopt them as part of the managed network or leave them as rogue devices.

Rogue mitigation takes detection one step farther, by letting the network administrator configure the AP or controller to take action against anything determined to be a rogue. Vendors may label their rogue mitigation with various sugar-coated branding efforts, but when it comes down to the ones and zeros, it's usually the same technique: a farewell attack. Yep, all our fancy wireless security systems leverage the vulnerability in management frame exchanges to launch a widespread disassociation attack against the rogue AP and any stations connected to it. If used properly in an organization, it's a good and effective security measure to protect the integrity of the wired and wireless networks. In the hands of a hacker, it's just a simplified nasty DoS attack that can be executed with a power outlet and a few clicks in a web GUI.

The best recommendation for network administrators is two-fold:

1. Monitor the wireless environment effectively with a WIPS system, and
2. Implement some controls on the wired side to prevent an attacker (or a dangerously misinformed user) from connecting a hazardous device to your network.

The latter is possible through the use of device registration, NAC solutions, wired 802.1X or MAC-auth port security, and monitoring the wire for new management traffic such as SNMP traffic.

Whack-a-rogue

• Exploiting rogue containment to launch a DoS

Low Tech Level 3

Similar to the rogue-on-rogue attack above, we can turn the tables and look at a related but almost reversed attack using rogue mitigation. Exploiting rogue containment gets a Low Tech Level 3 for an ease of execution but with the requirement of having wireless hardware at your disposal.

Many wireless security systems take advantage of the controllers and access points already installed throughout the environment. Using these existing devices, instead of overlaying an additional WIPS system, to help monitor and secure the wireless can be a great cost-saver, but it comes at some other expense. An AP can't be time-slicing and channel-hopping to serve wireless clients and monitor the airwaves at the same time. It can't contain a rogue AP while clients are attached, and it can't service clients when it's trying to contain a rogue.

Think of it in terms of a tractor beam. If the *Enterprise* is locked onto an object and containing it within a subspace/graviton interference pattern, the ship's movement and ability to perform other starship duties is hampered.

You can probably imagine, in an enterprise (lowercase enterprise, not the Starship *Enterprise*; we're past that) using this type of wireless security, an attacker can simply light up one or more rogue APs for the explicit purpose of causing the legitimate wireless controllers with WIPS to move APs from servicing endpoints to rogue containment mode. If the attacker places these APs strategically and times it well, he could affect a widespread DoS on the wireless. Even if some APs maintain their client connections, the additional load from clients that would normally attach to the affected APs (the ones containing the rogues) will likely overload the rest of the APs in the area and cause a domino effect of availability loss. In short, this hack can attack specific APs, but will have a domino effect and overload neighboring APs for as far as the wireless eye can see.

As with the rogue-on-rogue attack, proper monitoring systems with some manual verification and alerting is key to managing this risk. If your organization's daily operations revolve around wireless and you can't afford down time, I'd recommend a well-developed autonomous WIPS or monitoring system of your choice.

Bogus beacons

- Vulnerabilities in channel assignments

  Low Tech Level 4

This next one is a less popular but witty attack. This attack shares some traits of the farewell attacks presented earlier. In the bogus beacon assault, an attacker leverages the unsecured management frames again, but this time to send a bogus channel to a wireless station.

The attack is more properly known as *illegal channel beaconing*, and here's how it works. Your friendly neighborhood hacker sends a spoofed beacon to a station; it contains the same SSID the client is currently using, but the channel field has been manipulated with a bogus channel. As a point of reference, standard 802.11b/g wireless has 14 channels available. The hacked bogus beacon might tell the station to look for the AP on channel 0, 123, 456, or some other nonexistent channel. Many wireless NICs can't process the bogus channel field and they just croak and die.

This attack is relatively easy to prevent with updated firmware and NIC drivers. What am I saying? All your laptops are patched, updated, and in no way vulnerable, right? Organizations with WIPS can also leverage the RF monitoring feature and investigate suspect new devices or APs that have suddenly moved.

Flooding

- Attacks on capacity

  Low Tech Level 3

Flooding attacks are so last decade. But this is an attractive low tech hack, so I'll give the flooding attack the accolades it's earned for being *so uncomplicated a Neanderthal could execute it*. Similar to the bogus beacon attack above, attackers can form bogus probe requests, forcing a station to try to reassociate repeatedly. This attack is a probe response flood and is the first in a line of many flooding attacks. It's accompanied by more layer 2 DoS attacks that take advantage of unsecured management frames, including floods of AP client association tables by sending bogus association requests and exceeding the AP's limits, which may be the IEEE standard-designated 2,007 or an administrator-configured realistic limit like 20 clients per AP.

Decoy SSID

- Confusion and distraction with nonexisting wireless LANs

Low Tech Level 3

Several years ago, an application called *Fake AP* was started as a project by Black Al-chemy. The intended purpose of the Fake AP tool was to create a large volume of decoy SSIDs and fake traffic to confuse and distract would-be attackers. Hiding a tree in the forest or a needle in a haystack was the credo. As shown in Figure 4.16, the Fake AP project website (www.blackalchemy.to/project/fakeap) still asserts, "If one access point is good, 53,000 must be better."[3] I'm not sure about that, but it does pose an interesting opportunity for a DoS attack. The screenshot in the figure offers Fake AP site visitors a brief explanation of the tool and provides a little insight into how it's implemented.

Imagine an attacker using Fake AP, or a similar tool, that creates and advertises phony SSIDs that were remarkably similar, or perhaps even the same, as your cor-porate environment used. Or maybe it's a set of SSIDs chosen to specifically mimic a popular retail area with a Starbucks, Barnes and Noble, or other stores that love to advertise their free Wi-Fi. A hotel would be a smashing place to try this little trick. The attacker wouldn't need 53,000 phony APs and traffic; all that would be required is just a handful of strategically named ones.

If corporate users or hospitality guests opened their laptop and saw 12 to 15 dif-ferent SSIDs, all named to appropriately reflect the native wireless they're expecting, your one or two legitimate SSIDs would be buried in the chaos and probably only a small percentage of users would make it to a real SSID and AP. If the SSID is the same, and the hacker's signal is stronger, guess which network the laptop will latch on to. Any users connecting to the hacker's Fake AP would be DoS victims, con-nected to decoy SSIDs that lead to nowhere.

This attack is easier to prevent in enterprise environments with managed end-points, where the wireless network is authenticated and encrypted. In these environ-ments, the endpoints are generally preconfigured for the enterprise network,

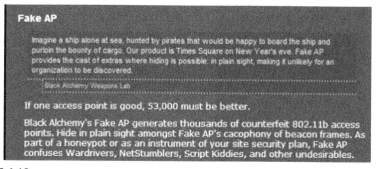

FIGURE 4.16

A screenshot from the official website of the Fake AP project, www.blackalchemy.to/project/fakeap/, describes how their utility works

including the appropriate security settings. The good news is, if an attacker tries this little hack on your network, someone is very likely to notice the sudden surge in SSIDs and sudden loss of service and the help desk will get some nasty calls that would alert you to the disturbance in the force.

Dead-end hijacking
• Man-in-the-middle attacks for DoS

  Low Tech Level 3

I'm especially fond of this attack because it takes the beginning of a complicated attack, assumes the attacker gets lazy and wants to stay low-tech, and turns a traditional hijacking into a DoS attack. Surely I wasn't the first one to dream this up, but perhaps I'm the first to take the time to type it up. This one gets a Low Tech Level 3 because although the hijacking could be done in a more graceful, technical fashion, we're going for duct tape and paper clips here and I'm keeping this one simple in execution.

In a real wireless hijacking, or evil twin attack, here's what would happen: Eager Ed (that's our hacker) would have software on a laptop that would let the laptop NIC look and act like an AP. He'd also have it configured to serve DHCP and maybe DNS. Ed would then plop down for a Hoffacino at the local coffee shop (yes, even the bad hackers like their tasty coffee beverages). He would tell his laptop to assume the identity of another legitimate SSID seen there. (If he's using some of the newer tools like Karma, the process is automated.) Eager Ed would use the farewell attack to send a disassociation to the other station(s) around. His honeypot of a signal would be stronger, so the victim laptops will immediately reconnect, but they'd unknowingly attach to his laptop instead of the real AP. At this point, Ed has all the access he needs to violate the victim laptops, deliver payloads, sniff traffic, or perform other malicious tasks. Voilà. And all before he finishes his coffee.

WARNING

One of the best real-world examples of the attack described above was Rich Mogull's demonstration of a man-in-the-middle attack on a Starbuck's wireless users. In his demonstration during Defcon Security Jam in 2008, Rich showed how he was able to package Eager Ed's attack (above) into a self-contained, automated package.

Among other tricks, several of the exploits used in this setup included:

• Exploitation of browser on splash screen
• Installation of a Trojan for later access
• Sniffing traffic and man-in-the-middle attack
• Injection of HTML
• Uploading of all traffic captures to a remote server

Overall this attack is clever and relatively simple in execution and would pose an extreme danger to users were it used in the wild. The fake coffee shop book contains everything needed to compromise laptops of unsuspecting guests. The rig inserts itself in the environment and appears to be the legitimate wireless network, broadcasting the local SSID (wireless service set identifier), but with a much stronger signal to entice the laptops to attach to the rogue stack instead of the legitimate coffee shop network. Once the users are attached to attack network, the possibilities are limitless. In Rich's attack, he sends users to a browser page (such as a captive portal) that he manages and uses it to deliver an attack payload to compromise the browser. A Trojan is also installed, allowing for remote access to the system later. This attack captures all the data going to and from the endpoint and sends it up to a remote server on the Internet.

Figure 4.17 shows just how unassuming the system is, cleverly disguised as a book that looks just as normal as a cup of Joe in the shop. When opened, as in Figure 4.18, you see the equipment concealed in the book, including an AP and router.

FIGURE 4.17

A faux book looks innocuous enough, but conceals the attack equipment

Image courtesy of Rich Mogull

FIGURE 4.18

When opened, the book enclosure reveals the attack gear, including a wireless AP and router

Image courtesy of Rich Mogull

Now, let's look at my lazy low tech hijacking. We have a similar scenario but a much less motivated hacker and the singular goal of a DoS. Lazy Lenny takes his laptop, and depending on how much Mountain Dew he's had, he may choose to just use the wireless management tools that came with his operating system or he may install the same free software Ed was using. He's okay downloading and installing the software maybe, but he doesn't feel like configuring anything. Lenny's not going to launch a payload attack and he doesn't care if the victims actually have Internet or not. He don't need no stinkin' DHCP server here. Lenny just tells his laptop to broadcast the same SSID as the coffee shop's and he sits, waits, and watches as the unsuspecting little lambs of coffee shop clientele pass in and out, befuddled as to why the wireless isn't working.

It's not the sexiest attack in the world, and I sure hate to ugly-up a perfectly beautiful automated attack, but sometimes we make sacrifices in the name of low tech. This attack could be pulled off with any device that can broadcast an SSID and has a stronger signal than the resident AP.

Attacks like this would probably be caught first by complaining users and second by your wireless monitoring system. Half-hearted attempts at an evil twin attack may be a little more obvious. If Lenny was so lazy he set up an ad hoc network with a spoofed SSID, the victim laptops would certainly identify and display it as an ad hoc (versus AP), but that doesn't necessarily keep anyone from connecting to it.

BACKDOORS AND CRACKS

There are a variety of attacks that take aim at passwords and encryption keys. Some of these attacks require a little more packet savvy than others, but almost every type of cipher or key attack has an automated tool available online. Other backdoor attacks make use of the wired infrastructure or additional wireless networks that may be more easily accessible to an attacker. Access to one less secured network is usually a nice backdoor to the juicy stuff.

Crack attack

- Sniffers and automated online tools for preshared key (PSK) cracks

  Low Tech Level 4

I'm giving this hack a Low Tech Level 4 rating right out of the gate. The underlying algorithms and behind-the-scenes processes are rather complex, but the application is on the Internet and readily available to hackers of all levels. Although I admire the cryptographic genius behind the attack, it loses cool points for being a relatively trite hack. Unless you've been hiding under a rock for the last few years, you already know that WEP and other PSK encryption schemes are broken. If this is your first time hearing the news, then I send my condolences and suggest maybe you skip this chapter and move on to the next one; you'll find it less disturbing.

Retract that last sentence; I just realized Chapter 5 is the Surveillance chapter. In any event, there have been a flurry of tools circulating that allow hackers to passively sniff wireless traffic, collect the data, and perform a traditional encryption crack. As we learned in WWII, the more times a password is used, the more vulnerable it is. These encryption cracking tools gather as many packets as they can from the wireless traffic passing around them to and from legitimate stations and analyze the initialization vector (IV) of each. It's estimated a hacker would need to collect about 500,000 IVs to crack a WEP key. While that may sound like a lot, remember those IVs are on every packet being sent. Still, in an enterprise environment, that could translate to days' worth of packet captures.

Hackers are not too keen on waiting, so they devise a better plan. Newer encryption cracking tools use injection attacks, usually in the form of ARP flooding, to force devices to generate more packets with more IVs, in a much shorter time. This catalyst allows hackers to capture enough IVs for a crack in a matter of minutes.

But, wait. It gets better. About a year and a half ago (at the time of writing), researcher Moxie Marlinspike launched WPA Cracker, a palpably named cloud-based service that offers a pay-per-use powerhouse of hacking. The online service has at its disposal 400 processors to check a WPA or WPA2 key against a sizable 135-million-word dictionary tailored for WPA cracking. How is it tailored? Read the side note on rainbow tables and WPA encryption. The hosted service costs just $17 and $34 per use, for use of half or all CPUs, respectively, and guarantees a response time of 40 or 20 minutes.

NOTE

What is a rainbow table? Most descriptions of rainbow tables reference a lot of crypto terminology, but it's really a simple concept. Many passwords are stored as hashes of the plaintext. Hashes are just one-way functions to turn legible plaintext into a fixed-length unintelligible string of characters. See the example in Table 4.3. The process is virtually irreversible, so the best way to crack a hashed code is to create a list of all possible plaintexts and their respective hashed output. If we just stop there, we're doing a dictionary attack. With a bit of cryptographic magic fairy dust, we have rainbow tables, which are like dictionary attack files, but instead include complete chains of possible hash strings that a hashed password can be dropped into and traced back to its original plaintext.

Table 4.3 Sample Output of Three Popular Hash Algorithms

Hash Example	Output
Plaintext	justsometext
MD5 algorithm	ae90755c088283403150f8711254aef2
SHA-1 algorithm	811388305d099e2e2953c2d624df451456335bad
SHA-256 algorithm	dd743a8eb27997dc289f02c99693654a9db2… 67a37a069a4e6bc8239dbd05785c

Continued

NOTE—cont'd

   Now, if you're curious how WPA Cracker is tuned for WPA/WPA2, those two algorithms take the ESSID and salt the pre-shared key with it. What that means is the hash will be a hashed value of the combination of ESSID and PSK, instead of just the PSK. The WPA Cracker rainbow tables take this into consideration and have included this variable in their lookups.

   Table 4.4 demonstrates the combination of the two individual elements used in WPA/WPA2 to create the hash. This table shows sample MD5 output using individual plaintext "myPSKcode" representing the pre-shared key and "linksys" representing the ESSID. The bottom row then shows the MD5 hash created in a WPA/WPA2 scenario where the two components (pre-shared key and ESSID) are used together to create a MD5 hash output. Notice the hash of the combined output cannot be derived from the MD5 output from the individual components.

Table 4.4 Sample Output Mimicking the WPA/WPA2 Operation of Salting of the Pre-Shared Key Using the Wireless System's ESSID

Component	Plaintext	MD5 hash
Pre-shared key	myPSKcode	6b2f0074d0e04a74078d886029f78028
ESSID	linksys	0c4c43c0a94fc3d2210fa58dca6e09da
WPA/WPA2, using ESSID + PSK	linksys+myPSKcode	0dc94bab6ff7b8b21eb56bf9ebc3050e

How do you protect against these types of attacks? First of all, don't use WEP. I don't really encourage anyone to use static (or even rotating) PSKs if it's at all avoidable. If the wireless should be secured in an enterprise, then 802.1X should be used for authentication and key rotation. At this time, the keys in 802.1X and the rotation have not been exploited.

It's worth noting here that there has been an attack named Hole 196 that exploits the use of shared keys, but it is the implementation that's vulnerable and not the keys themselves.

If an organization needs to support legacy devices that can't participate in 802.1X exchanges, it should use the strongest encryption algorithm supported and isolate that usage from the rest of the network with VLANs (Virtual LANs) that terminate at a firewall or a routing switch with ACLs (access control lists) that restrict those devices only to the resources they need. A great example is a handheld scanner. If the best it can do is WPA2 with a PSK, then use that, and put them on their own VLAN that only has access to the server they communicate with.

The third piece of advice is not to use default SSIDs, even if it's not YOUR default SSID. I've seen a lot of organizations with enterprise APs that use "linksys" as the SSID to trick would-be hackers into thinking it's a different type of wireless, with a different set of default passwords etc. This will make you more vulnerable to the WPA Cracker attack, which uses thousands (maybe tens of thousands) of popular and default SSIDs in their rainbow tables.

Tap, tap. Mirror, mirror... on the wallplate

- Using mirror/monitor switch functions to grab wireless traffic

Low Tech Level 3

Who's the fairest of them all? It's not Snow White; it's one of the evil dwarves. I'm pretty sure it's Dopey. There are a host of attacks we can launch on wireless networks, from wired networks. One such attack is a mirror/monitor attack. If you're familiar with switching at all, you've probably seen or used a port monitor to mirror traffic from key ports. The traffic is usually used for analysis, monitoring, and logging or to get specific types of information to network appliances, such as sending DHCP traffic to a network access control (NAC) appliance. I give this hack a Low Tech Level 3. With the right access, a hacker can very easily view all wireless traffic from an AP, set of APs, or entire controller system, without using wireless protocol analyzers and special drivers. It still takes some tech savvy to dig out the interesting pieces, so it doesn't quite earn a 2.

An attacker could also use this handy little switch feature to duplicate all traffic from an AP and send it to a laptop or other wicked hacker storage device. "But wireless traffic is encrypted," you might argue. It's true, but most wireless, if encrypted at all, is decrypted at the AP and passed in cleartext over the wire.

There are exceptions to this rule. Some wireless vendors offer encrypted tunneling from wireless stations all the way to the controller, and extremely security-conscious organizations may implement an IPSec tunnel for their wireless clients. To address the former, a strategically placed tap could be outside the controller and catch traffic after it's been decrypted by the controller but before it leaves the network. An attacker would more than likely get a deluge of other random traffic with this placement, but that's not necessarily a deterrent. To address the latter, there's little a low tech hacker can do to break your IPSec tunnel. The more affluent hackers might go after SSL certificates and trustpoints, but evil Dopey is unlikely to get into your tunnels.

As a network administrator, it's important to understand how your wireless system works, how the APs communicate to the controller, and how it integrates into the wired network. There are many types of wireless in terms of these variables. Some authenticate and then drop traffic locally on the designated VLAN at the switch. Others tunnel (but don't encrypt) traffic from the AP to the controller so you don't have to provision all the extra wireless VLANs throughout the infrastructure. A few wireless solutions offer an option to tunnel and encrypt from the APs to the controller, and those usually also offer wireless station to controller encryption.

Modifying switch configurations isn't as difficult as you may think. I'd say 90 percent of the time, I find some hole in the wired infrastructure management, whether it's a default SNMP read/write string or a web management interface left open. In this scenario, a hacker would have an easier time with physical access to the network, but this attack can certainly be executed remotely, should he or she successfully infiltrate the network.

Taps and unauthorized monitoring can be prevented with port access controls and mitigated with strict network monitoring. Network administrators should be aware of sudden traffic spikes on previously low-volume ports, and any configuration changes.

Guesssst who got in

- Infiltrating the network via guest wireless

    Low Tech Level 2

Garish Gary is a guest. You love my alliteration, don't you? You give Gary a guest login to your nice shiny new wireless guest management system. He connects, accepts the terms and conditions, and is browsing the Internet in no time. That's the access you wanted him to have, right? Just Internet; that's all he needs. You get called in to a quick meeting down the hall. Gary finishes answering a few emails and gets bored while he's waiting for you. He opens up a network scanner, pokes around the wireless as in the last attack, and then starts exploring outside the wireless network. He looks at the display on your new laser printer, sees the IP address, and uses that as the seed for his next target scan. He scans your internal network, runs NMAP (a free network mapper tool with a super-easy-to-use Windows GUI), finds a domain controller or two, and closes it all back up before you're saying your good-byes down the hall.

You're lucky Gary isn't a hacker, because he would have just scored complete and total network domination. I know this little trick works, because I've channeled my inner Gary on more than one occasion.

You're sure the guest network is the guest network and only has Internet access. But what you don't know is your network administrators didn't put ACLs on the routing switch. Or maybe they did, but they didn't add them to the new one installed last month. Maybe the ACLs were written for a specific guest scope and the DHCP scope was expanded and now serving addresses outside the IP range in the ACL rule. It's possible the guest VLAN terminated at the firewall and someone made an update or replaced it. Maybe the CFO came in and his daughter was having problems getting to some game she liked to play online, so the IT department temporarily removed the ACLs and forgot to reinstate them. Who knows how it happened, but the end result is your curious guests have unfettered access to your production network.

This attack gets a Low Tech Level 2 because it requires only a simple free GUI-based tool and minimal knowledge to execute. So easy, even a Gary could do it.

These types of attacks are easy to prevent but hard to maintain. A simple ACL on a switch would have prevented the attack, but keeping up with the maintenance and management of routing switches can be difficult for an IT team strapped for time. Everyone's putting out fires, and no one's teaching fire safety.

I encourage organizations to perform their own light pen tests internally from time to time. There are many tools out there that are easy to use, free or inexpensive, and that provide a wealth of information about vulnerabilities and misconfigurations on your network. I also strongly encourage network administrators and IT staff of all types to attend conferences, webcasts, and demonstrations of pen testing and hacking techniques so they can be familiar with the tools and methodologies.

> **TIP**
>
> There are quite a few white papers and best practice notes floating around the Internet, instructing people to use cloaked, or hidden, SSIDs as a layer of security for their wireless networks. Unfortunately, this practice does not increase security at all. To the contrary, it may even create an additional vulnerability.
>
> Before we talk about why SSID cloaking is bad, let's take a moment to talk about what it really means. On the client side, the SSID is what users see in the list of available wireless networks that their laptop (or other wireless device) provides. On the network side, the SSID is a wireless network, with specific attributes tied to it – such as the authentication method, the encryption type, the name, and probably the VLAN (virtual LAN) it's associated with on the wired side.
>
> When a network admin cloaks or hides an SSID, he's telling the access point not to broadcast the SSID. Broadcasting just means the AP is letting nearby clients know, "Hey, I have this wireless network." If the AP isn't broadcasting that the wireless network is available, then the clients are forced to ask for it. This happens by configuring the laptop's preferred networks manually or by pushing those settings via a management tool. Either way, to connect to a non-broadcast network, each client must know the SSID name and its associated security settings and be configured to look for that particular network, even if it's not being broadcast. In this configuration, the wireless client, regardless of where it is, will keep looking for that network.
>
> As an example, let's say there's an ACME Corp. that has their secured internal network configured to not let APs broadcast (cloaked SSID). The secured SSID is named "ACME-Secured" and it's using a pretty strong PSK. ACME's corporate office has close to 1,000 users, approximately 40 wireless APs, 800 laptops, and an estimated 500 other wireless devices, such as wireless-enabled phones, iPads, or Kindles. Most of the employees use the ACME-Secured network, but a few may hop on a guest network instead. With this scenario, each of the 800 laptops and 500 other devices that have used the ACME-Secured network will be looking for that network wherever they go. Outside the walls of ACME Corp., each device will be sending a beacon of "Hello, ACME-Secured network, are you there?" The devices will do this everywhere — at coffee shops, in airports, malls, and even security conferences.
>
> The vulnerability is twofold. First, the corporate network is at risk, because each of these devices is very publicly broadcasting key information about the network. The details broadcast by the endpoints are meaningless to most but pure gold for a hacker. Second, this beaconing puts the client at risk, because someone wishing to launch a MITM (man in the middle) attack has all the information they needs to spoof the client's preferred wireless network and lure the device in to a malicious rogue connection. For more on this attack, flip back a few pages to the WARNING on Mogull's MITM attack from Defcon.

Peer-to-peer-to-hack

- Attacking peers on the wireless LAN

   Low Tech Level 3

We're following the guest attack with another hack that takes advantage of a likely unintentional configuration that allows unfettered wireless access. In this case, the unintended access is not between the wireless and wired networks but between clients connected to the same wireless AP. In most cases, any stations attached to the same SSID on an AP are in the same VLAN and broadcast domain. There are a few exceptions, such as SSIDs that use dynamic VLANs specified by the authentication server, but still in that case, the users that authenticate and are assigned the same dynamic VLAN are in the same network. Sorry, I had to digress for the sake of accuracy. The important part is, you can think of devices that share a wireless network and AP similarly to devices on a wired network within a VLAN or broadcast domain. It's all layer 2; these things can see one another and talk using their MAC addresses, without having to consult a router for direction.

In terms of malicious activity, it means a hacker on the same network could easily get to, attack, and even deliver a dangerous payload (virus, rootkit) to any other vulnerable device within that broadcast domain. As we saw in Mogull's man in the middle attack earlier, access to the host device serves as a gateway for a variety of attacks. Viruses attack the applications and may spread to other devices on wireless (and possibly wired) networks. Rootkits provide attackers with back doors to the system. The bottom line is, once an attacker has access to the host system, many types of attacks can be launched, and the severity of the attack varies with the tools and intent. The only way to segment the traffic at layer 2 is to further VLAN the network or to physically separate the devices. There is simply no other control on a wired medium.

However, on wireless networks, we have the option of layer 2 protection not available on the wire. Here's the hitch: it's probably not enabled. Cisco calls the option *PSPF* (Public Secure Packet Forwarding), other manufacturers call it *interstation blocking, peer filtering, station isolation*, and other similar terms. Regardless of the name, it keeps wireless stations attached to the same network from being able to see and directly communicate with one another.

Many network administrators assume this feature is enabled by default, and while I think it probably should be, the fact is even in many enterprise wireless systems, it's not. Someone has to research that vendor's moniker for this feature, find out how to enable it, and configure each controller or AP accordingly. From a hacker's perspective, I give this one a Low Tech Level 3. It's pretty simple to execute and doesn't require any special tools or applications.

There are times when using interstation blocking is not appropriate. Networks supporting medical equipment, wireless phones, handheld scanners, and proprietary systems should check with their vendor before enabling this security feature. As an example, voice over wireless (VoWiFi) phones that have push-to-talk (walkie-talkie style) features need direct communication among the devices because the protocol uses multicasting. If a wireless system needs this type of communication, just make sure those devices are on their own SSID and segmented from the other wireless data.

Securing from this attack is pretty simple. To make sure your organization doesn't fall victim to a peer hack that uses this gateway, network administrators should clearly inventory all (read: ALL) wireless, including controller-based systems and any autonomous APs, no matter how inconsequential. Once they can determine which SSIDs are being used for what and determine that interstation blocking can be enabled on one or more SSIDs, that security can be pushed throughout the wireless infrastructure. As an added layer of security, it's always recommended that organizations use endpoint security tools that offer firewall protection at the host, thwarting attacks from peers, viruses, and spyware. Most modern antivirus providers offer standalone and enterprise-managed tools with this type of protection.

TIP

We anticipate a pretty monumental shift in wireless technology over the next few years as manufacturers realize the value of virtualized technologies. At the time of writing, Meru is the only enterprise vendor I'm familiar with that is offering solutions built on virtual AP technology. In this case, virtual AP means the wireless clients see just one set of SSIDs, from what appears to be one really big AP. When this setting is enabled and a client connects, all it's aware of is itself and the virtual AP. The technology lets organizations provision a single-channel wireless infrastructure without interference, so all APs could be on Channel 11, for example, alleviating the need for extensive maintenance, channel staggering, and reduced power so channels don't overlap.

This same technology also prevents attacks like the one mentioned above from happening. Because the client and AP are in their own virtual world, clients aren't susceptible to peer attacks or even the Hole 196 vulnerability released at Defcon in 2010. Hole 196 is an insider attack that leveraged group keys in 802.1X.

With the added security and ease of manageability, I think more wireless vendors will follow suit, moving to more virtualized technologies in wireless.

Ad hoc, ad finem

- Independent basic service sets (IBSS) and ad hoc networks

  Low Tech Level 2

Staying in the vein of peer attacks, let's look at the hacking potential with ad hoc networks. *Ad hoc* is defined as *formed or used for specific or immediate problems or needs*, followed with *fashioned from whatever is immediately available: improvised*.[4] In terms of 802.11, an ad hoc network is an independent basic service set (IBSS), which just means there is no AP.

Without an AP, everything connected in an ad hoc network is a peer; there's no master and therefore no one to regulate the chaos. Because of this, ad hocs are dangerous networks to have floating in an enterprise. You don't know who's connected to whom, what they're accessing, and you can't see or control the traffic or access. These unhampered connections cause less heartburn in homes and home offices where users are looking for the convenience of connectivity without the hassle of architecting a true network.

I've given this scenario a Low Tech Level 2 because it can be performed with a variety of wireless devices and only requires a small configuration change to implement. An ad hoc network gives a hacker surreptitious access to its peers, allowing the same type of attacks seen in the previous peer-to-peer hacks.

There are some obvious limitations to exploiting an ad hoc network, since a hacker would need to get close to your other wireless clients, as the antennas in laptops aren't as strong as those in APs. The warning to heed here: this attack is a great approach for an insider attack. The data he or she acquires, either wirelessly or via a wired bridge, is virtually untraceable. Your switches, routers, firewalls, IDS/IPS, and data leakage prevention (DLP) tools at the gateway will not see data stolen in this manner.

Organizations, especially larger ones, are strongly encouraged to use a variety of tools to protect against these types of attacks and possible data theft. Settings on laptops and forced configurations through group policy or endpoint security tools can prevent endpoints from participating in ad hoc networks. In addition, the protocol analyzer or WIPS can be used to look for IBSS traffic, which would alert you to an ad hoc network in the environment.

TIP

Acronym descramble: SSID, ESSID, BSS, IBSS. Here's how to decode the various acronyms used in 802.11 wireless.

- SSID (Service Set Identifier)
  The wireless network name. It should be unique to each AP and can/should be used on multiple APs if users are roaming between APs. The SSID is what shows up in the wireless network list on your laptop.
- BSS (Basic Service Set)
  A term used to describe basic 802.11 services and the standard mode for enterprises; wireless connectivity using an AP and stations. The AP controls the stations in its BSS. Think of each AP as a BSS.
- IBSS (Independent Basic Service Set)
  An ad hoc network with no APs, only stations that communicate directly to one another as peers.
- ESS (Extended Service Set)
  The set of interconnected BSSs with the same SSID (network name). When you add the same SSID to all APs in a building, they have the same SSID (network name) but are physically located on different access devices (BSS). The SSID that's extended across those APs is part of an ESS.
- BSSID (Basic Service Set Identifier)
  Unique ID for each BSS, includes the MAC address of the AP. In ad hoc (IBSS) networks, BSSIDs are per peer devices and are made-up MAC addresses based on a random number.

GOING ROGUE

Just a few months ago, in the first quarter of 2011, AirTight Networks (www.AirTightNetworks.com) released a report with findings gathered through extensive research on wireless security and vulnerabilities in the enterprise. The research was based on analysis of more than 200 cardholder data environments, all of which fall under regulations by Payment Card Industry Data Security Standard (PCI DSS).

One of the most significant findings from the data is that 24 percent of enterprises had rogue access points in their environments.[5] That number should be shocking to most. It's not to me, because out of the hundreds of sites I've worked with, I can count on one hand the number that I've encountered *without* rogue devices of some kind. The sites with zero rogues tend to be secured high risk facilities.

Almost one quarter of these organizations had rogue access points. Rogue APs are just one type of rogue device; rogue wired devices such as switches and routers may have been present, as well as rogue clients or wireless endpoints. With the recent consumerization of technology, enterprises are struggling to keep up with the latest wireless gadgets and strike a balance between productivity, employees' desire to bring new toys – I mean, tools—to the office, and an acceptable level of risk and assurance for the organization. There's a full gamut of rogue devices and vulnerabilities that pose security risks.

Following are low tech hacks involving rogue devices and rogue networks integrated into the existing enterprise network.

Marveling at the gambit of rogues

*   Introducing rogue access devices on the network

    Low Tech Level 2

An attack is an attack, regardless of the source or intent. If someone wants to take your stuff, destroy your stuff, or tamper with your stuff, whether that person is part of your organization or an outsider, is inconsequential. More often than not, rogue devices are introduced into a network by authorized users such as employees and contractors. Even if the intent of the user isn't malicious, his limited knowledge of technology probably means the added device has not been properly secured and is accessible by fiendish users who may connect for access, as well as connect to the management interface and make changes or reroute traffic.

A rogue device is any device—client or infrastructure—that attaches to your infrastructure without knowledge or consent by the organization. Rogue devices are a huge security risk in an enterprise. They open unknown and therefore unmonitored paths to data and critical resources. Someone could be siphoning data from your network at this very moment via a rogue access point, and you may never know it happened.

Should a hacker decide there are juicy tidbits on your network, he may not even need bother with breaking in to the authorized production network. Chances are, he can find an employee who's thrown a wireless AP in the office so he can move around more freely, get better signal or let his kids play online with their Internet-enabled games. I've assigned this hack a Low Tech Level 2, because our happy little hacker doesn't even need to hack much; your employee did the work for him.

In this scenario, a nefarious individual can attach to a rogue AP and 99% of the time he'll get right on the production network, instead of a guest network. Why? Because when the IT department adds wireless, it provisions the proper VLANs, networks, and settings to offer secured wireless for the organization, whereas the ignorant employee will simply plug an unconfigured AP in the most convenient wall plate (on the production network) and go on about his business. He may not even intend to leave it in place; perhaps there was some immediate and sudden need.

The key takeaway here is these rogue devices added haphazardly by non-IT employees won't have the appropriate configuration, security, and management controls. If you don't know about them, you can't manage or secure them. If you can't manage or secure them, they're at risk.

Mitigating rogue access devices, such as APs, is a daunting task. There are a variety of ways to prevent new devices from being inserted into the network or to monitor for devices after they're added. My preference is to be proactive and inhibit rogues, but if you can't do that because of logistics or budget, monitoring and reactive mitigation are acceptable. Organizations can:

- Use network access control (NAC) technologies to prevent new devices from attaching to the network
- Use dynamic VLAN assignments to force devices to authenticate before a wired port offers a production VLAN
- Use switch configurations to learn and lock to specific registered MAC addresses
- Monitor for SNMP and new devices on the wired network, matching OUIs or MAC addresses
- Monitor for new RF or SSIDs with a WIPS tool or with the existing wireless infrastructure

New SSID on the street

- Adding new networks to the production wireless

Low Tech Level 3

I'm never able to communicate exactly how insecure management access is for many organizations' network devices. Even in environments that have telnet disabled, SSH used, and web GUI access removed, there's usually some little back door. Perhaps an SNMP read/write string set to the default public/private. Many times one secure management feature is configured and enabled, but the less secure option is not disabled. For example, SSH might be set up, but Telnet was left on, or HTTPS enabled, but HTTP still accessible. It's possible in some systems that a manager password is set for the CLI, but the web GUI uses a different username/password combo, and it's still on the default.

Regardless of the specific vulnerability, nine times out of ten, there's SOME way to access the management interface of a switch or access point. And if a hacker can get to the management interface, they can pull many underhanded tricks. Unless the hacker affects the services, for example, launching a DoS attack, the changes he or she makes may go unnoticed for an extensive period of time.

One such sly trick is to add a new SSID on a wireless AP or controller. With this, the hacker has two options, depending on the culture of the IT staff. He can add an SSID with a completely different name (something that would appear to be a neighbor's wireless, if someone were to view the list of local SSIDs from a laptop), or he can add something very similar to a current enterprise SSID that might seem like a legitimate corporate network. The former works in a smaller organization that doesn't regularly manage, maintain or audit the wireless systems.

The latter works in a larger organization with a more segmented network management team. With divided responsibilities, one management team might not question a configuration change that could have been affected by another team. There also tend to be more turnover and movement of personnel within larger organizations, versus a small IT shop, with one or two folks who have built and maintained the networks for years. This hack gets a Low Tech Level 3 designation. It doesn't require special equipment, and it uses a relatively simple attack on device management, followed up with the extremely easy-to-execute process of adding an SSID.

If an attacker were to gain access to the management of an AP or controller (I've already explained why this is not farfetched at all), he could add an SSID that would be the least obvious to the users and IT team. By setting his own security options on the SSID, he wouldn't need to bypass any other security to get network access. The network wouldn't show a rogue device, because the SSID would appear to be rightly configured on an enterprise AP.

The rogue SSID would allow a hacker to access the network, possibly directly to the wired production network. You know, if I were performing this attack, I'd definitely put my rogue SSID on the production or management VLAN, depending on what my goal was. This type of access would give him entrée to the wired network, to other network devices or network users and to whatever data he configured the SSID to give him access to – servers, credit card info, HR records, etc. He'd have this access until someone noticed the additional SSID; it could be days, weeks, months, or even years.

How do you combat this attack? Handling this vulnerability is actually pretty easy, but most organizations don't think about it. I've worked with many enterprises and government offices that had a mish-mash of wireless equipment, layered with both controller-based and autonomous APs. With such a random jumble of equipment and usually a short-handed network team, these organizations rarely revisit or audit the wireless. It gets set up, it works, and it gets left alone until something breaks. Here are ways to combat this attack:

* Regular monitoring of the RF environment for new SSIDs
* Secured management interfaces for the APs, controllers, chassis hosting controllers
* Strict change management policies
* Monitoring and auditing configuration changes and alerts on changes
* Annual or semi-annual review of all wireless configurations

TIP

When reviewing wireless networks, I frequently find legacy SSIDs accidentally left in place after testing and after a migration to a different SSID. For example, an organization may have been using WEP or WPA2 with pre-shared keys (PSKs). They're moving to 802.1X, but they leave the PSK SSID up while they transition the endpoints and test, but no one goes back to de-provision the original SSID. I see it almost daily, and it becomes a risk in an enterprise. As noted above, regular reviews of the wireless configurations will help stifle these issues before they're a problem.

It's a bird . . . it's a plane . . . it's a ROGUE?

• Adding legitimate-looking rogue APs

Low Tech Level 4

This is a hack everyone can appreciate. It's a little twisted, elegantly simple, and quite sinister. The majority of new wireless networks are using controller-based systems. These use a central controller (or group of controllers) to manage access points across a single location or full enterprise. Controller-based APs come in many flavors, but one is particularly easy to implement and, for that reason, potentially dangerous.

The systems vulnerable to this attack are light-AP-based controllers that are configured to use a single provisioning VLAN. A provisioning VLAN is used between the controller and APs to communicate, and usually all wireless traffic is encapsulated in it. It's great for large organizations, because the IT department can add a wireless AP with different SSIDs without having to pipe through all the wireless VLANs. I'm going to use the HP WESM solution as an example. By default, it uses VLAN 2100 to communicate between the controller (HP WESM) and AP (HP Radio Port). If our guest VLAN is 99 and production wireless is VLAN 5, we still only have to extend the provisioning VLAN 2100 out to the AP. Traffic from VLANs 5 and 99 will be tunneled over VLAN 2100 with no additional VLANs on the switches along the way.

To make life even easier, many of these systems offer an auto-provisioning feature. I'm picking on HP here, because I know their VLAN assignments off the top of my head, but many other vendors do the same thing, and network administrators love it. The auto-provision lets the organization add an AP. The switch says "Hey, you're an AP, you get VLAN 2100." The controller then sees the AP pretty immediately and auto-adopts the AP. When it auto-adopts, the configuration is pushed out, with SSIDs and security settings, and the AP is ready to use in no time!

Sounds fabulous, right? It is. It lends to a more plug-and-play-style operation and saves the IT teams from the daunting tasks of having to identify every single interswitch link and add two or more VLANs.

There's a downside to all this auto-provisioning plug-and-play. If an outside attacker or mischievous employee wanted to extend the corporate wireless network to an area that was intended to have no access, the most inconspicuous way to do so would be to use the same equipment already in place, and simply add to it. The AP would most likely be auto-adopted by the controller, and the IT staff wouldn't think anything of it. If the network staff even noticed the new addition, it would seem innocuous – just an extension of the corporate wireless. If the IT staff didn't have alerting set for new APs, they might not even notice until they performed some type of refresh or coverage survey.

Extending wireless outside the intended boundaries can be troublesome; the SSIDs and access served may be intended only for specific groups of users, in specific locations. In some instances, they're provisioned for equipment in healthcare and manufacturing and not intended for general data use. Adding APs can disrupt RF planning, compromise security containment areas, and create a quality-of-service issue if the new users cut into bandwidth for the intended users of the system.

Preventing this type of attack is straightforward. In an environment where wireless containment is critical, network managers should turn off auto-adopt and auto-provision of APs and VLANs. All organizations should set alerts that report on new APs and keep a detailed inventory of where every AP is, with its MAC address and physical location. In addition, regulated businesses may also use WIPS and RF sensors throughout their facilities or locations to alert for the presence of new RF in the environment. PCI DSS standards require this, and it's a good practice if a location shouldn't have wireless, to offer assurance that there is, in fact, no wireless:

- Disable AP auto-adoption on the controllers.
- Disable auto-provisioned VLANs on switches.
- Set specific alerts to notify a network admin of new APs.
- Use WIPS or RF sensors to monitor for new RF in protected areas.

There are organizations that may have a business case for auto-adopt and auto-provisioning, so I wouldn't make the blanket statement that these features should never be used. The IT staff just needs to be aware of the possibility and keep a closer watch on the wireless network.

Bridge bereavement

- Abuse of bridged interfaces in ad hoc clients, printers, and cameras

    Low Tech Level 3

In the earlier section, Ad hoc, ad finem, we looked at attacks that took advantage of the vulnerabilities in ad hoc networks. Here, we extrapolate on that concept and dig one layer deeper to exploit bridged network access in these environments. Bridging lets devices connect two network interfaces—for example, wired to wireless and vice versa.

Wireless ad hoc networks aren't only menacing due to the lack of control of wireless access; they can also become gateways to the wired infrastructure in an enterprise. We've already seen how hackers can exploit ad hoc networks; think of the possibilities if they used that access to penetrate the wired infrastructure as well.

Users can bridge the wireless and Ethernet NICs, either deliberately or accidentally, through the use of self-configuring applications. In this scenario, an attacker would get immediate and probably undetectable access to your wired infrastructure, via an ad hoc network.

This attack doesn't stop at vulnerable laptops. Newer wireless-enabled printers, cameras, and other networked headless devices can also become gateways for destruction. These devices are designed with easy plug-and-play functionality, so without configuration they'll advertise and participate in ad hoc wireless networks. The other end of that printer or camera is attached somewhere to the wired network. With an 802.11-enabled printer as our example, an attacker can easily access the management interface via a web GUI, upload vulnerable firmware, and/or simply modify the settings so the wired and wireless interfaces are bridged. The same attack works on some camera and security systems as well.

Securing the network from hazardous bridged configurations requires a bit of tenacity and attention to detail. As suggested earlier, group policies and forced settings will protect laptops from misconfigurations and configuration tampering. Disallowing the use of ad hoc networks and forbidding interface bridging is a good start for laptops.

The headless devices, such as printers, are a bit more troublesome because they're so often overlooked and undocumented. The IT department should have an accurate inventory of ALL network devices and maintain an accounting of what it is, when it was added, where it is, why it's there, and who's responsible for it. Strength in enforcement can come from technology but will be more effective with organizational policy and strict regulation. To do this, the IT department must be monitoring the network regularly for new devices. The organization should have very clearly documented policies on adding networked devices, and those policies should be communicated clearly and often to all employees. If someone is discovered to have added a switch, AP, or even printer without permission, he or she should be reprimanded appropriately.

The technological difficulty for many organizations is not having the mechanism to be alerted on new devices. To this end, port access security, NAC, and MAC-based management systems offer the only enterprise-level solution. Other more manual techniques for smaller organizations may include switch-configured MAC-learn and MAC-lockdown features. These tell a switch to learn the MAC address (or addresses) of what's plugged in, and not allow anything else to be connected. Another manual option would be for the IT department to run a light network mapping scan every so often to identify devices that have been added. Free scanning tools such as NMAP can report on findings from scans to target networks. More advanced network management tools (usually paid) include advanced reporting, archival data, and comparative tools that are better at notifying the network team of changes. Just remember: knowing something has changed does no good if the organization's management team doesn't act on it and enforce policies.

- Create and communicate a clear policy on adding networked devices.
- Use directory group policy to enforce settings that protect computers from ad hoc networks and interface bridging.
- Enforce the policies by monitoring the network closely.
- Use tools to scan the network manually and look for new devices.
- Use network management applications that will monitor and alert on new devices.

ASSAULT BY DEFAULTS

I vacillated on whether or not to include this section. Avoiding susceptibilities of default configurations seems like such a no-brainer. That was my original thought, at least. Then I reconsidered. It's a problem often disregarded as being too mundane, yet I habitually see organizations fall victim to it. Besides, exploiting default configurations has to be a paramount low tech hack.

Open sesame

- Breaking in with default passwords

  Low Tech Level 1

It's like taking candy from a dingo! Wait, no. It's like taking a dingo from a baby . . . .
No, that's not right. The dingo ate the baby? Oh, never mind. This hack needs no
introduction. People have been using default passwords since before Al Gore
invented the Internet. Sometimes for legitimate uses, other times for malicious intent,
if default settings are left in place they will be exercised.

Within the realm of wireless, there are many default settings that are of interest to
a hacker, including:

- Default management usernames and passwords for APs, controllers, and WIPS
- Default management usernames and passwords for wired devices servicing wire-
  less access
- Default read/write network management strings
- Default management IP addresses
- Default serial terminal settings
- Default database accounts and passwords
- Default directory service accounts and passwords
- Default Bluetooth PINs, both on laptops and accessory devices
- Default RADIUS policies and common RADIUS shared secrets
- Default management access and absence of certificates out-of-the-box

Armed with one or more of these little gems, a hacker has the potential to modify
management settings, lock out legitimate admin users, reconfigure devices, launch
man-in-the-middle attacks on authentication, participate in 802.1X and other authen-
tications without an account, attach to a device, and/or engage in out-of-band device
management. These are more general assertions of possible hacks using default
settings, but the list is really limitless.

I don't have to tell you what the appropriate steps are to prevent this manner
of attack. (I will anyway, but I don't need to.) Always, always, always change default
settings and default accounts that are provisioned within any part of a wireless
system. This includes, but is not limited to, the controllers, APs, switches, endpoints,
authentication and directory servers and any management hardware or software.

As seen in Figure 4.19, simple Google searches can yield a wealth of information,
including default management passwords for just about any type of hardware (or
software) you can imagine.

Default WPA keys

- Default PSK lookup for ISP-provided WLAN

  Low Tech Level 2

Not long ago, several ISPs were offering wireless as an add-on to their Internet service and doing so by providing a branded wireless router with a default SSID and
default PSK for WEP, WPA, and WPA2. Figure 4.20 demonstrates the availability

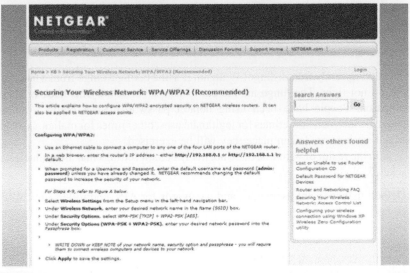

FIGURE 4.19

Screenshot of a Netgear Internet knowledge base showing default management passwords

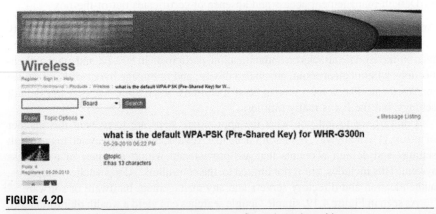

FIGURE 4.20

Another example of a different system with preconfigured preshared keys

of these preshared keys on the Internet in various knowledge bases and web forums. The preshared keys were generated from an algorithm that was later compromised. I'm not sure if the algorithm used by the ISP was accidentally shared or reverse engineered, but the end result was any preconfigured wireless PSKs were vulnerable to access by unauthorized users privy to the phenomenon. This paragraph sums it up:

The algorithm used by ▮▮▮▮▮ *to determine both the default SSID and corresponding WEP/WPA-PSK/WPA2-PSK passwords has been published on GNUcitizen.org. If you have a wireless router from* ▮▮▮▮*/*▮▮▮▮ *please use the tool below to determine if you are vulnerable. Though WPA and WPA2 are by itself pretty secure,* ▮▮▮*s implementation of generating default values has proven to be flawed. Unfortunately, some ISPs like* ▮▮▮▮▮ *are still distributing this router and allowing their customers to use the default (insecure) settings . . . .[6]*

This hack is assigned a Low Tech Level 2, because there's really not much to hack. If a hacker uses a simple wireless network scanning tool, knows the system is vulnerable to this attack, and simply uses a search engine to look up the algorithm converter, then bingo! He's in.

The obvious fix for this low tech hack is not to use default SSIDs and/or default PSKs. Most important, don't use the default PSK, but if you read the section, Crack Attack, you'll know why you shouldn't use the default SSID either.

More Google hacking

- Google hacking for wireless device mgmt interface

  Low Tech Level 3

One of the most entertaining (and revealing) gateway attacks is precision Google hacking. If you've read Johnny Long's *Google Hacking for Penetration Testers*, Volume 2 (ISBN: 978-1-59749-176-1, Syngress), you know exactly what I mean. The resources and examples provided in the book are rather exhaustive and appropriate for all types of information gathering and hacking.

For wireless, there are a few specific Google techniques that can serve as a launching pad to many of the other low tech attacks in this chapter. One of my favorite Google hacks is searching for configuration files stored on Internet-accessible servers. If you look into Chapter 4 of *Google Hacking*, you'll see specific examples for using the Google inurl operator with key phrases like "conf" or "config." Expanding on that search, you could also look for specific filename strings and file extensions, .txt, .pcc, .ini, and many others. Finding this information will give a hacker information about the organization (based on the IP or server found) and configuration of various network devices, including wireless APs, controllers, switches, routers, and more. Important information such as management configurations, SNMP strings, IP schema, routes, and VLANs could be gleaned from these configuration documents. I've also been successful in finding backup archives containing this information online. Along the same lines, you can Google foo to find log files, including Putty log files. Putty is a tool used to connect to CLI interfaces of devices, via SSH, telnet, or serial. They frequently contain technical troubleshooting output and therefore may be even more interesting and telling than just a configuration file alone.

FIGURE 4.21

Google Hacking for Penetration Testers, Volume 2 (ISBN: 978-1-59749-176-1, Syngress)

Chapter 8 of *Google Hacking* details specific strings for finding Internet-accessible network hardware. With Johnny's search strings, an attacker can easily find devices such as switches, routers, wireless hardware, printers, firewalls, cameras, monitoring systems, and more. Examples include searches for "intitle: DEFAULT_CONFIG –HP" to find HP Networking switches and "intitle:"switch home page," "cisco systems," " Telent–to," for Cisco switches. The list spans seven pages and includes juicy search tidbits for all types of devices. Clearly, finding live production network devices on the Internet opens up a host of attack possibilities that can be executed remotely.

Google hacks create a field day for hackers. Save yourself from Internet-launched attacks by making sure critical systems, backups, and configurations aren't accessible from the Internet, and perform your own Google hacking every 3 to 9 months to ensure you're not a search result. *Google Hacking for Penetration Testers*, the cover of which is shown in Figure 4.21, is one of the best, if not the best, resources I've seen on this topic.

BYPASSING SPECIFIC SECURITY TOOLS

In the great world of wireless hacking, there are even a few low tech hacks that can bypass very specific higher tech security mechanisms. In the examples below, we'll see how to bypass MAC filtering, port security, and even some of the newer NAC-based controls.

Going static

• Setting a static IP to avoid DHCP-enforced security

Low Tech Level 2

Here's an easy one. In our going static strike, a hacker simply uses a static IP address to bypass dynamic host configuration protocol (DHCP)-enforced security. Many monitoring systems and even NAC devices (whether in monitor-only mode or full enforcement) rely on DHCP and layer 3 configurations for security. Some network security solutions simply look at DHCP traffic to get a map of what devices are connecting, when and where. Other products use DHCP to serve containment IP addresses, default gateway and DNS settings to clients. You'll usually see this method of enforcement on wireless captive portals as well as NAC appliances that protect both wired and wireless network access. As an added layer of DHCP security, some access solutions also use DHCP fingerprinting to identify and verify the type of device requesting access. We'll tackle that attack in a later section, MAC Switcharoo.

In some instances, a static IP won't be enough to bypass the system; for example, NAC solutions that use a layer 2 (VLAN) enforcement may appear to be containing clients via IPs and routing, but in reality the system is flipping VLANs at edge ports or wireless SSIDs. Setting a static IP on these will just further isolate you from the network, since you'll have assigned an IP associated to the wrong VLAN and, therefore, have no way to access any default gateway.

It's hard to say how often this hack will be successful. It's so easy to test, it would be more of a trial-and-error attack than one heavily researched by a hacker.

You'll know if this attack works on your network. Even if you don't understand the operation of your access security enough to deduce whether it's layer 2 or layer 3, you can (like the hacker) just give it a whirl and see where you get (or where you don't get). You have the added benefit of knowing your IP schema, so you can be precise in your self-pen test and know for sure whether a hacker would also be successful.

Protecting the network from statically addressed devices is multifaceted. Believe it or not, there are many organizations that are still (intentionally) using all or partially statically configured devices. Each has its own reason for doing so, and many are trying to transition, but it's important to note that some of the protection against static rogues isn't suitable for environments with intentionally static-assigned devices. For DHCP environments, there are numerous options. Most name-brand enterprise switches have DHCP protection features, some of which look for MAC addresses that appear on the switch but don't match to the DHCP requests seen going through. That gives a very high level of assurance that the device was statically configured. Other solutions are software-based and plug in to DHCP servers and/ or directory services to correlate data between network devices and switches.

Organizations may also choose to provision different networks and access types for managed and unmanaged endpoints. The managed production network might offer access only to corporate assets, which can be more strictly controlled via group policy. Meaning, the IT department could set a policy to disallow employees from setting static IP addresses on any network interface. The guest, or unmanaged, devices would use another network that is perhaps less restrictive but doesn't offer access to internal resources that would pose a security risk.

Counterfeit MACs

- Basic MAC spoofing (and why it works)

    Low Tech Level 3

Good ol' fashioned MAC spoofing is a great way to get around a variety of security controls in place. MAC (media access control) addresses are unique identifiers for each network interface on a device. A laptop, for example, probably has at least two- one for the wired network port and one for the wireless card interface. They're hex characters (0-9 and a-f) displayed in the format 00:00:00:00:00:00 or 000000-000000 and are put on the hardware by the manufacturer at production. It's worth knowing the first six digits in a MAC address identify the manufacturer. Each manufacturer may have several unique identifiers. Although the MAC address is coded on the machine, it can be changed in the software, making it possible for a user to change a MAC address on his device.

For systems that use layer 2 enforcement on a wired or wireless network, the system uses a device's MAC address to uniquely identify it, and access is then allowed or denied to that particular MAC address. At the time of this writing, the majority of access solutions out today use MAC addresses to control access. Some more advanced solutions (like NAC) use a combination of criteria to identify and authenticate combinations of users and devices, but the vast majority of solutions aren't there yet.

MAC addresses can be changed on most devices with a few clicks of the mouse, making it an easy option for even nontechnical users. Traditionally, MAC filtering has been used more often in wireless networks than wired. There's some debate in the industry over whether or not MAC spoofing is a hack or not. Spoofing a MAC is an action usually affected on the attacker's own machine in an effort to subvert or circumvent security.

There's a current federal indictment against a programmer, Aaron Swartz, in Massachusetts, who is charged with illegally accessing the Massachusetts Institute of Technology (MIT) network in order to steal electronic documents from a nonprofit who hosted archives and provided access to colleges and their students for a fee. Over the course of many weeks, Swartz subverted the security mechanisms in place at MIT with basic MAC spoofing. The college would identify the bad behavior and block the MAC address of his computer(s). Swartz would then change the MAC address, as described above, to circumvent the filter. This process repeated several times and allowed him to successfully access the network and steal millions of pages of content. The full indictment from the U.S. Courts can be found at http://web.mit.edu/bitbucket/Swartz,%20Aaron%20Indictment.pdf.

MAC switcharoo

• Using a legitimate device to get past a profiler

Low Tech Level 4

Some of our NAC vendors are going to hate me for this one. This low tech hack gets a 4, because it does require some street smarts on the part of the hacker and physical access to devices and ports. If you fall victim to this one, maybe you should revisit Chapter 2 to see how Jack recommends you secure your facilities.

As mentioned in Going Static earlier, some network access solutions (NAC and endpoint security) use DHCP fingerprinting to identify and validate a type of device. I'm going to try to describe the behavior succinctly, but I think it's important to understand what happens so you know why this attack works.

In this incident, let's say there's a NAC solution in place, and it's configured to identify any iPads (current or new) on the network, register them in the NAC controller, and then allow them access to the production VLAN. DHCP fingerprinting is one of the most common methods for identifying common commercial network devices, such as printers, phones, handhelds, and even for identifying types of laptops and the operating systems they're running. I'm using iPads as my example because they connect wirelessly, and we're trying to hack the wireless in this scenario.

Here's how the attack plays out. George the hacker, through observation, social engineering, or good guessing, knows that iPads are allowed on the network without additional user authentication. George gets an iPad and connects to the wireless, and the iPad requests an IP address. The NAC system sees the DHCP request, knows it's an iPad, and follows its normal process of registering the device in the system using its MAC address. It's now considered a known device. George then fires up his laptop, spoofs the MAC address of the iPad, and BAZINGA: immediate access for George. Now, if George thought he was going to be abusing this wireless quite often, he could make a small adjustment to his hack and spoof his laptop's MAC address on the iPad before connecting the iPad to the wireless for the first time. This technique will work if only DHCP fingerprinting is in use to identify devices, but it may fail if the NAC is also inspecting the MAC address for the OUI (Organizationally Unique Identifier), which would divulge the manufacturer. If both are inspected and there's a mismatch between the results of the DHCP fingerprint and the OUI, then the attack variation would fail.

There's a key recommendation in network security that would save an organization from this type of attack. That recommendation is to secure appropriately and differently any portions of the network that are provisioned differently. So in this case, if iPads are allowed on the network without user authentication, then they should be segmented from the primary network, secured differently, and only allowed access to what they must have. An iPad may only need Internet access, for example, and a printer may only need to talk to a print server. With this design, an attacker could still bypass the system, but they'd have limited access to the network and likely give up and find an easier target.

< html >Free Wi-Fi</html >

- Pay for free: Hotel wireless captive portal HTML modifications and MAC duplication

Low Tech Level 2.5

Here are two admirable hacks for getting free wireless from paid access providers. We've all used a hotel or airport captive portal. You know how it goes—you read the agreement, promise to pay some exorbitant fee for an hour or a day's use of Internet, enter payment info, and you're on your merry way. This first free Wi-Fi attack requires a simple modification of the HTML in the payment agreement coding. Maybe that wireless is worth $1 or $0 to you instead of $12. Using any of a number of in-browser HTML editors, you make the appropriate change in the code, flip back to normal view, and hit the submit button. And . . . ta-dah! It's that easy, or so I'm told. I'm not going to share any specific details of this attack. Feel free to Google that one for more! This hack gets a Low Tech Level 2.

The second attack is a bit more work, and so is a Low Tech Level 3, slightly higher tech than the first HTML hack. In this attack, a corrupt user approaches the task a bit differently. Perhaps this fellow is more comfortable with his free sniffer tools than with the HTML editor. In many paid wireless portals, the back-end system keeps inventory of paid devices by MAC address. This is why connecting to a paid system via wireless and moving to wired may trigger a recharge.

This stingy hacker knows how to abuse the system, so he uses a wireless protocol analyzer to look at wireless traffic and find another wireless client already paid and registered with the system. That's the hard part, if there was one. All the hacker needs to do now is spoof one of the registered MAC addresses he sniffed out, apply that to his device(s), and hop right on. It's highly unlikely he'll get any type of captive portal page or notice of charge because the wireless system thinks he's a device that's already paid.

SUMMARY

As you can imagine, even with the breadth of low tech hacks described in this chapter, we're just hitting the tip of the iceberg. Wireless is a broad topic, with a variety of implementations throughout the world and in every facet of life. These technologies are found in at least one item, and probably dozens, in our daily activities; cell phones and hands-free calling tools, enterprise and hotspot Wi-Fi access, satellite communications, traffic and highway monitoring, wire-free audio and video technologies such as baby monitors and security cameras, RFID tagging and tracking in retail stores, and even medical devices in hospitals.

Now armed with a little technical know-how and the street smarts to protect against physical intrusions and social engineering attacks, you're well on your way to increasing the security of your wireless systems at home, in the office, and anywhere you travel along the way.

ENDNOTES

1. Wiles J, personal communication.
2. Nguyen T, Nguyen D, Tran B, Vu H, Mittal N. A lightweight solution for defending against deauthentication/disassociation attacks on 802.11 networks [Internet]. 2008 [cited 2011 Sept 10]. Available from: http://www.utdallas.edu/~neerajm/publications/conferences/attacks.pdf.
3. Black Alchemy Enterprises. Fake AP [Internet]. 2001-2002 [cited 2011 Sept 01]. Available from: http://www.blackalchemy.to/project/fakeap/.
4. Merriam-Webster Dictionary [Internet]. M-W digital online edition. 2011. ad hoc [cited 2011 Sept 10]. Available from: http://www.merriam-webster.com/.
5. Is Your Wireless Safe? QSR Magazine [Internet]. 2011 Apr [cited 2011 Sept 10]. Available from: http://www.qsrmagazine.com/outside-insights/your-wireless-safe.
6. SpeedTouch default wireless/wpa/wep password security checker [Internet]. 2009 [Updated 2010 Nov 11; cited 2011 Sept 10]. Available from: http://www.mentalpitstop.com/touchspeedcalc/calculate_speedtouch_default_wep_wpa_wpa2_password_by_ssid.html.

Low tech targeting and surveillance: How much could they find out about you?

INFORMATION IN THIS CHAPTER

- Initial Identification
- Property Records, Employment, and Neighborhood Routes
- Disclosure on Social Networks and Social Media
- Financials, Investments, and Purchase Habits
- Frequented Locations and Travel Patterns
- Third-Party Disclosures
- Use of Signatures
- Automated Surveillance
- Target Interaction
- Scanners and Miniatures

Back in the day, surveillance necessitated a great deal of strategy, research, time, equipment, vehicles, travel, disguises, and of course, bad coffee. If you've never had the opportunity to actually conduct surveillance operations, you have certainly seen the drill in the movies and on TV. Law enforcement, private security specialists, spies, military units, disgruntled spouses, and private investigators have been the typical characters on the big screen (and in real life) whose business it is to surveil, collect, and document information on their target(s). In addition to some of the movie protagonists, their adversaries have launched their own intelligence-gathering and surveillance techniques and counter surveillance measures.

In the past and certainly today, people still want to find out about people. Historically and psychologically the search for people and the motivations to find information about them has remained consistent over time. Whether you are a celebrity, high profile person, fugitive, or just an average Joe, someone may be looking for you. The surveiller may be as innocent as a former classmate who has not seen you in years or a lost relative or more threatening, such as an angry ex-spouse, cheated business partner, or stalker. The good news was years ago, for someone to really surveil you, a lot of time, expertise, energy, and perhaps money would have had to be invested in conducting that type of activity. The bad news is . . . today, anyone can do it with just a laptop, iPad, or Smartphone and an Internet connection.

The surveillance techniques used over the past several decades have required "feet on the street" operations. Years ago, if you wanted to find someone or additional information about them, you would have to start with the basics and then typically launch into the classic tailing and documenting of evidence. But even the basics, the presurveillance activities and preliminary information collection, took time. The research conducted revolved around finding hard copy records, usually in libraries, courthouses, county repositories, or archives. Additional records could be obtained through sifting through miles of microfilm and microfiche. Once foundational information such as name, address, or phone number is located, then other parts of the operational plan had to be considered and investigated—by foot, by travelling, by doing more hard copy research (e.g., reviewing maps). Even if you were fortunate enough to have access to law enforcement databases to obtain the first layer of information, at some point if you are going to do surveillance, you have to get out there and actually monitor, tail, collect, wiretap (of course with a warrant!), photograph, videotape, run audio collections (of course within the legal constraints of your state or jurisdiction), or dumpster-dive the target(s). Thus, the second level of operational planning is needed and likewise time consuming—getting to know the target and the environment before establishing the surveillance plan.

During this second phase of planning, surveillers know it is important to understand the operational environment. What is the neighborhood like? Where does the target work? What would be the likely routes? How much foot traffic? How many autos and what types? What appears to be normal and what will stick out? Is a disguise needed? Is changing vehicles needed? How should the surveillance detection routes be planned? What vantage points are needed to attain photos? Video? Audio? The preparation list goes on and on, including considerations such as "What is the cover story?" and "What if the operation is blown?"

Now that all the preparation is completed and the surveillance plan is selected based on the target, the location, the environment, and the goal of the intelligence collection, the actual surveillance can begin. While some investigators feel this is the most interesting, challenging, and exciting part of the operation, it can also be long, tiring, deadly dull, and dirty work at times. Spending night after night, lurking in a van in some neighborhood ready to surface with a stealthy click of the camera in order to collect the one or two incriminating photos, can be exhausting. Too many cups of coffee, fast food, and lack of sleep just don't help to put you in the mood for the next joyous exercise of waiting for the target and all the neighbors to leave for school and work in the morning so you can rifle through their garbage. Don't forget to watch for Mrs. Smith: she only comes out of her home to garden and she may notice you even though you have changed vehicles three times. This lady won't buy the world's best cover story if she sees you going through the trash. Although all the time spent tailing, observing, listening, watching, photographing, and videotaping can provide very thrilling results that are crucial to the investigation, you are exhausted. Understanding the patterns of the targets, where they go, what they eat, who they talk to, who their friends and business associates are, and who they love and hate, becomes an integral part of the puzzle and the investigation.

All of the data and intelligence collected while conducting surveillance can then be distributed according to the parameters of the investigation: presented to the client, delivered to the prosecutor or defense team, or used as personal fodder for some other agenda. Again, that was a lot of time, effort, travel, sleepless nights and planning needed to achieve stellar surveillance results. Using the open source tools available on the Internet today makes the art, science, and expansion of surveillance so much easier than it was in years past.

The methodologies and techniques of surveillance have expanded over the last 5 to 10 years by the amount of information that is available on the Internet. Over the last 2 to 3 years, with the explosion of social networking and social media sites, the available sources of information to conduct surveillance have likewise proliferated. So, what does that mean exactly? Basically, anyone, in any place, at any time can now conduct some of the preliminary and secondary data collections on a target, and then actually conduct surveillance of that target from the comfort of their own home, cybercafé, coffee shop, or office by using a laptop, iPad, or Smartphone. The information is there to collect in the open source, meaning that no one needs to hack, crack, break encryption, or otherwise compromise servers to collect information on a target. The information is out there on the Internet, on blogs, on social networking sites, on social media sites, on microblogs, and on websites. So how much information is out there on you? What if you were surveilled online?

This chapter focuses on methods surveillers can use to gather information about you. Presented in the coming pages are some basic collection techniques used by anyone who wants information about you, your organization, your company, or your family. In addition to providing some of the methodologies used in online surveillance, this chapter provides recommendations to reduce your Internet footprint and better preserve your safety, security, and privacy online. This chapter only scratches the surface on all of the creative methods, techniques, and sources used in online surveillance, but it should provide you a good overview of what can be collected from the convenience of any location, with a cup of great coffee, adequate sleep, and no dumpsters.

INITIAL IDENTIFICATION

Most investigations start with a name. If someone is going to surveil you, the most obvious and easiest place to start is with your name. In some cases, the surveiller may just start with an address, a phone number, an email address, or a screen name. In any case, starting with just one piece of data is not unusual and it is the job of the investigator/surveiller to build on that single piece of information. Let's start with your name. There are literally dozens of Internet sites in which to attain more information from than just your first and last names. For example, the following websites offer up information such as home address, home phone number, cell phone number, or email address by just putting in your name. In some cases, the sites, such as pipl.com and isearch.com will also provide lists of your potential relatives or associates:

- http://www.peoplefinders.com
- http://www.people.yahoo.com/
- http://www.anywho.com/
- http://www.411.com
- http://www.phonenumber.com
- http://www.zabasearch.com
- http://www.pipl.com
- http://www.123people.com
- http://www.ZoomInfo.com
- http://www.spokeo.com
- http://www.intelius.com
- http://www.whitepages.com

For example, http://www.peoplelookup.com offers several types of look-ups via tabs on the same site, including reverse phone number search, background check, criminal check, social networking check, email look-up, property check, and civil record checks (i.e., court records, death records). Zabasearch.com is another interesting site. Anyone can enter your name and the state in which you live (which in many cases is a very educated guess if it is not readily known). The results of Zabasearch produce home addresses, home phone numbers, and in some cases the history of where you have lived. The useful thing about Zabasearch is that if your address is found, a "Find" on the page using your address can be conducted to see if others are also listed living in your home. This is a great way to find spouses' names or children's names.

Another good alternative is https://www.knowx.com (which is a Lexis-Nexis company). This site offers information and records pertaining to bankruptcy; judgments; lawsuits; liens; criminal records, certificates (i.e., death, divorce, marriage, birth); vehicle ownership, which may include aircraft, real estate, and watercraft; business profiles; and professional licenses. The number of sites that offer a variety of personal information are too voluminous to provide a comprehensive list. New sites keep coming out and the existing sites adapt to offer more options.

TIP

Please note that some of these PeopleFind sites require a fee to obtain additional information. Be mindful and careful about providing credit card numbers or personal information such as your email address to some of these services. In many cases, the additional information is not worth exposing your name, credit card details, or email address. If you do select to use the pay-for services, use a throwaway email address and pay for the services with PayPal or a credit card that can be monitored for fraud. It may be safer to be persistent with the free sites. Someone who is looking for you and is determined will, however, use every tool available and purchase the information with throwaway email addresses and stolen credit cards.

Using one or multiple PeopleFind sites can yield a great deal of information. It is not unusual to at least obtain some additional pieces of information such as a home address or email address. Then the surveiller may use open source search engines such as Google, Google Advanced, Google Groups, Google Blog, Ask.com, Yahoo, and Bing, to name a few, to enter your name, email address, screen name, address, or phone number to see if any other information or records surface.

> **WARNING**
>
> Our team was provided the name of one woman who happened to be the wife of a high profile CEO of a Fortune 500 company. Just by using Zabasearch, Pipl, and Yahoo People Find, we were able to attain the home address of the target. Moving on very easily to just a rudimentary Google search using her home address, three additional pieces of information popped up immediately: 1) a copy of an "approval" document from the city to allow her to build a swimming pool in the backyard, which contained her cell phone number; 2) photographs of her (and her family including children) at a charity event (even more was collected using a simple image search); and 3) sites that showed her political donations over the last 5 years, along with an additional address in the same state (but this one turned out to be a vacation home). These findings led to more findings, led to more findings, etc… This is the type of information an adversary or protester may use against her, her husband (and his company), or their family. In this case, the executive's wife did not post any of this information herself and she did not know it was out there.

Once information in addition to your name is collected (e.g., your address), there are additional state-by-state searches and databases that can be accessed to see if you or your activities have been catalogued. For example, if a Google search turns up some information that you were involved in a small claims case in New York, it simply takes a few more clicks of the mouse to find out what the case entailed. By going to http://www.nyscourtofclaims.state.ny.us/decisions.shtml, anyone can do a search on your name, the judge's name, the case dates, or some key words to bring up more details.

If you are in a certain profession (e.g., physician) or are former or current military, some searches can be conducted specifically for you. By just Googling "find military personnel," a set of possible sources of information is presented. Some of these sources require a login or an account, but most of them are free. For example, Military.com requires the user to put in their service branch, status (which can be "other"), email address, and a zip code. Again, with a throw-away email address and entering a non descript status, anyone can surf this database. Just with this first step of searching and digging, a lot of information can be uncovered about you. To gather a better idea of your neighborhood, your property, and your job, let's move onto finding and viewing your property, job, and routes.

WARNING

A typical question is, how can I get this information removed from the Internet? The truth is, you really cannot get any of your information actually removed from the Internet. For example, some sites offer a "remove me" service in which you fill out a form and in theory you are removed from their site. While that may be true and ABC.com did take you out of their database, the problems stem from crawlers, spiders, indexing, archives, caches, and other people who copy, reproduce, repost, or resurf for the information and keep it alive on the Internet. In many cases these PeopleFind sites will remove you from their data, but then when their Internet spiders go out to collect another round of information about people, your name and affiliated information may get scooped again and displayed on their site. These are automated collections that are difficult if not impossible to stop. There are techniques available to "bury" some findings on the twentieth page on Google instead of the first page, but even those methods don't guarantee that you won't be found. Just be warned that, once it is out there, it will live and it can be found.

PROPERTY RECORDS, EMPLOYMENT, AND NEIGHBORHOOD ROUTES

Extending the search about you, the next step is to do some virtual drive-bys of your home, find out where you work, and then theorize on some of the local routes you may take to work, the nearest grocery stores, the movies, and restaurants. In traditional surveillance, it is best to understand the environment—the target's neighborhood; what the homes look like; the routes in and out of the neighborhood, the year, make/model, and upkeep level (or lack thereof), of neighborhood cars; and what access to the target's home and/or garbage may be available. Attaining additional information about other properties, assets, and vehicles would also be highly useful in many circumstances.

Once your address is known and validated, it is very easy to attain additional information about that property, even before you have been the resident. By using some of the real estate and property-find search engines, anyone can gather more detailed information. Take these sites, for example:

- http://www.netronline.com/
- http://www.homeinfomax.com/
- http://www.realestate.yahoo.com/Homevalues
- http://www.zillow.com

Zillow.com provides maps, home values, photos, mortgage information, and links to local area information such as grocery stores, schools, parks, and gas stations. Gathering all of this information from one site is pretty good. But, if the surveiller then places the address information into Google Maps for a satellite view and for a street view, a real view of the home is provided. By using street view, anyone can walk around the home, the neighborhood, and assess the cars, property, roads, distance between homes, and other details. By closely assessing the details. on street view, an enormous amount of information can be attained about the environment. Granted, the virtual maps are not in real time, but an excellent cursory review of the home and environment can be ascertained without actually driving anywhere.

Once the neighborhood is reviewed, Google Maps (or any online mapping program or Smartphone app) can guide the surveiller to the local stops—the grocery stores, the post office, gas stations, and coffee shops—that you might frequent. While these techniques will not provide the level of detail of live activity in the neighborhood, the information can be coupled with additional online intelligence to indicate where and when you come and go.

> **WARNING**
>
> Do research on your own home to see how exposed you could be. It is possible that the home you live in may have been photographed, currently or in the past, by a prior owner. Some real estate agents present not only photos but also virtual tours of homes highlighting the interior and exterior of homes. If your home is high profile, it may have been documented in an architectural magazine or design journal with full blueprints and architect drawings. Now armed with not only basic street view information but also actual video and blueprints, the surveiller has information about the residence in overwhelming detail including the furniture and blueprints. Maybe there is even a panic room.

One place you probably go is to work (or school) or some other location (i.e., a friend's home, a relative's home, volunteer work facility). If you are "easy," meaning you attend and/or speak at conferences, have a website, have a web presence, participate in public relations activities, or do press conferences, you are probably very easy to find with a Google search. Your company, your organization, and your marketing personnel will have posted information about you on the company website (and in some cases which conferences you will be attending next or where your next press conference will be). If you are not that public in terms of your organization, let's revert back to some of the information already found through PeopleFinders and other techniques. Using a found email address or phone number, again, a very simple publicly available search engine can potentially detect where you may have posted your email address, phone number, or screen name. Do you use eBay or Craig's list or post information to forums, message boards, or news groups? Have you ever posted your phone number because you are selling an item, renting an apartment, or just reaching out to someone for assistance? While some people do use hotmail, gmail, or other nonwork-specific email addresses to post online, it is surprising how many people in a moment of convenience or through habit will provide their work email addresses, work phone numbers, or other information that discloses their employer. If you have a website or are responsible for your employer's website, doing a domain search for registration information may also provide contact information or validation of an employer.

OK, now that we know where you live and where you work with some rudimentary idea of places you may frequent, we still need to know your habits, your behavior, and your comings and goings. The first place to start collecting information on the patterns of your behavior is to target social media and social networking sites.

DISCLOSURE ON SOCIAL NETWORKS AND SOCIAL MEDIA

Social media and social networking sites (i.e., LinkedIn, Facebook, MySpace, Twitter, Flickr) are filled with information. The membership of these sites is growing and new ones are popping up every day. Some of the self-disclosure that occurs on Facebook, for example, is amazing. These sites are chock full of demographic information, photographs, names of others such as friends, family, and survey data. Yes, survey data. One very popular thing to do is to share and post surveys with the answers to very personal questions—Where do you work? Do you like your boss? Do you do drugs? When was the last time you got drunk? Do you suffer from mental illness, and if so, what are you diagnosed with? And, yes, even more remarkably, people answer these questions and post the whole survey on their social networking page.

Remember years ago when people had diaries. With the little lock and key? Younger brothers everywhere made it their mission to crack into their sisters' diaries to find the secrets. No need now. People just put it right out there on Facebook for everyone to see. What about your Rolodex? Those used to be coveted compilations of information: your network, your confidential business contacts, your close and extended family members. The Rolodex was personal intellectual property. Jobs were given to salespeople who had the best personal contacts. Power, status, and success were perceived and guided by who you knew and who you personally had access to. No more. Enter LinkedIn. Like the diary, LinkedIn is just a huge disclosure of your Rolodex. LinkedIn is one of the prize collections of the surveiller and again, so easy to get access to even if the majority of your account is closed. That's right, even non members of LinkedIn or Facebook and those who are not in your friend network can have a peek into what you post and what is on your Facebook wall or who your network is on LinkedIn. A number of available search engines provide that "view through the fence," so let's look at Whostalkin.com.

By entering search terms into Whostalkin.com, you can see a host of findings from a variety of sites. For example, if you enter "America" in the search box, a lot of results will popup and some will be from Facebook. A few lines of text from that Facebook account will appear in the search results. However, if you click on the link to that specific Facebook page, you will be sent to the Facebook login page. So without actually logging into Facebook or being a friend of that poster, you have that peek into his or her commentary. Other useful and available searches into social networks include:

- http://www.yoname.com/—people search across social networks
- http://www.zuula.com—search for web, blogs, Twitter
- http://www.icerocket.com—search for web, blogs, MySpace
- http://www.tweetscan.com—search on Twitter
- http://www.youropenbook.org—search on FaceBook

Each of these search engines is a bit different and can provide distinct results. Tweetscan is interesting and can be more fruitful than going directly to Twitter.com for a search of your Tweets and Twitter names. For example, if you are the Tweeter and you Tweet, "I hate my boss Bob. I think I will slash his tires on my way out" (Note: Yes, these types of Tweets do exist and are posted every day), as the Twitter account owner, you can retract your Tweet. What this means is that if a search is done on Twitter.com for "+hate + Bob" your Tweet will no longer be available to view and will not be in your page of Tweets. However, if Tweetscan.com is used and "+hate + Bob" is placed in the search bar, results will reveal your retracted Tweet. This phenomenon occurs because Twitter.com keeps up with changes made by their users. Tweetscan archives and indexes Tweets and once they are indexed, they live and thrive and can be searched. Always remember, nothing really disappears or can be deleted from the Internet. Likewise, if there are some older Tweets that need to be uncovered to develop that target profile, there are several archive engines available, two of which include BackTweets and Snapbird.

NOTE

This example is a real-life case study. The job was to surveil a specific businessman to assess what his next investment strategy or business plans would be over the next few months. In addition to following him on Twitter, which mostly provided benign data, it did provide information about his speaking engagements. Knowing where he spoke provided the "in" needed to send him a LinkedIn invitation, which he readily accepted. Now insight into his network was available. What became very revealing was the combination of information—Tweets provided information that suggested this businessman had traveled to City X several times over the past month (interestingly enough, his main competitor's HQ was in City X). Next came the new LinkedIn associates, who were two attorneys. Typically this target did not have a lot of lawyers in his network. A quick Google search on these attorneys showed that they were prominent M&A attorneys. Now, $1 + 1 = 2$. The next business move was that the target was probably in merger or acquisition discussions with his main competitor. This was significant intelligence and found so much more easily than following him around in unmarked cars, skulking around large plants in restaurants to see who he was meeting with, and where he was going.

The beauty of these social networking sites is that they are meant to network people. So, in many cases people present a link to their Twitter account on their Facebook page or links to their Facebook and Twitter pages on their LinkedIn profile. This makes the job of information assemblage so easy. The key to really gathering insight into a person is not to evaluate the person by an isolated Tweet, one blog, or a comment on Facebook, but to compile these postings over time. The surveiller wants all of your Tweets over time, months and months of your blog postings and a collection of all of your friends and associates. Thus, the amassment of all of this information over time is what provides a very nice picture and profile of the target. Supplementing all of this text-based information with images, video, and photos from Flickr, Photobucket, and YouTube can also add to the overall profile.

> **TIP**
>
> Problem: the surveiller is not a member of LinkedIn, Facebook, or Twitter or doesn't want to login with his or her real account data. No problem. There are sites that will allow the surveiller to use someone else's login data. For example, http://www.bugmenot.com contains login data to approximately 14,000 different sites. Bugmenot includes login credentials to popular sites such as Blogspot.com, Foursquare.com, Myspace.com, Xanga.com, Intelius.com, and Blippy.com. While certain sites are blocked from Bugmenot.com, such as Facebook.com, Linkedin.com, and Twitter.com, the surveiller can still target you by going to other login share sites such as http://login2.me and attain access to Facebook, Twitter, and LinkedIn.

It is difficult to exhaust the potential information that is available on social network and social media sites. The process of surfing, searching, and digging does take time. There is an art and a science to knowing which search terms to enter, how to use Boolean strings and search punctuation, and tricks within Google Advanced to narrow down searches. However, as much time and energy as surfing may take, it can still be done by anyone, anywhere. Implementing the right Boolean strings using "OR" "ADD," or "-" between terms is experimental until you find the right combination. And then applying those strings in Google Advanced, for example, to narrow the date fields or the domain fields and determining what "exact terms to use (or request be removed from the search) make up another layer to the overall search and decision-making process. For the surveiller who now may have more than just cursory information about you, digging deeper is still necessary. Finding out about your finances, purchase habits, and maybe more about your job and salary is next on the agenda.

FINANCIALS, INVESTMENTS, AND PURCHASE HABITS

Financial data may be very critical and useful information for a surveiller to attain on you. There are a myriad of ways to collect this information online and a number of ways people unwittingly disclose this information. In other instances, it is someone else or another entity or organization that is revealing this data. Many people may be interested in your finances, everyone from a curious neighbor, to a new employer, to an investigator who is trying to determine if you are hiding funds. Let's look at just a few ways this type of information is made public.

First, some of the PeopleFind sites do offer financial checks and background checks but they are provided for a fee. Some sites provide worthwhile information and some don't. It is a bit of the luck of the draw whether or not you end up receiving valuable information. The fees are not high—ranging between $29.99 and $99.99, but the bigger risk to the vendor may be providing a credit card number to purchase the financial report. As mentioned earlier, some unscrupulous surveillers will provide a stolen credit card's number to purchase the needed information. The assets that are registered for tax or license purposes, such as houses, property, vehicles, boats, and aircraft may be the most straightforward to search for and identify. For a free search, there are hundreds of free sites dedicated to boat owners, airplane enthusiasts, and real estate entrepreneurs. If the surveiller has your email address, screen name, or other information, these sites are worth checking as asset owners typically love to discuss the make/model/purchase date of their cherished item, and with that data, the estimated value of the asset is easily determined.

There are other ways to gather salary information online without paying for services or worrying about credit card numbers. One starting point may be the government databases that offer salary information for government (city, state, and local) employees. If the target is employed by the government, it is easy to find their salary. For example, if you are the target and you are employed by the Kansas City government, a search of the state database for salary is available. Searches can be done by first and last name or by the target's position. In this example, the database link is provided by the Kansas City Star online news source at http://www.kansascity.com/2008/04/09/568285/search-the-kansas-city-salary.html.

It just takes a quick Google or Bing search with +"target city" OR +"state name" + "government salary data" as the search terms and lots of resources will be presented. It may take a few tries to get to the correct database, but each state/city has one and they are all online.

If you are not a government employee, there are other techniques to collect your data. One search that can be conducted is to use Peer-to-Peer (P2P) network searches for disclosed documents, specifically for tax records. If at any time you have saved your tax filings and records on your home computer and then allowed that computer to access a P2P network (either with or without your knowledge—teens are notorious for downloading free movies and music), it is possible that without the correct settings the contents of your hard drive were also exposed to the P2P network. Basically this means that all of your files are now on the loose on P2P for anyone to see. Using any of the popular P2P networks, search for "1040," "1099," "W2," or "tax form" and the name of the target—even if the target's tax file does not pop up, you will be surprised how many others do. Of course, this piece of information discloses not only annual earnings and taxes owed or refunded but also social security numbers, a treasure trove of information. Likewise, searching for other documents related to insurance claims (using the standard claim numbers) can also be done on P2P.

WARNING

Poking around on P2P can be a bit dicey. These platforms are wrought with pirated and free versions of music, videos, and other free ware. The time spent surfing and reviewing P2P files is one concern. However, the bigger concern is acquiring some type of malware by clicking on these findings. Use a virtual machine environment if possible.

If the target is an investor or dabbler in the stock market, they may post to a variety of financial newsgroups, chats, or forums. Sites like YahooFinance are the places to check. Some people even have their own blogs dedicated to the stocks they own and follow, and they provide their own advice about investing. Typically, these bloggers divulge their own investments and all of the smart investments they have made. Followers or commenters to these forums or blogs may also present information about the target. These followers may be fellow investors, former or current business partners, relatives, or old college chums. At any rate, sometimes it is not the target who discloses their own network but a close friend, family member, or colleague. In fact, the disclosure could accidentally come from the target's company, benefits organization, or human resources department. While it is rare (thankfully), at times new company databases or web pages are not secured and are left open. Or spreadsheets are left visible on the open Internet or placed on fileshare sites such as DocStoc.com or Slideshare.com. All of these vectors are worth checking.

Blippy.com is of the most lucrative sources of financial data because it is combined with shopping habits and expenditures (time, date, and location included). People sign up for Blippy and then allow a copy of their credit card records be sent to Blippy so they can be posted. Yes, this is real. The credit card numbers and true names on the credit cards are removed, but all of the expenditures remain, revealing what was purchased, where it was purchased, time/date of the purchase, and the prices of the items purchased. While the true names on the credit cards are removed, most people set up their Blippy accounts as they do their LinkedIn or Facebook accounts—with their real names. An account that is set up on Blippy.com, an alias or screen name can also be linked to the user's real-named social media sites, thus giving away the identity anyway. Why, you ask, would anyone sign up for such a thing? The philosophy behind Blippy is to help others get the best price available for any given item. So, if you are looking for the best Sony 42" HD TV, you could scan Blippy to see who has purchased one, where, and what the best price was for that TV. Users of Blippy have used the records of others, presented at their stores, to get the lowest price possible. Obviously, there is a high degree of disclosure by any Blippy user. First, your spending habits are revealed. Second, your shopping habits—time, date, place, etc.—are exposed. In combination with other data picked up from Twitter, Facebook, blogs, LinkedIn, potential routes to work, school, grocery stores, etc., the surveiller is now getting a much better picture of your overall habits and behavioral patterns. Over time, it may become obvious that every Saturday you are charging tickets to a baseball game or buying something from the home improvement store. At any rate, during those times, you are not home and it can be estimated with mapping apps, GPS, and online driving directions how long your commutes are and when you will be away from home.

> **WARNING**
>
> Personal bank account amounts and line items are very difficult to attain online, unless you, the bank, or a third party has somehow exposed otherwise secured information. Some surveillers have tried illegal and unethical methods of attaining bank account information. For example, one trick is to mail a check to the target for a few dollars, calling it some type of rebate or prize. If the surveiller knows your spending habits on Blippy, the ruse of a rebate check for

that new HDTV may work. When the target deposits the check, the back of the cancelled check will contain the bank routing number. From there, inquiries about the account can be made. However, it is not legal without the express permission of the account holder to disclose this information to another party. If you find yourself the recipient of a curious award, rebate, or prize, investigate the source and verify that it is real.

Acquiring financial data, and if you're so lucky as to acquire spending patterns and behavioral shopping patterns, is just the start of actually starting to track and tail a target. By now the surveiller may have your basic background data, insight into your social and familial networks, work location, basic travel routes, some financial data, and some idea of how you come and go from various locations. But now it's time to drill down on locations and travel patterns.

FREQUENTED LOCATIONS AND TRAVEL PATTERNS

As indicated earlier, sites such as Blippy provide some data regarding frequented locations and the times/dates they are visited. To add to this information, there are other ways to attain more detailed behavioral and travel patterns. Let's take a look at Foursquare.com and GoWalla.com. Both of these sites allow you to sync and link with Twitter and Facebook, but the real purpose is to announce your location. With a simple sign-in for membership and an app download, you can Foursquare your location to friends, family, . . . and the public. These sites were developed to provide social networking for their users but also to allow restaurants, coffee shops, and bars to be part of the Foursquare or GoWalla network. Therefore, if you are a frequent visitor to a coffee shop and that coffee shop is part of the network, the vendor may offer free coffee or snacks to the "Mayor" of the coffee shop. The Mayor is the person who frequents the shop the most and announces their presence in the store via the app. There are also other points, prizes, etc. that you can attain. While this is great advertising and marketing for the vendors, and maybe a good way to get a free beer or cup of coffee, exposing this type of data is announcing to the world that "I am not home right now. I am at the coffee shop." In addition, when a Foursquare user's profile is visited, it has a list (much like a user's Twitter page with all of his or her Tweets) of all of the locations that have been visited. This data also comes readily equipped with time and date information. Looking at a user's profile over time, it is fairly easy to put together a behavioral pattern. We used to be told, years ago, that when the family went on vacation, "don't tell anyone." Only one set of neighbors would know so they could water the plants and check the house. It is curious that in the current age of Amber Alerts, triple locked doors, and home security systems, people are publicly releasing such private data. But to the surveiller, this is golden.

Even if GoWalla or Foursquare are not used, a less obvious site to look into is Yelp.com. While Yelp is typically and innocently used to read and post restaurant reviews, this too can be used as additional intelligence. Yelp also posts directly to

Facebook and Twitter and it can tell you when the target visits a particular restaurant. Moreover, the posted reviews by the target might reveal which restaurants he or she frequents.

WARNING

There are sites dedicated to posting about those individuals who are using GoWalla and Foursquare or otherwise announcing that they are not home via Twitter or other sites. Check out http://www.robmenow.com/ and http://www.pleaserobme.com/.

While this type of data collection and surveillance may impact personal safety and security, there are cases where trolling and surveilling online can produce a target. Some of you may have clearances, classified jobs, or careers where you come in contact with very sensitive information in the form of trade secrets. Those who are interested in competitive intelligence, corporate espionage and state-sponsored intelligence gathering could employ some of these techniques—if for no other reason than to identify a good target.

WARNING

During a case investigation, a woman (Jane Doe) was identified as an employee of a certain organization. Through some rudimentary searches of the name of her employer, the results showed that Jane was an avid user of Foursquare. In fact she was the Mayor of her employer's facility, dutifully checking in on her app every morning as she arrived for work around 8:15AM. Assessing her other frequented locations on Foursquare, it was determined that every Thursday she went to her favorite tavern, on Saturdays she did laundry at a local laundromat, and while the clothes were washing, she went to the sandwich shop next door to the laundroy mat. On her Foursquare account, she also listed links to Facebook and Twitter where more information was uncovered. At the end of the investigation, it was revealed that she had a security clearance, worked at a very sensitive and secured government installation, was fluent in a few languages, and did not like her job. Pictures of her and her friends were also available. Combined with her behavioral patterns of where she goes and when, she is a perfect target for foreign operatives, state-sponsored spies, or other adversaries. These adversaries basically had enough information to target her and make an approach at a variety of locations. Should this type of social networking use be assessed as part of an active clearance process? Currently, in order to obtain or update a U.S. government clearance, even though traditional background checks are still conducted, no online check is even considered.

Those of you who do not use GoWalla, Foursquare, or Twitter. to announce your locations, there are a few inadvertent ways your locations may be disclosed. Most of the apps available on Smartphones that take photos include in the meta data of the photo a GPS location and a time/date stamp. One technique of also collecting information about the travel and behavioral patterns of a target includes the analysis of posted pics. Anywhere you can find photos and images online, whether those images are on photo sites such as Flickr or Photobucket or are found through social networking sites or simply through an image search on any publicly available search engine, there is a high probability that they contain GPS and time/date stamp meta data. So even if you do not meta tag your photos with a name or label your photos on these sites, you still may be disclosing location-related data that can then be assessed for patterns. With the speed of taking the photo and uploading, for example, to Flickr or Facebook, the disclosure of additional location data could be happening in near real time. Doing an assessment of all posted photos could again line up a timeline of activities, habits, patterns, and travel that you may not want disclosed.

WARNING

An assessment was conducted of a high-profile executive to determine how exposed he and his family may be online. This executive has received several death threats and was concerned about his family's safety. While the executive did have some basic background information available (i.e., home address, home phone number, alumni funds, charitable donations, some photos, including his family at a sports event, and some details on his recent divorce), it was his daughter who escalated the level of risk for him and the rest of the family. On her MySpace page was not only a blog posting which read, "Yeah, 5 more days in NYC! Staying at the XYZ Hotel—it's awesome! Dad lets me do whatever I want, so while he is at a boring meeting, I am going to hit 5th Ave shopping." The blog included photos that verified their location in NYC and the current time and date. It appeared she was engaged in some tourist activities, took photos, and uploaded them from her phone to her accounts, so her friends could get a blow-by-blow of her exciting trip to the city. Looking further on her MySpace page and the friend's comments revealed the time, date, and location of the next sleep over as well as details about her school events.

While photo, image, and location apps can provide some good surveillance data, you cannot forget about YouTube and the other sites that allow users to post videos. It is possible that someone has already "cased" your target environment. YouTube is filled with all sorts of crazy, silly, ridiculous, . . . and useful videos. Much like the virtual tour a real estate agent may have posted on the home you live in now, people are easily taking video of anything and everything they see. Similar to Google street view, sometimes neighborhoods video their block parties or their drive to the dry cleaners, or kids are running around on their scooters with Smartphone video camera rolling in hand.

WARNING

In some cases the target of surveillance is a place. During a red-team exercise in which the goal was to assess some of the safety and security standards in a U.S. city and conduct surveillance of the city completely from online sources, a number of interesting findings were made. One of the more interesting findings is who we refer to as "Graffiti-man." In a series of over a dozen YouTube videos a very industrious "go-green" environmentalist packed up his backpack full of spray cans, along with a template that read, "Save the Planet, Ride Your Bike," he jumped on his bicycle and took off to stencil his message across the city. On his bike helmet was a mounted camera in which he recorded his activities. He spray painted his message on a dozen locations across the city, including the courthouse, the sheriff's office, the public library, and other government buildings. Watching Graffiti-man's

---

Continued

> **WARNING—cont'd**
>
> videos provides an adversary some interesting and telling intelligence. While the actual defacement activities of Graffiti-man may add up to no more than misdemeanors, his behavior and methods of operation would be valuable to an adversary. If there is a need to disperse some type of devices, canisters, or other planted items in multiple locations throughout the city following this man's pattern may represent a somewhat undetectable operation as he was never detected, even while defacing city and government buildings. Graffiti-man is an example of how to blend into the culture of the city without raising any concerns, and his camera provides valuable reconnaissance and surveillance of the city.

If you have read this far and don't use social media, social networking sites, or even log in to the Internet, you are still at risk for some surveillance techniques and data gathering. Information about you is still out there to be collected by anyone.

THIRD PARTY DISCLOSURES

Remember the old Kevin Bacon Game, six degrees of separation? The goal being that if you knew one person, who knew another person, you could actually social network your way to Kevin Bacon. If the surveiller wanted to get to you, and find someone who was one or two degrees removed in order to collect additional information on you, it would take some legwork. But now with the Internet, there aren't six degrees of separation between you and anyone else but six hundred degrees of inclusion. For those of you who do not use the Internet, you don't Facebook, you don't Tweet, you don't post, you're not on LinkedIn, and you certainly don't blog, the others—the other 600 people removed from you just might.

Take, for example, an initial list of people with whom you do come in contact and who are probably Tweeting and blogging and Facebooking and Foursquaring:

- Children
- Spouses
- Significant others
- Other family members
- Friends
- Home staff (interior and exterior)
  - Nannies, au pairs, babysitters
  - Housekeepers and maid services
  - Gardeners and lawn services
  - Repair services
- Teachers, coaches
- Parents of children's friends
- Religious affiliations and leaders
- Vendors

These are the people that come in contact with you and may be posting information about you—your contact information, your life, your travels, your problems, your successes, your home, and your family—without your knowledge. Even innocent disclosures, conversations, and comments you make may end up on someone else's wall or blog. In a previous example, you saw how the executive's daughter ended up posting a lot of family and personal information on her MySpace page. So you need to consider, what is the nanny posting? Does the babysitter Tweet that she is sitting for the Jones family because the parents are out for the weekend? Does the housekeeper have access to the mail? The bills or any financial records around the house? Any of this information can end up on the Internet in the open and it does.

WARNING

The CEO of a small company was having a problem with his web and email service provider. His IT staff indicated that all of the calls to the help desk for their vendor were going overseas and they were not receiving the needed assistance. One critical server was completely down and they were losing business. The vendor's HQ was in the United States, and the CEO wanted to talk to someone in the United States. So, the collection of information on the Internet commenced. First a list of U.S.-based executives off the vendor's own website was pulled together. Then the name of a likely target was chosen: the VP of customer service. And as luck would have it, he had an unusual name, so sorting through a myriad of "Bob Smiths" wouldn't be necessary. The VP did not Tweet, or blog, or even do press conferences. But, his personal cell phone number—not his work cell phone number—was found. It was found in two places. The first was on his synagogue's website as the VP is also the coach of his son's soccer team. Apparently the rabbi decided it was prudent to post the cell number of the coach so the other parents would have access if they needed to contact him. In addition to the synagogue's site, a mother of another young soccer player also posted it on her Facebook page, "If your kids are on the team, here is [named the VP] cell number. He lives down the street from me at 1052." Searching around on her page, one of her friends posted her full address on his wall 6 months ago to let people know where her birthday party was taking place. So, with personal cell phone and home address in hand, the CEO called the VP of customer service. To say the least the VP was surprised and taken aback by the ability of anyone to get his personal number. The disclosure was by one person he knew and some other parent whom he did not know.

If someone you know isn't posting about you, maybe someone you don't know is posting. There are a number of sites that dedicate themselves to eavesdropping. Loud talkers in airports, on trains, and in restaurants are all susceptible to others listening in. Take notice next time you are on a plane, train, or even at a shopping center. People are just talking out loud on their cell phones as if they are in the privacy of their own home. They are giving out their phone numbers and credit card numbers for reservations, talking about their jobs and their accounts, and in some cases even spelling out their first and last names to operators or whoever is on the other side of the line. There are also listeners out there who take all this in and post it. Some of the interesting sites that post conversations and other comments include:

- http://www.overheardinnewyork.com
- http://www.overheardintheoffice.com
- http://www.overheardeverywhere.com

In addition to those above, there are similar sites for London, Dublin, Washington, DC, Chicago, Indianapolis, and other cities around the world.

Be careful to whom you text message and what you write in those texts. If people are interested in your conversations, they are also potentially interested in your text messages. Those who post your texts may just find them amusing or because it is easier to disperse a piece of information (like the address of the party that is hosted at your home) to a group of people who are followers of Twitter or Friends on Facebook. The site http://www.textsfromlastnight.com, for example, lists funny, embarrassing, or otherwise potentially sensitive texts. On this site, the texts can be sorted by user, area code, or keyword.

USE OF SIGNATURES

Some intelligence collection jobs and surveillance jobs are more difficult than others. When the target is not readily identified, it is hard to even get a starting point. For example, you receive a threatening email but it is pretty obvious that the email address was spoofed and the headers indicated that the IP address is coming from a server that also could have been compromised. In this case, the language used in the threatening email is most useful. We are all creatures of habit and even our emails contain bits and pieces that could lead to an identification. Think about how you open your email messages. Do you say "Hi Joe" or just "Joe" or nothing at all as a greeting? How do you sign off on your emails? Do you type "Regards" or "Sincerely" or "Thanks" or "Thx"? To different people you may use different pattern. To a spouse, you may always sign off "Love" or "Love ya" or whatever your personal pattern happens to be. Likewise, we choose our words and phases and write in grammatical and syntactical styles that differ ever so slightly. It is those distinctions that are important.

Once a distinction is found, an unusual colloquialism, an odd acronym, or maybe the email contains one of those sayings people put on the signature line like "A wise man doesn't need advice and a fool won't take it." These peculiarities are what can be identified. An investigator can put these terms and phrases into search engines and see what happens. With some luck, other instances of these phrases will appear, and with a lot of luck and persistence, the target may be found. It is not unusual that people will reuse their vernacular. They will post the same language with the same linguistic constructions in email as well as on blogs. Even professional and organized criminals have a hard time altering their natural language patterns.

> **WARNING**
>
> This case was an investigation of a criminal network of people selling fraudulent and black market goods on the Internet. One seller in particular was of interest as he was difficult to identify except by his online handle. The goods that were being sold were also advertised and sold online. The first bit of business was to collect all of the suspect's ads and known postings. It became apparent that more than a handful of his ads contained some of the same words, same phrases, and one consistent misspelling through all of the known ads, even the ones that didn't have some of the same phrasing. An Internet search was conducted using that one misspelled word plus some key concepts from the products for sale. Five new ad pages popped up, all using another name, but in this case the name was of a known suspect. It was investigated further (using other means) and it turned out that the unknown seller was actually one of the known suspects. He changed his name and tried to hide his tactics, but he could not disguise his rhetoric.

If you do have a signature phrase (e.g., Emeril has "Bam," Ryan Seacrest has "Seacrest Out," and Arnold Schwarzenegger has "I'll be back), be judicious about using it online. Even if you don't post your real name, your real profile, or other identifying information, your language may identify you. It is from that initial point of identification that all of the other discussed techniques to gather information and intelligence and to conduct online surveillance can be implemented.

AUTOMATED SURVEILLANCE

In the interest of keeping up with the target, there are some quasi-automated tools available. A lot of techniques can be used to collect information about you, but the surveiller also has to practice good operational security—even in the cyber world. A sloppy surveiller can get snagged by a thorough webmaster. So, it is important to consider speed, disguise, and stealth while gathering intelligence and conducting online surveillance.

While the majority of the initial data gathering may be conducted manually, once the surveiller knows what to look for and where updates are possible, a more automated collection of ongoing or updated information may be in order. Available RSS feeds or Google Alerts can alert the surveiller to additional and new information. If you are being monitored and you are a Twitter user, the surveiller may become one of your followers. Therefore, every time you Tweet, the surveiller will be notified. Likewise for other social networking sites. RSS feed aggregators can also be used to push all of the potentially relevant information to one place, which can be web based, email based, or mobile phone/Smartphone based.

Some browsers have add-ons or plug-ins that can make the searching and ongoing collection easier and faster. For example, Firefox offers a number of add-ons that allows the user to customize searches and ongoing searches without re-entering the search terms. Safari and Google Chrome also offer different flavors of RSS capability and browsing and navigation tools. Browser add-ons may also offer some specialty items that could be of interest to a surveiller. For example, one add-on for IE7 is Videoronk. This allows the user to search on eight video-sharing sites simultaneously. All of these feeds and add-ons can save time for the surveiller and make the collection more targeted and hopefully robust.

An additional concern for the surveiller, much like in the traditional sense, is the use of disguise or stealth to conduct the online intelligence collection and surveillance activities. One consideration for the surveiller is how to conduct the information collection quietly and in alias. Many different products and services can be used. The very simplest method is to conduct the searches at a neutral location—a cybercafé, a coffee shop, or a library. Do note that some of these locations require a payment for Internet access and/or have cameras on site. So hiding in plain site may not be an option. Other considerations include the use of anonymizers, encrypted Internet connections, virtual private networks, proxy servers, and IP port proxies. Other browser add-ons may also assist with achieving some level of anonymity or disguise while surfing. An add-on called Ghostery (can be downloaded for IE, Safari, Chrome, and Firefox) detects trackers, web bugs, pixels, and other types of beacons placed on web pages from Facebook, Google Analytics, and hundreds of other web publishers.

An additional consideration for the surfing surveiller is to use some form of virtual machine software or VM ware. Because of the amount of clicking, opening, searching, viewing that a surveiller has to do to collect the needed information, inevitably a virus or piece of malware will be downloaded. If this does occur, it is easier to just end the VM session and start anew rather than scrub the machine.

TARGET INTERACTION

So far this chapter has focused on passive intelligence collection and surveillance. But sometimes, additional information may have to be collected directly from the source—you. Just as in the physical world, certain intelligence or surveillance operations may necessitate actual contact with the target or someone who knows the target in order to gain or verify information. Because a passive intelligence collection has already been conducted, the surveiller has all the needed information to make a swift and believable approach on the target. If you are the target, you now may be a target of social engineering, spear phishing, whale phishing, Smishing, or Vishing.

Using some of the stealth and anonymizing techniques, along with email spoofing and the information that has been collected on you, it is not too difficult for a determined surveiller to target you specifically. Let's say the surveiller wants to watch what you are doing on your computer or get access to your banking logins. In order to get that type of access the surveiller may need to drop some malware on your computer, such as a Trojan. While this type of activity is not legal, it is not beyond the realm of possibility for a head strong and unethical surveiller. The goal of the spear phish maybe to get you to click on a link and open or download a document. By knowing your background, your activities, your family names, friends' names, and work affiliations, it is quite straightforward to construct a believable and very personal email or other correspondence. Imagine that the spear phisher has found information about your home, your daughter, and your alumni affiliation. By spoofing the correct or a facsimile of a sending email address, potentially believable emails could be sent from your homeowner's association presenting new rules and regulations for the neighborhood, your daughter's school district, or your university with information from the alumni association.

WARNING

It does not take a lot of hacking technical skill to spoof an email address and make it appear that the email is coming from a legitimate source. In about 5 minutes, anyone can go on YouTube and search on "Spoof Email" to find quite a number of tutorial videos to choose from.

Other techniques that could be used to target you or your family may include more direct contact. A social engineering attempt could come via phone, fax, text, instant messaging, or a knock at the front door.

WARNING

Last summer, just outside of Washington, D.C., in suburban northern Virginia, a couple went away on vacation and had a house-sitter take care of the pets and plants. One afternoon, a nicely dressed young man came to the door with a clipboard and a form. The house-sitter was informed that the sanitation service in the neighborhood was under new ownership and that all the accounts would be moved to the new company as soon as the forms were completed. The nice man explained that if the house-sitter filled out the form right now there would be no delay in service and the garbage would be picked up on schedule in two days. The house-sitter politely took a form and indicated that she was in a rush and would have to do the form later. She left the copy for the couple and explained the interaction. As it turned out, the form was a fake and a scam, as an announcement came out from the local police department. Information requested on the form included name, address, SS#, and credit card information, and sadly dozens of neighbors fell for it. In this case, the neighborhood was targeted, but this social engineering attempt could have easily targeted one person or one family.

If the surveiller was able to pick up information off of Foursquare or GoWalla, or if you are in the habit of Tweeting your locations, it would also be uncomplicated for the surveiller to target you at one of your frequented locations. Armed with additional background data and intelligence, striking up a conversation or finding a reason to interact would be pretty straightforward.

SCANNERS AND MINIATURES

Certainly a great deal of information can be collected over the Internet and the surveiller can remain safe and secure in comfortable location. At some point, some surveillance operations might require the use of tools, equipment, and devices, and the surveiller may actually have to get out from behind the computer to resort to more traditional techniques. Years ago, surveillance equipment was highly specialized and fairly expensive. The equipment was sometimes heavy and obvious. Fortunate investigators and those conducting surveillance as law enforcement or intelligence officer may have had the privilege of using specialized scanners and miniature devices that were tailor made for their operations. However, the average household or citizen did not have spy equipment on their person or at home. Now nearly everyone with a Smartphone has some ability to record audio and video and take photos on the spot. Do you even give a second look to an iPhone or Droid sitting on a conference room table while everyone is having a meeting? People join the meeting, sit down, put down their phones (or iPads) and start the meeting, checking their phones periodically during the meeting. But do you ever wonder if someone is using that Smartphone to record? Is anyone running an iPad app to record or transmit the conversation? Does anyone seem overly alarmed if a Smartphone is left in that conference room? A typical reaction is to ask, "Hey, is this anyone's phone?" and if there are no takers, to just put it aside until after the meeting and give it to a receptionist or office manager who can try to find the rightful owner.

Beyond carrying the built-in phone capabilities, anyone can go to the mall, an electronics store, or surf the Internet for miniatures and spy gear. Even Toys-R-Us carries spy gear toys for children, and some of the police listening devices, "special agent" night vision recording gear, and CSI kits are pretty good. The toys today are better than what was readily available to the public 10 years ago. The jewelry is actually quite impressive. Even in locations that mandate X-ray security checks or are classified as a sensitive compartmented information facility (SCIF), how many brooches, earrings, or watches are checked or suspected as anything but jewelry?

WARNING

The miniature cameras and audio/video recording gear come in all shapes and forms. Use a publicly available search engine and you will find stuffed animals, jewelry, pens, coffee cups, and a host of other household and office items. Some innocent-looking office lamps are fully equipped with hours of full audio and video coverage triggered by a motion sensor, transmitting all coverage via a wireless and/or Bluetooth connection. Bug-sweeping is a bit of a lost art and practice. However, with all of the very small, benign objects that don't arouse suspicion, the practice of bug-sweeping may need to be reconsidered for sensitive areas, board rooms, offices, and meeting rooms.

Not only are the serious surveillers using the widely available miniature devices, but so are your neighbors, your children, your children's friends, etc. Remember the idea of 600 degrees of inclusion. If your neighbor is spying, your conversations may end up on the Internet. If your neighbors are very bold, you may be the star of your own YouTube video unbeknownst to you.

Wi-Fi scanners are another easily accessible tool for any wanna-be surveiller. These devices can be acquired as their own stand alone device that come in a variety of shapes and sizes including those that fit on your keychain. Otherwise, just download a scanner app on a Smartphone or iPad. What you need to be aware of is war-driving. In general, war-driving is the activity of driving around neighborhoods looking for an open Wi-Fi network. In the process of searching, the scanner does see all of the networks in the area and their names—even the ones that are secured. In some cases, open, unsecured homes are "war-chalked" meaning that their home is tagged as an available wireless hotspot. If you have never driven around a neighborhood with a scanner, it is an interesting exercise. Many people don't secure their wireless networks. Many people name their home networks with their last names, nick names, or with their address. If you are being targeted, this is another way in which a surveiller could gain information about you and your home network or take advantage of a home network if it is left unsecured.

WARNING

The goal of the exercise was to identify the home addresses of as many military personnel as possible in one particular city. It made sense to start searching around the base itself. While part of the team was digging up information online, another team just drove around in neighborhoods surrounding the base where it would make sense for military personnel and their families to reside. With Wi-Fi scanners on, numerous homes were identified immediately. Home networks were named "CaptnJoe," "2LT," and "semperfi." In addition to the network names, CaptnJoe and 2LT also had Army and U.S. flags hanging outside their homes. Most of the neighborhood from the artifacts and other network names seemed to house Army officers. The biggest question was how did the Marine (broadcasting "semperfi") end up living in this predominantly Army neighborhood!

SUMMARY AND RECOMMENDATIONS

One of the most important aspects of targeting and surveillance is to put all of the collected intelligence together. This is perhaps the more artful step in the process. Creating a working profile of the target based on open source information may lead the investigator to consider different avenues or strategies if traditional surveillance needs to be conducted next. It is very difficult not to find information on any given target. However, if the target is rich, the amount of open source intelligence can be rather astounding.

This chapter has focused on some of the techniques and methods used by online surveillers. While the information has just skimmed the surface on all of the ways to target, surveil, and compile intelligence from the Internet, it should give any online surveiller a good start. But what if you are the surveillance target? There are some precautions you can take to reduce your Internet footprint and decrease the amount of information someone could collect on you. Remember, just staying off the Internet doesn't work because your closest 600 friends, family, and strangers will continue to post information about you regardless of your participation on Twitter, Facebook, or any other social networking site.

Recommendations

Don't allow yourself or your family to become a surveillance-rich target. There are several things that you can do to create a stronger safety and security profile online. It is not wise to just never go on the Internet or use social networking sites. Using and communicating using the latest in technology is where the world is moving. But you can be vigilant and safe. Here are 10 basic recommendations:

1. Beware of real estate transactions, fund raisers, school functions, charity events. These organizations may share your personal information inadvertently or through the normal course of business without realizing the dangers. Get throwaway cell phone(s) numbers and email addresses. When you are sharing your contact information with coaches, teachers, parents, and others not in your circle of trust, provide those parties with a throw away number. If you are compromised and this number is posted to the Internet, you can simply get another throwaway phone.

2. Consider using PO box(es), your corporate address, or the address of another service provider (i.e., attorney, accountant) for bills. Since most billing is done online now, in some cases a physical address may be provided that is different from your real home address. Even if in other circumstances you have to provide a real address, when the PeopleFinds spider and compile your addresses, at least there will be some question as to which one is real. Anything to deflect or to introduce confusion provides just one more layer of privacy.

3. Purchase gift cards for use (i.e., VISA, AmEx, iTunes). Never download music, videos, or documents from P2P sites. P2P sites are notorious for malware and unless your settings are correct for each P2P network, you can risk being exposed. No one needs to illegally download free music. Most songs are 99 cents with an iTunes membership or gift card.

4. Check your wireless network at home—choose network/server names that are generic and don't contain your last name, address, or any personal identifiable information (PII). On any wireless networks, change defaults, use encryption, and name your network anonymously.

5. Children's' participation/interaction on the Internet is age and maturity driven. However, children must understand how to use technology and social networking safely—it is critical to their developmental skills and knowledge base in the 21st century. Not allowing usage may impede academic, social, and professional success later in life. So it is very important to provide children and teens specific education on social media and social networking. There are available DVDs and training kits for children. Check out what is available from the National Center for Missing and Exploited Children and from the FBI's website. Adults may benefit from some of the materials also.

6. Never click on any link in any email, IM, or other message from someone you don't know. For all emails, use the "mouseover" test on all links. If the visible and actual don't match, don't click it. Be suspicious of anomalous communications even from a familiar email address (it could be spoofed). Use another vector of communication to validate the email, such as a phone call. Type and bookmark the sites you normally visit. Don't use links found online or in an unsolicited messages.

7. Be cautious when accepting invites on LinkedIn and other social networking sites. Review your own LinkedIn account to see if you are comfortable with everyone in your network. Ask yourself, what does your network reveal about you? Are you disclosing anything you shouldn't? In some cases, a salesperson may have a huge LinkedIn network filled mostly with their customers. But what if the customer-vendor relationship is under an NDA? The salesperson has just violated the NDA by exposing all of the customers to each other.

8. Safety lessons for using the Internet should be given the same amount of time and energy as for how to interact in the physical world. On Facebook, MySpace, and family websites, always keep you and your family disclosures to a minimum:
   - No last names or identifying information
   - No photos/videos (unless password protected and check for metadata if needed)
   - No disclosure of age
   - No disclosure of locations, visits, trips, or events. There is really no need to use sites like Foursquare and GoWalla . . . unless you are the surveiller.
   - Set the highest level of security settings. On Facebook, this may take going through 35 to 40 settings and these settings may change periodically as Facebook updates their services. Remember, the social networking sites want you to network as much as possible. Sharing and security don't always go together and it is more important to keep yourself and your family safe.

9. Install VMware or isolate an existing computer to use for suspicious or risky actions and aggressive searching. These precautions will help you stay free of malware.

10. There is never any reason to divulge financial data. Using sites like Blippy is not necessary. If you need to find the best prices available for products, there are plenty of comparison sites to visit that post pricing for items from both retail stores and online sources.

Over time, targeting, surveillance, intelligence collection, and human behavior have not changed that much. Our tools, devices, and techniques have adapted to the available technologies of the day. But at the end of the day, a quote from Jane Austen made over 200 years ago still stands the test of time, "Every man is surrounded by a neighborhood of voluntary spies."[1]

ENDNOTE

1. JaneAusten.org [homepage on the Internet]. [Cited 2011 June 08]. Available from: http://www.janeausten.org/jane-austen-quotes.asp.

Low tech hacking for the penetration tester

6

INFORMATION IN THIS CHAPTER

- The Human Condition
- Technology Matters
- Staging the Effort
- Getting Things in Order
- A Useful Case Study

Up to this point in the book, you've read a lot about physical security, social engineering, and surveillance (with a touch of Wi-Fi thrown in for good measure!). And these are all great topics, especially if you're working from the perspective of someone who is physically present at the location in question. But what about low tech hacks for penetration testers or those of us who work in the world of red teams? There really are no limits to what you can achieve in a penetration test if you use a bit of creativity. Everything you've read about, up to this point, can play an integral role in your work as a penetration tester; all you need is your own imagination and the ability to consider how "normal people" react to your actions.

There are literally dozens of books about penetration testing and red team operations. They all go into the use of software tools, usually within a Linux platform, to conduct the standard steps; information gathering, exploitation, escalation, migration, and exfiltration. But what most of these books fail to cover are the low tech activities that not only benefit your normal penetration testing but also can often stand on their own when working these types of projects. As you'll see as you progress through this chapter, we're taking the concepts of social engineering and combining them with easy-to-use technology to create valid and effective attack techniques.

Penetration testers tend to agree that the end user is the weakest link in any information security chain. This is mostly due to the fact that we've gotten better at using security tools and appliances. They're tangible; you can reach out and touch them. They come with an owner's manual and support groups in online forums to help you troubleshoot. But humans are social animals, and we've trained ourselves over the generations to help people and to trust people. It's always been a mechanism for the survival of our race. More individuals prefer to believe the best in others and their intentions. At the very least, we don't want to be the person who slows down the organization or stops progress altogether. But that aspect of being human also makes our employees vulnerable to compromise by creative and enterprising attackers. As we've mentioned in the previous chapters, everyone could use a healthy dose of suspicion.

Additionally, humans tend to have physical, emotional, and mental limitations that impact how we process information. Our brains tend to take shortcuts, which makes reading a book more of an exercise of understanding the key concepts in the book versus one of reading every single word in the book. That same ability to generalize data from our surroundings makes us vulnerable to specially crafted attack methods. A great penetration tester can achieve high success rates by introducing slight variations in a target's environment without arousing suspicion. As an example, we can introduce a new person into an environment and play that person off as an employee if we can create a feeling of confidence and trust in the target. This could be as simple as ensuring our new employee wears similar clothing to other employees in the organization, like a uniform used in a hospital or hotel chain.

This chapter will cover some of those aspects of our human employees and how they can be used against the end user to provide access to the penetration tester. We'll also provide a case study example of techniques that have worked in the past and describe why those techniques worked so well. There are as many possibilities as there are creative thinkers in the security business, so this chapter doesn't pretend to cover every possibility. But you should still walk away with a better understanding of what's really possibly, what really works, and why it works. We'll cover the basics in the first part of the chapter and then walk through our case study to demonstrate how effective these techniques really are in the real world. Let's start with *why* these techniques work.

THE HUMAN CONDITION

Despite the natural urge we may have to disagree, the human being and the human mind are not perfect. We're normally born with a plethora of tools intended to help us survive and live long and happy lives. From our base senses, such as sight, smell, touch, and hearing, to our ability to solve problems, it looks as if we're prepared for almost anything. But although we use the resources available to us efficiently, we have basic flaws that are built in and can be taken advantage of by an attacker. Before we delve into the penetration testing aspects of this chapter, let's examine some of the flaws that make us vulnerable. This is analogous to complex computer systems that can perform extremely difficult tasks but, due to their sheer complexity, introduce any number of other flaws as well.

Selective attention

In 1999, two psychology professors from different universities performed an experiment called the "Invisible Gorilla." Their names are Christopher Chabris and Daniel Simons, and the premise behind their experiment was that human beings are naturally quite selective in what they pay attention to during a normal day. That selectivity can actually be tuned so targets will see what you what them to see and, with a high degree of success, not see what you'd like them to ignore. This is called *selective attention*.

In the experiment, you, as the observer, are watching six college-aged kids passing basketballs in front of some elevators. Three of the players are wearing white shirts and three are wearing black shirts. You're asked to count how many times the players in white shirts pass the basketball. And while the task sounds simple enough, and you're likely to get the correct answer to the question asked of you, you're also likely to miss the fact that a person in a gorilla suit walks right through the group of students, pounding its chest before moving off the opposite side of the screen.

You can find out more about the experiment, and watch some of the videos at www.theinvisiblegorilla.com. But since you, the reader, are already aware of the outcome, it might prove more fun to have one of your friends watch the video without telling them the punch line.

In reality, selective attention is a great way to engineer people's reactions and motivations. As a more practical example, consider for a moment why casinos in Las Vegas make you walk through the gambling areas and high priced shopping to get to your hotel room after check-in. Additionally, when you're bored, standing in line at the grocery store, how many times did you buy the candy bar? Or how many times (if you can count that high) did your children desperately want that toy on the bottom shelf at the checkout line? These are methods for keeping your attention elsewhere, to increase the chance that you'll spend more money and forget your wait in line.

Generally speaking, great hackers can use this to their advantage as well. If I can draw your attention to one thing, it means you're not paying attention to something else. This can also be referred to as *distraction*.

Magic is distraction

One of the core concepts of magic is to distract your audience so you can do something else while they're not paying attention. We've discussed magic in this book previously because it ties in well with what we're trying to test for in the security world. When was the last time you watched a magician perform a trick live? Can you recall the reaction of the audience? Was it surprise? Shock? The great part about this example is that the audience *knew* this was going to be a magic trick, and it *still* took them by surprise.

Let's take this one step further and not tell the audience about the trick or the magic. In fact, let's not even tell them they're an audience or we're a magician. At this point, the trick, when performed correctly with distraction and practice, should go completely unnoticed. Remember, our goal is to get the user to do something (help us install malicious software and bypass security mechanisms) while ignoring something else (the threat we could pose to the organization as an unknown person with unknown motives).

Building trust and influencing behavior

In a 2004, Robert Cialdini wrote an article for *Scientific American* entitled "The Science of Persuasion." In his work, the author discusses the underlying interactions between human beings that can be manipulated in such a manner to increase the chance of a positive response from a target. As a penetration tester, we can use these same concepts to ensure our efforts are rewarded with success.

In the article, Mr. Cialdini states, "Six basic tendencies of human behavior come into play in generating a positive response: reciprocation, consistency, social validation, liking, authority, and scarcity."[1] So, from our perspective, in order to best penetrate an organization, we'll want to utilize these human tendencies when interacting with the employees of an organization in ways they'll understand instinctually. This touches on the social engineering concepts we've covered previously in this book. As you'll see in the case study later in this chapter, we use this concept to limit the chances we'll be confronted during our work. For example, actions as simple as looking and acting as though we have the appropriate level of authority to conduct an action, giving the target something tangible (such as a USB drive or CD), and being polite by offering the target a compliment help build trust and allow us to influence the behavior of the target. You'll see a demonstration of how a team can use these methods when we cover the case study later in this chapter.

TECHNOLOGY MATTERS

Since this book is all about low tech methods for penetration testing and red teaming, we'll keep the technology to items and software that are easily and readily available to the layperson. These are typically items that won't require too much heavy lifting by the reader but will still provide useful results as well as a decent learning experience.

When we discuss technology in this chapter, we're discussing delivery and communication methods. Delivery methods allow us to get users to install our communication methods for us, simplifying the process of bypassing the security mechanisms in place at the target. In the most basic sense, delivery methods can be normal, off-the-shelf technology, such as USB thumb drives or a CD-ROM. In a more complex attack we might also utilize techniques involving drive-by web attacks or email phishing attacks. But let's start with the basics concerning our possible delivery methods.

USB thumb drives

At this point, if you've been around the security industry for any amount of time at all, you've likely heard the tale of "the guy who knows a guy that scattered USB thumb drives through a target parking lot, only to have the users pick up the drives and plug them into their computers." It's a consistent story, and it's been around for a while, even if no one is actually certain who started it.

This technique has worked fairly consistently in the past. Your team buys some inexpensive thumb drives, installs some nefarious software on the drives, and places the drives in conspicuous places in the parking lot. USB drives have value to users because they're small, they hold data, and, frankly, they're cool. Over time, however, as this story has spread and been introduced into security awareness discussions and training, users have grown suspicious of random, unknown USB drives. As a penetration tester, that means we need to adjust our attacks to appear trustworthy to the users again, and we'll cover more about this later in the chapter.

First, let's look at some basic USB storage devices that might be useful to us during our testing. The first is the normal USB thumb drive. They range in size from about an inch to an inch and a half long, as shown in Figure 6.1. The storage capacities of these devices is sufficient for small payloads (such as a self-loading Trojan or key logger), or they can accommodate entire bootable Linux distributions. The payload you use should be determined by your end goal and your rules of engagement. And since these devices are so popular, most operating systems will auto-mount, auto-load, and/or auto-run content from them without much in the way of user interaction. This will be important later, when we're considering our strategic options for compromising the organization.

The next type of USB device is much smaller, and in my opinion, much more dangerous for users. If you recall from Chapter 1, we discussed the use of key logger devices that attach to the keyboard plug on the back of the computer. These devices look as if they belong there and don't draw attention to themselves. But, from my perspective, they're still larger than I'm comfortable with during a penetration test.

Looking at Figure 6.2, we see another version of the USB drive that is significantly smaller and can actually utilize a variety of storage chip sizes. This means

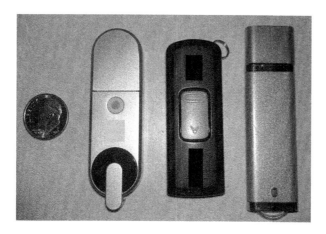

FIGURE 6.1

Standard size USB thumb drives

FIGURE 6.2

MicroSD USB storage device

we can create an 8 GB, a 16 GB, or even a 32 GB USB device without ever changing the actual hardware. And the storage cards we use in the device can be preloaded with specific types of deliverables, based on our needs.

In Figure 6.2 you'll see an image of the small USB device (it looks like those small USB dongles used for wireless mice and keyboards). Next to the device, I've placed several different micro SD cards, which are used as the memory for the device. One of the micro SD cards is shown sticking out of the slot, so you can get a better idea of how the memory slides into the device. And finally, I've included a dime so you get a better perspective of the size of the device.

NOTE

I'm sure you've already guessed, but the two different USB devices we've discussed here will likely be used in two entirely different ways. For example, a full-size USB device dropped in a parking lot will still be seen by people walking to and from the office building each day. The smaller device is probably too difficult to see if it's lying on the ground, based on its size and color. And since the goal of this exercise is to ensure people see the device, pick it up, and use it, we'll have to consider a different attack method.

Also, bear in mind the USB devices themselves aren't the dangerous part of this setup. They just happen to be a convenient medium for delivering our actual content to the user's computer. We'll discuss more about how we can use these devices later in the chapter.

CDs and DVDs

CD-ROMs and DVDs are a popular medium for users. They can store music, documents, pictures, or other digital media, and they're fairly inexpensive. Most modern computers can utilize these discs without any extra software, and most operating systems can auto-run these types of devices.

For comparison purposes, CDs can hold up to 700 MB of data. This would be a great size for storing data with embedded Trojans or other malware, even with a fully bootable Linux operating system. On the other hand, DVDs have a capacity of roughly 4.4 GB, once all is said and done. In this instance, you can create the same bootable Linux operating system and include a much larger store of software that allows you to bypass any operating system—level restrictions or to compromise the data on the hard disk itself.

Again, which one of these options we end up utilizing depends entirely on the mission goal. If we're looking for a quick, user-level compromise, then we're probably better off using the less expensive CD-ROMs. If we're going for a full system compromise, where we intend to exfiltrate or modify data on the hard disk and need the larger collection of tools, we'll probably want to use the DVDs.

STAGING THE EFFORT

Up to this point in the chapter we've focused on why humans are vulnerable to our efforts and on the medium we can use to finalize the compromise. The reason we haven't touched much on the actual penetration/red team portion yet is that I needed to set the stage. In this section, I'll talk a bit about how we can stage our effort, depending on the target organization, and then, in the case study, we'll cover more specifics.

Remember, this is a low tech approach to penetrating a target organization, and we'll cover this stuff in more detail later in the chapter in our case study. We're not using specially crafted exploits that we've written ourselves. Our goal is to keep this process as simple as possible and use suitable tactics for the job. So let's consider the information we need to know, generally speaking, to make this happen.

Target organization

One of the first things to think about is the target organization itself. What type of organization is it? Where is the organization located? What are the primary organizational mission goals? Where will the team move in on the target? Will it be at the office building itself? Is it at a conference location? What types of employees will we likely encounter during the work?

Location considerations

If we're hitting the organization on its own soil, then we need to know where the building is located and what the physical security is like. We won't cover that here since we've already covered it in Chapters 2 and 3. But it's an important consideration that we can't skip.

What if the organization is larger in size and has an annual conference, perhaps in Las Vegas (that is the convention capital of the world, right?)? This presents us with similar issues but with a few advantages. For example, if we were working from the target site itself, we would be more likely to encounter physical security mechanisms. But from a conference site, there is so much foot traffic that we can better blend in with the other folks in the area.

NOTE

As noted previously in the book, we need to look the part. And that look depends entirely on the site we're working from during the initial compromise. Consider a corporate wide conference being held at a hotel. We have multiple options for how we dress and act. We can pretend to work for the organization itself, the hotel staff, the conference planning staff, or even a third-party vendor that has come in to provide discounts on local attractions to the employees. In many cases, we'll find that a mix of these will be useful. Regardless of how your team decides to deploy that initial compromise, never underestimate the value of *looking the part*.

Organizational culture

Another consideration for your penetration team is the culture of the target organization. Working within a medical environment, for example, is going to be entirely different from working in a conservative, non profit environment. Your attitude, personality, clothing options, and more should conform to the expectations of the target. If you recall from earlier in the chapter, people naturally want and need to trust other individuals. All you have to do is fit into the confines of their expectations.

Let's look at a quick comparison of two disparate organizations, so we can get a clearer picture of what might be necessary. Our first organization is a financial and investing firm based in a large urban setting. The employees dress professionally, with business casual attire for the worker bees, and suits and dresses for the executive staff. If we're looking to fit into their normal, everyday expectations, it would behoove us to avoid dressing in blue jeans and a t-shirt. Briefcases are more common than backpacks. Looking the part is critical here.

The second organization is a tech company that believes creativity is based on providing as few limits to the employees as possible. Workers are allowed to wear shorts, t-shirts, and flip-flops to work. The company is a green organization, stressing the recycling and reuse of as many materials as possible. In this instance, not only will we need to consider how we look and act within the organization but we'll also need to take into account how we deliver the media to our target. Over-the-top plastic or cardboard packaging could be detrimental to our cause.

GETTING THINGS IN ORDER

Once we've collected this basic information about the organization and where/when we should attack, we can put our project together. This part is where we get to use our imagination and decide what will work best. Will we initiate the project at the organizational headquarters? Or will we interface with the users directly in a more informal setting, such as a conference or public location?

Based on this decision, we'll decide what technology we'll use and how to launch our attacks. I use the plural term because we're likely to encounter more than a single user when implementing these techniques, and each one will require an attack. And location, time, and technology aren't the only decisions. There's always room for a wardrobe change as well. If you'll be working in a hotel environment, where all the hotel staff wears a green casual shirt with black slacks and black shoes, it should be easy to imitate the wardrobe. Name badges are also easy enough to mimic, since most are white or gold plastic with printing on them. The right clothing and accessories can create a sense of trust within your target because you blend in with their expectations.

Deciding on location

Users tend to be more relaxed and less on their guard when they're off-site than when they're at work. Now, that doesn't mean users are going to be alert and reliable when a stranger is in their work area; it just means they're likely to care more than they will when working off-site. So the best location to target users will normally be outside their normal working environment. Conditions are different and new. And most users won't know what's normal for those environments, making them less suspicious.

If you're forced to conduct the project at the customer organization, your team will need to be more detailed in planning stages and conform more to the cultural norms of the organization. Your language, manner, and approach will have to be tailored to match the environment. When done correctly, on-site penetration projects shouldn't be much more difficult for a seasoned professional.

Another alternative is an off-site meeting or gathering of employees. Good examples are fund-raising carnival days, team-building exercises, and even charity work performed by employees as a group. They still work for the organization, but they're out of the office and less likely to be security conscious.

Choosing the strategy

The strategy is our game plan. It's how we'll approach the users, gain their trust, and get our software installed on their computers. The strategy *has* to take the location and the mood of the users into account. A good example of this would be a product convention in Las Vegas versus an executive meeting at an Atlanta hotel. The product convention is likely to include employees from all ranks of the organization, whereas the executive meeting is more likely to be attended by folks in formal business attire. Also, Las Vegas tends to foster that "what happens here, stays here" mentality, where employees are more likely to let their guard down and enjoy themselves. An executive meeting held at a nice hotel in Atlanta is less likely to foster this type of attitude.

> **WARNING**
>
> When we use the term *approach* to describe our initial interface with the users, it doesn't necessarily entail walking up and having a conversation with them. There are a number of methods for introducing our payload in formats that will be trusted by employees. Printed flyers, gift bags, special offers, and other approaches can be utilized to gain the user's trust. And each one of these has benefits and disadvantages that you'll need to weigh as you create your strategy. Just don't make the mistake of assuming you need to interact with the employees face-to-face for your penetration test to be successful. You might find the employees are more trusting of a printed flyer presented with a benign-looking CD to the random stranger handing them something they never asked for.

The strategy we choose needs to fit with the location, target audience, time, and wariness of our targets. We can snail mail our payload to the target in custom packaging that makes it look more official (thus more likely to be opened and trusted). Another option to get the payload into our target's hands is to present it as a perk of a conference or convention. In some instances, we can use our newly developed social engineering skills to get third-party individuals to pass along our surprise for us (hotel staff, conference staff, human resources, etc.).

Since our penetration projects will be different, each of our approaches will be customized to the organization we're targeting. Your team will need to be flexible and creative. Consider all possible alternatives, because you can be fairly certain the target organization hasn't.

> **NOTE**
>
> Many people have issues with approaching strangers, and their lack of confidence shows when they're forced to carry on a polite, friendly conversation with someone they've never met. To compound those anxieties, the individuals we'll be approaching are actually targets of our project. And while the end goal of our project is to educate the organization and its employees, there may still be an uncomfortable sense of anxiety that impacts the way we interact with the individuals with whom we're communicating.
>
> I'm pointing this out because it's incredibly important to be relaxed in your interactions. Most people haven't studied body language, but they do have instincts that react to body language and can alert them to situations that could be dangerous or misleading. In our case, we're not actually a danger to them, but we want to reinforce that *safe* feeling in our target with friendly smiles, free-flowing and casual banter, eye contact, and a sense of professionalism. All these cues will be picked up by the target and will reassure them of our intentions, even if they don't actually stop to think about it (which is technically the point of this exercise).

Choosing the technology

The technology should fit together with whatever plan you've decided on. They're like pieces of the same puzzle. If you try to use technology that doesn't fit into the story you've created and that you're walking your target through, it will stand out and is more likely to look suspicious. CDs may be more useful in situations where it's a public venue and needs to appear mass produced, such as coupons, tourist information, or home business opportunities.

USB thumb drives cost more, and people will know that, so trying to hand someone a USB drive with "Atlantic City Tourist Information" on it will appear suspicious. We want to save the high-cost deliverables for those instances when we're working with a smaller target audience, and we want the impression to be *personal*, as if we're trying to earn that person's business.

In those cases where we have physical access to the target organization's building, we can use the micro USB drives, CDs, or something similar. These allow us to plug into the USB port on target systems and either automatically install our own software or reboot the computer into a customized operating system that will allow us to mine data from the resident hard disk.

Automated attacks vary

When we look at our technology, we need to consider our attack method. Are we looking to perform a one-time data mining effort and have that data exfiltrated to an external system on the Internet? Or are we hoping to compromise a target host with a Trojan or backdoor that calls back to a server, providing us with a tunnel into the target network? It really doesn't matter which of these you decide to pursue, but you need to take into account the hardware and networking requirements of your attack.

Users are able to skirt most of the security technology that protects the organization. This is due to the legacy belief that all attacks will come from outside the network, from the Internet, and users are allowed free reign to come and go from their own network. But one of the most annoying technologies for penetration testers is the proxy server. Proxy servers force users through a single tunnel for their traffic, restricting the ports with which they can communicate. Trojan software tends to utilize set port numbers for communication, and a proxy server can break that connection, making all your effort up to this point fruitless.

Since this book is about low tech hacking, your best bet for pre compiled, ready-to-go Trojans and exploits is Metasploit and some of the other software on the Internet, such as Beast or Theef. Metasploit is your safer bet and provides mechanisms for wrapping the malicious software around executables, Internet documents, etc. As a bonus, the source codes for these payloads are normally available to the capable penetration tester, for free. Many Trojans, outside of consolidated tools like Metasploit, are written and released on the Internet, and the source code likely isn't available for you to review before using. If you pick a bad one, you could actually be doing much more harm than good for your client.

I should point out that using off-the-shelf payloads increases your chance of detection by security software on the user's end. Because these tools are so readily available, antivirus and security software vendors have created signatures that detect the tools and quarantine them almost immediately. They'll still work in many cases, but your chances of failure are increased. In some cases, you can find *wrappers* that will help obfuscate the code structure from detection systems on the user's side. But since we're limited in scope to low tech hacking, start out by practicing with the more readily available tools.

TIP

A wrapper is used by many hackers to obfuscate the code signature of a piece of malware so that it won't be detected by anti virus software once it's been installed on a user's computer. Most wrappers have an extremely short life span, since anti virus vendors search the Internet for them and adjust their tools to detect the artifacts/signatures left behind by the wrappers themselves. You can test your attack payloads against the various anti virus software products to find a wrapper that works, or, if you're a programmer, you can simply write your own.

A USEFUL CASE STUDY

Now that we've covered many of the basics of putting together a great low tech penetration test, it's time to put it all together. This case study will show how a possible low tech hack can be used to gain access to target computer systems. As you read through this example, it's important to remember that all of details in this penetration test can be changed and manipulated to fit your needs. This is less a step-by-step recipe than a demonstration of what's really possible.

The target in question is a large organization, with various offices in different cities around the country. The organization is large enough that it's difficult to tie together employees from different offices, who work in the same field, to communicate and strategize. Because of this, it was determined that an annual conference of human resource workers from all the offices would be held in Las Vegas, Nevada.

The goal of the conference was to get human resource employees from different offices to share solutions to common problems, to reinforce corporate human resource policies, and to foster relationships across the organization so employees have people to call when confronted with a difficult situation. The venue was chosen based on costs, proximity to the Strip, and the willingness of the hotel staff to help coordinate the effort. The HR manager at the corporate headquarters was the lead for the planning of the conference.

To aid in the planning of the conference, a list of potential attendees (numbering roughly 75 employees) was posted to the corporate website on a page linked from the corporate human resource page. While the link was not specifically advertised, it was still accessible from the Internet. The information on the page included name, phone number, email address, position, and location of each HR employee attending the conference. The page was updated automatically as each individual registered for the conference.

Based on all this information, it was decided that the best way to approach the employees would be through deception of the hotel and conference staff. Our team would stage two levels of attack, one against the hotel and one against the conference itself, but both aimed at the HR employees. Each of these two strategies required separate planning, but the two would dovetail into the same outcome.

The goal of the penetration effort was to get HR employees to install Trojan software onto corporate resources, allowing the team internal access to the corporate network. Two different approaches would be used, one via USB drive, and the other via CD-ROM. Where one medium might fail, the other might be successful.

Approaching hotel staff

The penetration team members decided that they would attempt to look like employees of the company holding the conference and approach front desk personnel with gift bags for employees checking into the hotel for the conference. It was easy enough to provide a list of employees who would be checking in, since this information had been provided on the corporate website. Each gift bag would contain a welcome letter from the conference organizers, valid corporate flyers (also downloaded from the corporate website and printed out), and gum, mints, candy bars, and a custom USB thumb drive that would have the corporate logo printed on it.

In order to approach the hotel staff, the penetration team members needed to look the part of employees from the company. A high resolution image of the corporate logo was found on the website and used to embroider corporate-colored polo shirts. Team members donned these shirts, along with slacks and nice shoes, and approached the front desk. A few minutes later, the hotel registration manager had gladly agreed to hand out the bags to incoming conference attendees.

Each USB thumb drive had been loaded with Trojan software that would install itself on the employee's computer, hiding behind the actual driver installation process that normally pops up when a new drive is plugged in. The Trojan would then attempt to call back to a specific server address on the Internet, alerting the penetration team that a new connection had been created. The information transmitted by the Trojan included the computer's IP address, machine name, and date/time of its installation.

> **WARNING**
>
> This type of activity is considered illegal, unless you've been granted specific permission by the organization to target their employees in this manner. And in many cases, you could still run into legal issues if the Trojans are installed on personal computers. Much of the legality of these activities depends heavily on what policies are in place at the organization itself, what the employees have been notified and trained on policies and expectations of the organization, and the state and federal laws that may apply.
>
> In ALL circumstances, be sure to consult with appropriate legal experts to determine where your boundaries are and how best to proceed. Don't take a chance with this type of work. While in some organizations it may seem cut and dried, in others you may find yourself in hot water if you don't do your homework first!

Approaching conference staff

The second method of approach would put the penetration team in direct contact with the conference staff. This time the attack would come in the form of custom-printed CDs that contained information on tourist activities in Las Vegas, including brochures, flyers, and coupons. Included on the CD would be the Trojan, which would auto-load when the CD was put into a computer.

This time, the penetration team would need to emulate hotel staff. The goal was to deliver the CDs to the conference staff while pretending to be from the hotel and state that the hotel likes to provide these CDs to conference attendees as a way to help them enjoy their stay in Las Vegas. Emulating the clothing of the hotel staff was simple, since most employees wore a black polo shirt with tan slacks. Generic gold-colored name badges (that were similar to the ones worn by hotel staff, just without the logo) were created with fake names for each member of the penetration team.

In the morning, on the day registration was supposed to begin, penetration team members donned their uniforms and went downstairs to meet the registration staff. The plan was carried off without problem. The conference staff was immediately drawn into the story provided by the pen test team members and put the CDs on the registration table next to their own handouts. This way, when employees registered for the conference on-site, they could simply pick up all the conference materials and the tourist CD at the same time.

Conclusion

This particular penetration test worked out quite well. And while the scenario itself has been fictionalized to a degree to protect the innocent, it's still valid. The penetration team in this case had set identifiers into each of the two Trojan delivery mechanisms so we could discern how each computer was compromised, by the USB drive or the CD-ROM. The success rate for this attack was around 12 to 13 percent. That means that roughly 10 people installed the Trojan on their computer system so that it reached back across to the Internet to our custom server. That's 10 separate footholds on computers that process, store, or transmit that organization's sensitive information.

Now, what I haven't told you yet is that this particular organization was very security friendly. When I use the term *security friendly*, I mean to say the organization has a robust security program with annual security awareness training for all employees. This particular target should have been a tougher nut to crack. But as I mentioned earlier in the chapter, a successful low tech hack depends heavily on where and when you approach your targets and how the payloads are delivered. We created a false sense of security using social engineering tactics and delivered our payloads in a manner that was trusted, allowing us to gain access to the target network in all the organization's various geographic locations. Imagine the success rate for an organization that was less prepared and poorly trained.

SUMMARY

Conducting penetration tests doesn't always have to rely on a great deal of technology. This chapter presented a methodology for using the concepts we've learned in this book to conduct such a penetration test. And while more technical payloads may help improve your success rate, it doesn't imply that your test will be entirely unsuccessful. Off-the-shelf software products, including some highly regarded free products, can often provide all the tools you need (along with your imagination) to do some low tech penetration testing. Also, keep in mind as you plan your test and start working through the steps, that you'll need to ensure you're playing by the rules. There are legal constraints that need to be addressed and managed.

ENDNOTE

1. Cialdini, R. The Science of Persuasion. Scientific American [Internet]. 2004 Jan [cited 2011 Sept 12]. Available from: http://www.scientificamerican.com/article.cfm?id=the-science-of-persuasion.

Low tech hacking and the law: Where can you go for help?

INFORMATION IN THIS CHAPTER

- Meet Mr. Tony Marino
- Meet Special Agent (SA) Gregory K. Baker, FBI

In addition to all of the other problems that can be caused by low tech hacking, you may also be dealing with a crime scene if you are a victim. For the past 10 years I have been working closely with local, state, and federal law enforcement agencies in many states all over the country. These low tech crimes have added a new dimension to the ways that companies and law enforcement deal with these crimes. Thousands of members of industry and law enforcement who have joined forces in the groups that I will discuss in this chapter have come to realize something very important. We definitely need each other, and neither law enforcement or industry can do this alone.

Many of these low tech hacking–associated crimes can be considered high tech crimes by law enforcement agencies. They are high tech in the sense that they don't normally involve a gun or someone physically breaking into a building. Physical trespass can certainly happen as I discussed in Chapter 2. With the crimes where technology or intellectual property are the targets, physical trespass is simply the way that people get to the information they are targeting.

This chapter will introduce you to a couple of senior members of law enforcement and the organizations that they belong to where people can go for help.

> **WARNING**
>
> Computers are interesting in that they can be used to commit a crime as well as be the victim of a crime. An employee or a family member could use a computer to commit a crime such as possession of child pornography. The same computer could be the victim of a crime should someone attempt to break into it to gain access to intellectual property. As virtually everything that's important to us is becoming completely automated, it is important to understand the types of crimes associated with computers as well as knowing the respective law enforcement agencies to contact for help.

MEET MR. TONY MARINO

Mr. Marino has been a tremendous resource for me and for all of the members of the North Carolina Electronic Crimes Task Force for many years. His willingness to share his decades of experience in the fields of electronic crimes investigation and in personal protection have been invaluable to the entire task force. He has been an excellent example of how beneficial it can be for non–law enforcement members to take the time to get to know and learn from these senior federal agents. Let's ask him a few questions so you can get to know him.

Low tech hacking interview with Tony Marino, U.S. Secret Service (retired)

Jack: Give me your best low tech hacking war story for how the bad guys might be using low tech tools and social engineering skills.

Mr. Marino: There may be several examples of basic low tech methods of attacks that utilized social engineering as the main ingredient in the application of an attack. The one I will recount here I found interesting because there was a perfect storm in effect that allowed the success of the attack. I will not divulge the parties that were victimized in this scheme, but I can say that the vulnerability has been remedied through hardware upgrades, internal procedures, and the advent of know-your-customers regulations that have been adopted.

- The background of this attack centered on a flaw in the design of a specific brand and model of ATM machine.
- The individuals exploiting the flaw obtained the information from the company involved in the manufacture of the equipment. The flaw was that a transaction could be canceled up until the moment that the customer physically pulled the bills from the dispenser. However, if the bills in the middle of the dispenser could be extracted, leaving the top and bottom bills, you could cancel the transaction, and the bills were placed in a transaction canceled bin without the number of bills being counted. The machine in effect presented the currency into view and allowed tampering with a check that the number of bills recycled into the bin was the number initially dispensed. The individuals who perpetrated this scheme traveled around the country to conduct the fraud.
- The last component was a convenience procedure in place at the particular financial institution in which a canceled transaction at the ATM did not affect the availability of funds for withdrawal on that date.

The enterprising criminals simply opened an account at the large financial institution with cash in an amount slightly above the daily withdrawal limit. They obtained a temporary ATM card, then after the branches had closed for the day, drove up to the ATMs, asked for the daily maximum they could withdraw, extracted the bills from the center of the stack, and cancelled the transaction. They then repeated the process, usually staying at the same ATM for hours, until the ATM had no more funds to dispense.

There are some other low tech social engineering schemes that come to mind. There was one where the subject used a phone book to come up with names and then called a major department store credit department posing as an associate of one of the stores. He would say he had a customer in front of him who forgot his credit card and would provide several addresses until he hit on an actual customer in the system. He would then use the information to make in-store and online purchases.

Jack: Do you think that the bad guys such as foreign spies and possible terrorists use many low tech tools for gaining access to critical information or locations?

Mr. Marino: I think it would be naïve to think that attack vectors would not follow low cost high success paths. Over and over again we have learned of critical information, or access, obtained though the most low tech methods, the most basic of which is the propensity for human beings to willingly provide access or information to those not entitled to have it. It could be from the granting of excess privileges to someone within the organization with no need for the additional access or more nefarious schemes from those seeking intellectual property, financial data, national security information, or any other thing of value. Being able to gain information socially has been around probably since verbal communication was invented. I would call it, if it has not already been called this, "the art of the talk." Skillful communication most often results in gaining pieces of information that are key to success in whatever line of business or social environment that we humans engage in. So it comes as no surprise that skilled criminals use these same skills of social engineering to advance their schemes. It also comes as no surprise that often when more sophisticated attacks occur they are conducted using already identified weaknesses. There is sometimes this misconception that in order to be successful the criminals have to do expensive engineering to target my enterprise. In fact what most often transpires is that they either go for the weakest link, the human being, or they use already available tools.

From an enterprise perspective an attack may simply consist of a call to an employee getting them to relinquish logon credentials or could involve having them take an action that infects their system with malware. Even with good procedures and practices in place an enterprise may be only as safe as how well their employees adhere to these policies.

The attack may also take the form of harvesting public information on the systems in use and using known vulnerabilities to gain access. Unknowingly providing too much information on our systems provides a clear blueprint for a possible compromise.

Closer to home and directly related to us as individuals, I can think of many examples where in spite of wide-scale public education programs and public media articles, both print and television, people still fall prey to low tech schemes, many coming in the form of what is termed 4-1-9 advance fee fraud. To briefly recap what 4-1-9 stands for, it was the criminal code section in Nigerian criminal statute that addresses these financial schemes. These schemes, meant to extract financial payment from the victims, are probably hundreds of years old. Our modern communication methods have just made them cheaper and easier to perpetrate. There are a variety of schemes, the complexity of which are fairly basic, but the results are the same, to extract funds from the victim utilizing social means. Common variants are using a counterfeit check for purchase of an advertised item or for payment of a required fee to receive funds being secreted from a faraway country, lottery winnings, to receive an inheritance, romance angle, fraud recovery, job offers, just to name a few. Victims come from all social, educational, and economic backgrounds. However, they all share the same component, which is that they have to willingly take the action of sending money or goods to the criminal.

Jack: In Chapter 1, I showed a picture (Figure 1.12) of a portable credit card reader that I found at a flea market. I have been amazed at the number of people that I meet who have been victims of credit card fraud. Do you have any recommendation for people regarding the low tech threat of skimming that seems to continue to grow?

Mr. Marino: There is always the obvious: do not let your credit card take a stroll with another person. Skimming is still an extremely effective and profitable activity. The variety of devices that can be deployed are now leveraging multiple technologies, including Bluetooth, for rapid compromises of affected accounts. Where once we were more likely to encounter a handheld device used at a restaurant or similar establishment to harvest accounts, we now have devices that are specifically customized to particular point-of-sale locations. The effectiveness of this cannot be overlooked. The customer has a certain level of trust that the ATM machine at their local branch, the gasoline pump, or grocery store point-of-sale terminal is secure. Unfortunately this is not always the case. Skimming parasites have been deployed at all these locations in spite of inherent security measures in place. I do not mean to scare people away from using technology in completion of a transaction and reverting back to cash, but instead to use measures that will significantly reduce the probability of becoming a victim. You notice that I said "reduce the probability." I meant to say that because there truly is no way to completely eliminate the risk. Technology alone has yet to completely eliminate the deployment of skimming parasites. From a technology perspective in the United States we still use legacy credit card technology. By this I mean that point-of-sale terminals at the millions of businesses in the United States are not capable of reading more advanced card data such as found in embedded chips in credit cards used throughout much of the world. These cards usually require a pin number used by the customer that authenticates the user at the time of transaction. Bringing all these legacy systems up-to-date is expensive for business owners. I will also note that these systems in use throughout Europe are not the magic bullet because other vulnerabilities can still be exploited.

Skimming to a certain degree is still an activity that succeeds in part on the ability of the criminal to socially engineer our actions. If you wonder why I make that statement it is because during the use at an ATM machine or a point-of-sale terminal where the card never leaves our possession we tend to relax. We come to believe and have faith that the transaction is secured. To a large degree it is secure, after the card data leaves the terminal, that is. However, if I inject a skimmer right here, at the card swipe location, you do the skimming for me and I simply intercept your transaction. Remember when I said earlier that the devices are customized?

Skimmers may be manufactured specifically for the specific target, whether to be inserted into a point-of-sale terminal or gasoline pump or made to go on top of a legitimate reader such as on an ATM. They may come in the shape of false fronts that can be placed over a legitimate ATM machine with an incorporated camera that, via Bluetooth, will transmit first the card data, and also the pin code, to someone or something nearby. I would suggest that when you walk or drive up to an ATM, examine your surroundings. Do so not only for someone "shoulder surfing," (a "shoulder surfer" is a person who attempts to intercept your pin simply by looking over your shoulder as it is keyed) but also for an ill-fitting face on the machine or a small pinhole. Why not use one hand to cover the numbers on the pin pad while you enter your pin?

The solution to safeguard oneself against an embedded skimmer in a point-of-sale terminal or the use of wireless technology (encrypted or not) by the merchant to pass the credit card data to their system are much more complicated issues. We can ask questions of the merchant, we can choose to use a credit card with a strict limit, we can use gasoline company only credit cards at the pump, and of course we can follow all the steps recommended by the Federal Trade Commission in the publication "Take Charge," securing your good name, which include opting out of pre-approved credit cards and monitoring of your credit history through the free yearly reports available from each of the three (3) credit reporting companies.[1]

Jack: You know that I have been a firm believer in the value of groups (not technically associations) like the Electronic Crimes Taskforce started by the U.S. Secret Service. Tell us how the ecTaskForces got started and when.

Mr. Marino: I am very proud of my service with the Secret Service. I truly feel that it is a great organization rich in history and tradition. The Secret Service is an agency not only responsible for the security of the President and his family, the Vice President and his family, former Presidents and their spouses, and foreign Heads of State while visiting the United States, but also in safeguarding our financial infrastructure. Every law enforcement officer, state, local, or federal, I am sure is equally proud of their service and importance of their duties, and well they should be. However, what I truly loved about the Secret Service was that it relies on the expertise, cooperation, and goodwill of other law enforcement professionals and private sector partners to accomplish its dual role mission. In the investigations arena, this is so very evident in the Electronic Crimes Task Force initiative. Born out of an experiment by the New York Field Office to eliminate some traditional mistrust between law enforcement and those in academia and the private sector, it rose to life in the aftermath of September 11th. The Secret Service office at 7 World Trade Center was destroyed during the attack, and immediately offers of assistance came from their academic and private sector partners. The benefits of these relationships cannot be overstated. So much so that the Bush Administration took note and mandated as part of the PATRIOT Act that the Secret Service continue and expand on the Electronic Crimes Task Force initiative.

The office to which I was assigned in the aftermath of September 11th was one of the initial offices to expand on this model. The number of private sector companies that participated is too many to individually name here, but it encompassed individuals and companies from financial institutions, energy, telecommunications, technology companies, and many more. Today throughout the United States and Europe the Secret Service has approximately thirty (30) such task forces with representatives of all the critical infrastructures, leading academic centers, and of course many state and local law enforcement partners. It is an initiative I was honored to participate on.

NOTE

Here is some information about the U.S. Secret Service (USSS) Task Forces taken directly from the USSS website. If there is an ecTask Force in your location, I highly recommend that you join them. Here's the link to their web presence with links to the respective groups throughout the country: http://www.secretservice.gov/ectf.shtml.

"The concept of task forces has been around for many years and has proven successful. However, traditional task forces have consisted primarily of law enforcement personnel. The Secret Service developed a new approach to increase the resources, skills and vision by which local, state and federal law enforcement team with prosecutors, private industry and academia to fully maximize what each has to offer in an effort to combat criminal activity. By forging new relationships with private sector entities and scholars the task force opens itself up to a wealth of resources and communication. The agency's first Electronic Crimes Task Force (ECTF), the New York Electronic Crimes Task Force, was formed based on this concept and has been highly successful since its inception in 1995.

"While the Secret Service leads this innovative effort, the agency believes in partnerships with strong emphasis on prevention and education, in addition to traditional law enforcement measures. The task forces provide a productive framework and collaborative crime-fighting environment in which the resources of its participants can be combined to effectively and efficiently make a significant impact on electronic crimes. Other law enforcement agencies bring additional criminal enforcement jurisdiction and resources to the task forces, while representatives from private industry and academia bring a wealth of technical expertise and research capabilities."[2]

Jack: As you know, my business partner at TheTrainingCo., Don Withers, and I are certified Personal Protection Specialists (PPS), Nine Lives members, and graduates of the Executive Protection Institute. As a part of our training, we learned of ways to help prevent our protectees from becoming victims of low tech hacking exploits. Since most people won't ever have or need a personal protection detail, they will need to know how to protect themselves. Can you offer any personal suggestions from the protection side of your years of experience?

Mr. Marino: Personal protection is something that everyone should take extremely seriously. We are faced with many situations in which we assume nothing will happen and we take no precautions. The threats that exist are financial and physical in nature. Wearing a seat belt in our automobiles has not only become the law but a routine habit that most of us exercise every day and take for granted. However, some other behaviors may not come naturally. For instance, many of us travel routinely whether for work or pleasure, yet do we always take the time to familiarize ourselves with evacuation routes? To highlight what I mean I will use two examples.

The first is when we board an aircraft. During my career I boarded hundreds of airplanes, if not more. I notice how many travelers, probably because this is not their first flight, simply ignore the safety briefing; we all know how to buckle and unbuckle a seat belt after all. An early lesson learned in protection, personal or of a dignitary, is to train like we want to react and do not take anything for granted; prepare for the worst case scenario. I recommend that you place attention to the briefing, planes are built differently, emergency doors use different mechanisms. However, an additional detail that I focus on during the safety briefing is when the flight attendant states, "Locate the nearest exit, it may be behind you." I not only locate that exit but I count the number of rows that are between me and the exit. I prepare myself, as should you, to maneuver in the dark by simply feeling the way in a cabin that could fill with smoke very rapidly.

The second example mirrors the first in that I repeat this same exercise when I check into a hotel, in this case by simply counting the number of doors from my room to the nearest emergency exit. To rely on a lighted sign at the ceiling level where smoke accumulates makes it extremely difficult in an emergency to orientate oneself to find the stairwell for quick evacuation. Extremely basic measures the likelihood of which we will never have to use, but one time that we are unprepared may be the last time.

There are also some very basic things that we can do to minimize the possibility of financial loss due to low tech hacking. The theft of personally identifiable information from the person of the victim is one of the most common attack vectors. Someone with the benefit of a personal assistant or physical security professional has safeguards and sometimes insulation between themselves and the general public. I recommend that under no circumstance, should one ever respond with personal information from an unsolicited, letter, telephone call, or email. Set limits for yourself as to the amount of information that is available on social media sites. When presented with the opportunity to opt out, do so. (Many "people search" websites that contain information about us allow you to opt out and have your information withdrawn, albeit with limited success especially in the case of state public records).

Practice physical security considerations that assist in safeguarding your personal information. Minimize the possibility of becoming a victim of petty crime. We are most at risk domestically and, even when traveling internationally, of succumbing to a property crime such as presented from a pickpocket. The amount of sensitive personally identifiable information or access to financial resources that we carry should not only be minimized, but also should be compartmentalized and placed in a not easily accessible location. For me it means lose the "George Costanza wallet" (a reference to the Seinfeld show where in one episode of the show Costanza's wallet was so full it made him sit on a slant and one day it exploded, sending all its contents into the street), maintain the minimum amount of information, minimum number of credit cards, never a social security card (unless you are on a job interview or starting a new job). If you travel internationally, keep your passport locked in the hotel safe and carry a photocopy instead. Many of the interactions that the U.S. State Department has with U.S. citizens abroad center on replacing a lost or stolen passport. Lastly, make sure that you maintain your personal financial belongings in a non–easily accessible location, which may mean not in your back pocket or a purse slung over the shoulder.

TIP

For excellent training in the field of executive protection, visit the website for the Executive Protection Institute at http://www.personalprotection.com. I have made this statement at briefings and presentations for many years: "If you don't have your own personal protection team (and few people do), you need to at least understand what a protection detail would be looking at while protecting you and your family, and do as much of it as you can for yourself.

Jack: I'd like to ask you one final question about the growing problem of identity theft. I suspect that much of that involves some form of social engineering and other low tech hacking exploits used to gain enough information to take over someone's identity. Is the threat continuing to grow in your opinion, and do you have any suggestions for our readers preventing becoming a victim?

Mr. Marino: Absolutely, as I previously mentioned the theft of personally identifiable information is very common and very profitable as well. The Federal Trade Commission (FTC) maintains the statistics on the number of victims of identity theft and the sheer numbers, their estimate is nine (9) million Americans are victims each year, are in my opinion staggering. I also have to believe that to a certain extent these numbers under represent the actual number of victims. Many people are not aware that should they be a victim of identity theft it should not only be reported to the police jurisdiction in which they live, but it should also be reported to the FTC as the central depository of the information.

We hear in the news about a large database compromise at a particular location and start to think that is where the problem lies. The truth of the matter is that low tech hacking and social engineering attacks are extremely effective and require little to no technical skills. A great location to scour for information is what we place on social networking sites. You may be thinking, "but my site is private." Password strengths vary by the individual, no different than the lock we choose for own home. If the password, or lock, is weak the criminal can enter your home or enter your computer and can become in essence the user or the "man in the middle" ("man in the middle" refers to a computer attack whereby the criminal sits in between the two intended users and controls the conversation or session). Besides the lock or password controls, risky web surfing habits can expose the user to any number of system vulnerabilities. The technical skill needed to deploy that vulnerability is really zero; you can buy off the shelf software tools (programs). So you see there are a number of ways that criminals could harvest entire address books in order to attempt social engineering attacks. The strength of any network, including our social networks, is only as strong as the weakest lock. One of the common attacks I have seen is where in this same scenario of the social network compromise, the address book was used to "spoof" (masquerade) an email pleading for cash, via a money remitter. The email appears to come from someone you know and they are pleading for funds because of an unforeseen travel emergency. Low tech, but effective, because of the human nature propensity to be trusting and helpful.

Make no mistake, however; methods used for identity theft are usually low tech, and unsophisticated. Though there may be variations to the schemes, the sources remain pretty constant. They include old-fashioned phishing attacks; theft of mail from our own mailboxes; rummaging through the trash; cold call pretexting, which is social engineering in the truest sense; and old-fashioned stealing of financial data by an insider with access or from our own person.

A lot of the power to protect us from identity theft resides with us. We can exercise good practices, some of which I mentioned earlier, and we can also exercise our own due diligence with tools at our disposal. The primary tool is our vigilance.

Jack: Thanks for always being there for us, Tony.

MEET SPECIAL AGENT (SA) GREGORY K. BAKER, FBI

Over the past few years, I've spent a fair amount of time with Special Agent (SA) Greg Baker of the FBI. As the InfraGard coordinator for the two largest chapters located in North Carolina, Special Agent (SA) Baker has proven to be a very dedicated federal agent as well as a friend to several thousand North Carolina InfraGard members. In the following interview I asked him a few questions about his thoughts on low tech hacking.

Low tech hacking interview with Special Agent (SA) Gregory K. Baker, FBI

Jack: Give me your best low tech hacking war story for how the bad guys might be using low tech tools and social engineering skills.

SA Baker: Malicious executable attachments to email continue to be the most prevalent low tech hacking threat. While social engineering strategies have changed somewhat, the hacker's goal of convincing unsuspecting victims to open and view email with malicious attachments remains the same. Changes in social engineering strategies include the increase in "Whaling" also known as "Spear Phishing" activity as opposed to traditional "Phishing." The difference in terms being that "Whaling" aka "Spear Phishing" specifically targets executive managers and decision makers within private and public sector organizations rather than utilizing the more traditional means of randomly distributing malicious code through bulk email "spamming" activity. Another social engineering tactic that has gained tremendous momentum preys on the explosive popularity of social networking sites. The strategy utilizes a slightly more sophisticated model of masking malicious .exe files with .jpg or .txt file extensions. An example would be that the victim opens the file to view a photograph or picture (.jpg) and running behind the photo is malicious code (.exe). The most significant difference when comparing the low tech hacker or "Script

Kiddy" to the more sophisticated lone wolf or state-sponsored hacker is that the low tech hacker will likely utilize malicious tools readily available for purchase on many hacker forums. These tools most often target known operating system (OS) vulnerabilities and rely on the complacency of the victim to be successful. This is very important to understand from the victim perspective and emphasizes the points of 1) utilizing updated system security software 2) utilizing the default system setting of "daily" to "patch, patch, patch" vulnerabilities identified by your OS provider.

Jack: Do you think that the bad guys such as foreign spies and possible terrorists use many low tech tools for gaining access to critical information or locations?

SA Baker: Jack I will keep my responses more broad in perspective. The points I make above are the points that I make in every cyber security–related presentation that I do. While it is possible that low tech hacking tools can be deployed by individuals involved in espionage and terrorism, the most important concepts for the users to embrace are: 1) the need to educate themselves on the current threats and tactics utilized by the criminal hacker and 2) how to protect themselves, their sensitive information, and their networks from these types of attacks.

Jack: Tell me more about "Spear Fishing" and what people should know to prevent being a victim. Our readers would also like to know when the FBI would get involved if someone thinks that they have been targeted.

SA Baker: The term "Spear Phishing" is a hacker term which indicates that the hacker is specifically targeting an individual for attack as opposed to a bulk spam mail approach. The significance from a law enforcement perspective is that it shows a significant shift in philosophy, sophistication, and most importantly, in criminal intent. As an example, a hacker utilizing a spam mail approach does not know what the return on the investment will be at the time of delivery. Often, the hacker is simply looking to disrupt or disable service connections for individual users, to incorporate the individual machine into a network of compromised machines known as a "bot net" or "bot herding," or in some instances to steal the personal identification of individual but unknown users. A hacker utilizing a "Spear Phishing" method has researched a private or public sector entity, identified a potential target based on position or perceived access, and specifically attempts to deliver a malicious payload to that person by way of email. The motivations for "Spear Phishing" are numerous. The hacker's motivations can be total network disruption, utilizing the network to store illegal or illegally obtained documents and images; theft of trade secrets; theft of classified material; theft of personal information; or financial motivation. The best defense against becoming a victim of "Spear Phishing" is do not open email and email attachments unless you are positive you know the sender. If you receive an email that appears to be from someone you know but the email has no entry on the subject line or the subject content is not consistent with the person you know (i.e., the email asks for information that is not normal for the known contact or the email contains content that is not normal or appropriate for the known contact), take caution. Discard the email to your "trash" folder. Often, but not always, the suspect email will ask for a response. If so, before you respond to the suspect email, telephone or initiate a new email from your contact list to the known contact that the email appeared to come from and ask them if they sent you an email.

If the receiver already opened the email and the email contains content that is obviously not from a known/trusted contact—the email contains photos, videos or other attachments that are obviously not from the known/trusted contact and/or the email contains illegible content—immediately close the email and contact your network administrator or IT security personnel. Some of the factors the FBI considers in determining whether to initiate an investigation regarding an apparent "Spear Phishing" attempt would be 1) Was the target an elected official? 2) Did the target hold a security clearance and/or have access to sensitive or classified data or networks? 3) Was there a loss of data, and if so, was the data classified? 4) What was the monetary loss or value of data lost, altered, or destroyed? 5) Did the intrusion result in damage to network or infrastructure or otherwise cause in the entity's inability to operate resulting in economic loss?

Jack: What can companies do to help law enforcement reduce the threat of low tech crimes?

SA Baker: Whether an individual or private entity, the best offense is a really good defense when protecting against the low tech hacker. By that I mean, now more than ever before the public sector is willing to share the most recent threat-based intelligence regarding cyber crime with private sector partners. Organizations such as InfraGard share threat-based intelligence at scheduled meetings as well as via a userid/password protected VPN where the most recent threat-based intelligence bulletins are posted for review by the membership. Individuals and the private sector as a whole should ensure that all of the stakeholders are well informed regarding the most current threat-based intelligence available. Companies should ensure that not just the IT staff are aware of the threats but rather all of the employees should have access to the threat intelligence. Generally speaking, the individual user is the most vulnerable and most targeted for compromise by the low tech hacker. Most states have adopted cyber crime laws similar to those enacted at the federal level. If a person or entity suspects they are a victim of cyber crime, they should contact the FBI, state, or local law enforcement agency nearest to them for advice.

Jack: With some of these low tech crimes, it can be difficult to know who in law enforcement a possible victim should call. If in doubt as to who to refer a potential crime to, should the FBI be contacted directly by individuals or companies?

SA Baker: Great question. Often it is confusing for victims to determine the appropriate agency to contact with information regarding hacking events. The FBI has taken significant strides in the past 10 years to remove some of that confusion. By creating organizations such as InfraGard, the FBI established a community outreach organization for the private sector. The most important aspect of the organization is that the FBI created a systematic method to distribute relevant information to a large audience of members. Members are educated on current cyber threats; provided with suggestions on protecting personal and sensitive industry data; and the jurisdictional responsibilities local, state, and federal law enforcement. InfraGard also provides for an identified FBI point of contact should a member need further explanation on jurisdictional matters. Another resource sponsored by the FBI is an FBI-managed website for cyber-related criminal complaints. This site is www.IC3.gov. The FBI provides this website as a service to persons and entities that wish to report instances of cyber-related criminal activity. Individuals can visit the site to report or research the latest cyber scams and other methods utilized by cyber criminals. Lastly, individuals requiring specific information or wishing to personally report information on cyber-related crime, specifically "Spear Phishing," are welcome to contact their local FBI field office either by telephone or in person.

NOTE

InfraGard exists as a private-sector FBI partnership dedicated to the protection of our nation's critical assets. Specifically, InfraGard is a nationwide organization consisting of over 60 chapters and over 40,000 members from the public and private sectors. Members interact, exchange information, and mitigate current threats through open dialogue at regularly scheduled chapter meetings. Members also communicate and exchange information through a nationwide Virtual Private Network (VPN) managed and funded by the FBI.

Each chapter is hosted by an FBI Field Office. Some field offices, such as the Charlotte, North Carolina, FBI Field Office host multiple InfraGard chapters. Each FBI Field Office has a designated FBI Special Agent who acts as the coordinator for the InfraGard program within the field office territory. The coordinator is responsible for developing a meaningful and productive relationship with private industry, allowing for a two-way flow of relevant information.

The FBI divides the entire InfraGard membership into 18 categories that represent all of our nation's critical assets, resources, and services or most appropriately, critical infrastructures. Critical infrastructures are best defined as "those assets, resources and services that if debilitated, could have a devastating impact on our nation's economy." This definition emphasizes the ultimate mission of the FBI's InfraGard program, which is helping to promote and protect the economy of the United States from physical threats, cyber threats, economic espionage, and terrorism.

Jack: How is the FBI working with local and state law enforcement agencies to help spread the word about these low tech crimes? One of the best Charlotte Infra-Gard meetings that I ever attended was a meeting where the FBI brought in all of the local and state agencies from the surrounding counties to share their current threat knowledge with our members. It was amazing to see how many of the same kinds of crimes were on the rise in each respective geographic location.

SA Baker: The FBI works closely with local, state, and other federal law enforcement agencies primarily through FBI-sponsored Cyber Crime Task Forces (CCTF) located throughout the country. In doing so, the FBI sponsors local and state officers and agents for federal deputations. The federal deputation affords the local and/or state officer the same federal investigative authority as an FBI Special Agent. This is extremely important in cyber crime investigations. First, most states have concurrent jurisdictional laws that mirror those established by Congress at the federal level. Also, most law enforcement agencies actively involved in cyber crime investigations are experiencing the same criminal acts to a varying degree. Because there is substantial interest among the general citizenry, cyber crime has become a priority to local and state law enforcement agencies. Investigative personnel resources for cyber crime matters, however, are generally very limited at the local and state levels.

The FBI CCTF therefore serves as a "force multiplier" to local and state agencies that are willing to commit their limited resources to the CCTF effort. Secondly, cyber crime effecting citizens in a particular community are seldom committed by an offender residing within that community. In fact, the offender oftentimes does not even reside within the United States. It is important to note this fact when considering the importance of the federal deputation. Without the FBI sponsorship of the federal deputation, the jurisdictional boundaries of the investigative agency would stop at the city, county, or state line where the investigating agency resides. An example would be a city police detective investigating a scam perpetrated on a person or persons responding to items listed for sale on an online personal advertising site. If the investigative detective was required to work without a federal deputation, her or his authority would stop at the city limits or other jurisdictional boundary established by the department.

The detective would then have to rely on her or his established professional contacts outside the jurisdiction or attempt to make contacts within the jurisdiction where the investigation might lead. Lastly, the detective would have to consider forwarding the investigation to federal authorities for investigative consideration. All of these issues are resolved with the FBI sponsoring the federal deputation, which allows for the Task Force Officer (TFO) to travel anywhere within the United States or its possessions in pursuit of evidence of the crime. Further, the TFOs are able to leverage the close working relationships that the FBI has established with its international law enforcement partners in pursuit of cyber criminals around the world. Last but certainly not least, participation in FBI CCTFs affords the deputized officers with extremely valuable cyber training at the FBI's expense. TFOs can receive numerous IT certifications at no expense to the participating agency.

Jack: Thanks for everything that you do to keep us safe, Greg.

SUMMARY

—Low Tech Jack

One of the main things that I wanted to accomplish with this brief chapter was for readers to get to know law enforcement. About 10 years ago I was honored to be asked to start the InfraGard chapter in Charlotte, North Carolina. I am happy to see that this has grown into a network of law enforcement and industry members exceeding 1500 in North Carolina alone.

Regarding the U.S. Secret Service electronic crimes task force, I have been doing things for and with them since 1989. This was well before the task force itself existed, but I began to learn some interesting things about working with local, state, and federal law enforcement agents. I can honestly say in the decades of being closely involved with so many of them, I have never seen the proverbial "talk to a federal agent and they'll make a federal case out of your conversation" myth. To the best of my knowledge, that has never happened in anything that I've been associated with. What

I do know is that I now have dozens, perhaps hundreds, of known trusted good guys whom I can call should I see a suspicious situation or simply need advice on who to refer a particular crime to. I'm proud of my association and friendship with so many members of the law enforcement agencies that keep the peace.

I used to ask this question at our InfraGard meetings here in Charlotte: "How many people sitting here in this meeting have never met a federal agent?" I was surprised to see that initially most hands went up. The meetings were the first time that a number of these members were able to have personal conversations with federal agents. This turned out to be pretty much the case when we talked about local and state law enforcement members as well. I have seen the relationships that can develop through these meetings grow into very strong personal friendships as it has between me and the two very senior federal agents that I interviewed for this chapter. They are some of the finest people that I have ever met, and I'm proud to call them friends.

ENDNOTES

1. Federal Trade Commission. Take Charge: Fighting Back Against Identity Theft [Internet]. [updated 2010 Sept 15; cited 2011 Sept 9]. Available from: http://www.ftc.gov/bcp/edu/pubs/consumer/idtheft/idt04.shtml.
2. United States Secret Service. About the U.S. Secret Service Electronic Crimes Task Forces [Internet]. 2010 [cited 2011 Sept 9]. Available from: http://www.secretservice.gov/ectf_about.shtml.

Information security awareness training: Your most valuable countermeasure to employee risk

INFORMATION IN THIS CHAPTER

- An Introduction to Information Security Awareness
- Designing an Effective Information Security Awareness Program
- Implementing an Information Security Awareness Program
- Making Security Part of the Company Mindset
- Measuring Your Program's Success

On May 24, 1844, the first telegraph message was sent from Baltimore, Maryland, to Washington, DC. The message, from Samuel Morse, was a simple, but prophetic one: "What hath God wrought?"[1]

Fast-forward almost 170 years and we find ourselves living in a very different time, but facing many of the same risks. Back then Indians and "unknowns" cut wires to disrupt the flow of information or patched into telegraph lines to steal information. Today "unknowns" disrupt business communications, steal sensitive information at a magnitude that costs billions of dollars annually to the world's economy. The Internet, as wonderful as it is, is "What hath God wrought?"[2]

Suppose there comes a day when the entire world goes silent at exactly the same time. Governments around the world, television networks, stock exchanges, banking systems, communications, transportation, electrical grids, cell phones, anything that relies on the Internet and electricity would go silent at exactly noon Eastern Standard Time around the world. We would be catastrophically pushed back to a time just prior to "What hath God wrought?"[3]

If you think this is a farfetched scenario, think again. The world has become so reliant on the Internet that it has become its own worst nightmare. Business continuity plans would be useless as the last ounce of fuel and batteries died. The world would fall silent except for the chaos and fears that would take hold.

Could this actually happen? Yes! Is it more likely to happen at your company? Depends! Is there anything you can do to avoid such a calamity? No! There is no safe haven unless you can get in front of the risk. Unfortunately, as in Morse's time, the risks existed, albeit not as severe as we face today. The "unknowns" only need to get it right once. Your company needs to get it right 100% of the time. The question is: "How do you stop the 'unknowns' from getting it right once and to what degree?"

"Is it luck?"

They do it through excellent understanding of systems, networks, applications, and they do it the old-fashion low tech way. They simply walk into your business and steal information—sensitive information left lying around, the password taped under the keyboard, the printed data left at the copier, the sensitive information in the trash basket, the cupboard left unsecured, the laptop left unattended. Yes, they do it the old-fashion way by making a call and simply asking for sensitive information. These are the "unknowns" who look or sound like they belong, make themselves appear to be credible with a valid need to know. These "unknowns" are often referred to as social engineers. Adept, smart, they use the employee's desire to provide good customer/client service to gather sensitive information.

Kind of a bleak outlook, wouldn't you say? But there are ways to minimize the risks posed by the "unknowns" and what the potential "wrought"[4] would be to your company. You must pay attention to your weakest link, and that is your people. It is your own employees' unintentional actions that are the greatest risk to sensitive information assets at your company whether customer, employee, business clients and that of the company.

AN INTRODUCTION TO INFORMATION SECURITY AWARENESS

This chapter is an overview on how to design and implement an effective information security awareness program. One chapter will not cover all you need to know, but it can serve as the foundation for starting a program or making an existing program better. In this chapter you will learn why an information security awareness program presents the best benefit, low-cost countermeasure for safeguarding sensitive information properly at any company, regardless of size. You will learn the critical steps and components to implementing a successful program.

The people and personalities of information security awareness

There are many essential characteristics needed for those involved in designing and implementing a successful information security awareness program. The following sections detail these attributes.

The information security awareness specialist

The need for an information security awareness specialist is emerging. This person has a good handle on marketing, communications, media, design, and project management. This individual doesn't necessarily need to be a subject-matter expert, and though having CISSP credentials would be helpful, it is not a requirement. A lot of what they must have is common sense and the ability to put into people-speak information outlined in the company's information security policy, standards, and other sources of guidance. An information security awareness specialist needs the creative ability and license to design a robust program and the maturity to implement it successfully.

What additional skill sets should you look for when hiring someone to design and implement an information security awareness program?

- Previous experience in implementing such a program is certainly an asset.
- Good writing skills.
- Someone with good people and presentation skills who is comfortable interfacing with all levels within the company. Often he or she will directly support the corporate information security officer (CISO) and other senior leaders in their presentation needs and craft emergency awareness messages too.
- Good project management skills.
- An entrepreneurial spirit.

The intrapreneur

An intrapreneur[5] is someone who embraces the principles of an entrepreneur when working for a company. In other words, the intrapreneurs works within the confines of a company as if they are running their own business, willing to be a risk-taker as they advance the awareness program through the company's political environment. During the 7 years I was with Bank of America designing and implementing the information security awareness program, I had seven bosses. If each of those managers had decided to change the direction of the awareness program, my position and responsibility to implement the program would have been futile. Awareness programs must follow a consistent path that leads to greater employee awareness on how to safeguard sensitive information properly at the company.

This is not to say my managers did not give me input and valued suggestions. They were great team players. What I appreciated more than anything was their willingness to be enablers versus hands-on managers. I have never worked with a more wonderful group of people in all my life. To implement a successful information security awareness program, especially in a large corporation, you must "own the program," be responsible for it and have the authority to implement it. The risk is *not* taking the responsibility and running with it. Never underestimate your capabilities to do so. If your manager is more of a hands-on person, you may feel less in control. You may not be able to create and implement the program you envision. However, you will still benefit from this chapter. The tools and techniques I will share with you will help anyone, and any company, start or improve an existing information security awareness program.

WARNING

There is a tendency for management to redirect those who are responsible for designing and implementing the company's information security awareness program toward other projects. This often can become the death knell for your program. That's why it's important to have a business plan in place. You can point out to your manager where you are in the process of implementing the business plan, and why your efforts should not be redirected to other projects that do not support your plan. Of course, if your manager still wants to redirect your efforts, that's their call.

Data theft and employee awareness

If data theft is as important as everyone seems to think it is, then why aren't all companies providing information security awareness training to their employees?

The answer is simple. They do not understand the risks. Here is a simple analogy you can use when someone asks why an Information Security Awareness Program is so important to have at the company: When driving to work, everyone knows the rules of the road, but there are those who feel it's alright to run a red light or endanger others by multitasking while behind the wheel. When "driving" information through your company, the expectation is that employees will follow all the rules of the road you put in place. When they don't, the company's exposure to risk increases.

Using a cell phone, checking Facebook, or tweeting as you drive down the road are just not acceptable behaviors. I know you've seen people talking on cell phones, eating a hamburger, putting on lipstick, even reading a newspaper or book while driving. Somehow, these behaviors have become pervasive in our society, and they put all of us at risk.

Some people simply believe their actions are acceptable because they do not believe their behavior will cause an accident. Go figure. The same is true in your company. Recently I was with a group of lawyers at a deposition. During the lunch break, every lawyer left their laptop computers and iPads in the conference room. Not one lawyer stayed behind to insure that they were not stolen. These are intentional behaviors without a clear understanding of the risks. If each lawyer's company had an Information Security Awareness Program that focused on this simple risk, an unintentional behavior (risk) could have been easily avoided. I have seen the exact same risk lead to a lost laptop in a secure area within a company's facility.

A common example of unintended risk is a laptop with unencrypted sensitive data left behind in a cab, at an airport, unattended and stolen. The employee who fails to secure sensitive information or properly destroy that information has put the company and its customers in jeopardy. Many companies today simply state in their standard that if your laptop is stolen, regardless of reason, it is grounds for termination. It is a serious problem that rivals that of tweeting while driving and other nonsensical behaviors.

IT specialists know the biggest risk every company faces is employee failure to safeguard sensitive information properly. All the security applications in the world will not stop unintentional employee security mishaps or premeditated events by a disgruntled employee. I sometimes wonder whether an Information Security Awareness Program should be called an information security risk avoidance program. That way, more senior leaders will better understand the importance and support the program. For some specific examples of these vulnerabilities, read Chapter 6.

The cost of noncompliance

The Ponemon Institute's 2010 "Cost of a Data Breach" report said: "The average organizational cost of a data breach increased to $7.2 million and cost companies an average of $214 per compromised record."[6] That is up from $192.50 per record in 2007. How much of this lost information was attributed to employees? We don't really know, but the data suggests that employees represent 80% to 85% of all data breaches. I stress this is not documented data, and, of course, not all data breaches are reported. Suffice it to say, unintentional incidents by employees due to a lack of awareness or improper behavior is a big issue.

A look at cost risk benefit

So, why don't companies look closer at the cost risk benefit ratio when it comes to training their employees in safeguarding sensitive information properly?

The following observations will give you insight to some of the prevailing thought patterns.

Not all senior leaders and managers understand the risk. Unfortunately, it isn't until an incident occurs that management becomes fully engaged in the need for a viable program. When the loss is staggering, the risk becomes reality. Often, the perceived cost to implement a program becomes a barrier. It only takes one data breach incident, costing $7.2 million,[7] as indicated by the Ponomen Institute, to get senior leadership's attention. Almost immediately, management wants to know what the company is doing to educate employees on the risks. Then the cost of implementing a program is no longer a factor. An investment of $1.00 to $2.00 per employee into a program each year that reinforces employee awareness on how to safeguarding sensitive information properly is far less costly than an incident caused by unintentional actions.

NOTE

Risks come in many forms, and the process of litigation and eDiscovery is a major risk. I have seen depositions wherein emails that were written 10 years previously are entered as exhibits. If your company does not have a document retention and destruction policy in place, it should consider one to ensure incriminating documents are not forgotten in the system only to raise their ugly head down the road.

Another reason companies do not implement an information security awareness program is that management may have the impression that employees are adequately reviewed and vetted during the hiring process. The prevailing thinking is, "We have good people. They have a vested interest in the company. They are loyal, honest, and law-abiding citizens of the enterprise. So why do we need to train them in safeguarding sensitive information properly?" Sounds a little stupid, I know, but, employees are also *human*, and *humans* make mistakes. Never assume that new employees understand how to safeguard sensitive information properly. It is the unintentional mishaps due to a lack of knowledge that present the threat. A solid Information Security Awareness Program assures all employees, new hires, and existing employees clearly understand and exhibit the right behaviors to protect customer, employee, business, and company sensitive information. These information assets, when in the wrong hands, generate a significant risk to the company. Thus, a good Information Security Awareness Program is not only a risk avoidance program but also a significant countermeasure to low tech hacking activity that every company faces today from inside and outside the company's walls.

DESIGNING AN EFFECTIVE INFORMATION SECURITY AWARENESS PROGRAM

An awareness program incorporates the company's defined behaviors regarding its policies, standards, and other guidance into easy to understand, commonsense protocols on how to safeguard sensitive information properly at the company. Components of the program should include, but not be limited to:

- Information classifications at the company (confidential, proprietary, etc.)
- Examples of each classification
- Classification marking and labeling
- Proper transmission of information
- Proper storage and retention of information
- Proper destruction of information
- Use of security tools (user IDs, passwords, password guidelines, and how to change a password)
- General guidelines (privacy, document protection, physical security, laptop security, workstation security, remote computing, social engineering, downloading software, use of USBs and other storage devices, cell phones, use of Internet applications such as Facebook and Twitter, etc.)
- Internet/intranet/email usage (general Internet/Intranet practices, electronic mail practices, email monitoring policy, eDiscovery)
- Incident reporting process
- Information security resources at the company (where to find specific information security guidance)

Information Security Awareness Programs will vary according to a company's resources and the level of risks it faces. There is no one solution to fit all situations, and each program needs to be customized to the organization.

Repetition is the aide to memory

When you give a presentation, there is an old adage attributed to Aristotle that says "Tell them what you are going to tell them. Tell them, and then tell them what you told them." In other words, repetition is the aide to memory. When implementing an Information Security Awareness Program, that same adage holds true. An effective awareness program is not a one-time event. It is a program designed to change a culture from one of noncompliance to compliance in exhibiting the right safeguarding sensitive information behaviors. The program repeats the same message seven different times and seven different ways through a logical progression of touch points. Our goal is to enhance employees' awareness so that information security will become a cultural value exhibited throughout the company.

Touch points

When designing your program you MUST take into consideration all the existing and potential touch points available to you. Touch points are other resources within the company that you can utilize to support or deliver your awareness program. Some good examples are in-house periodicals, training platforms, media development capabilities, and other such communication avenues. As you look around your company, you will find many groups, such as personnel, supply, compliance, training and development, and communications, who will want to support the implementation of your program. Other divisions or groups within the company may not be as supportive. Too often, divisions or groups silo themselves, thinking that their operation is the most important, and thereby do not communicate effectively with other groups in the company. Your people skills in expressing your willingness to partner with others for the good of the company and its stakeholders will be of huge benefit to you in this process.

NOTE

Never underestimate the needs of other group(s) within your company to support your awareness program. And never underestimate your ability to interact with those groups to provide services. Often, they need you just as much as you need them. You just need to help them see it. For example, if your company has a privacy group, they would be a great resource to partner with and support your awareness program. An in-house video production facility is always looking for ways to support internal clients, and so is training and development.

The first product I released in my program was a quick reference guide (QRG). I initially had a QRG sent directly to each employee in the company. For new hires,

I partnered with the people in personnel who handled the new hire post-acceptance package. Each time the company hired a new employee, the employee received a package of materials such as a welcome letter, benefits information, corporate mission statement, etc., prior to their start date. The group that managed that process was excited to include the information security awareness QRG in the package.

NOTE

As your program develops, you will discover that there is an administration component. The more you can relieve yourself of these responsibilities the more time you will have to concentrate on and move your program forward. For example, if you manually survey employees on an annual basis, who within the company can help with an electronic solution? Are they willing to run the survey for you? When I was creating our survey, I looked for individuals within the company who knew how to write good survey questions. There was no one. But, 2 years later, the need for surveys throughout the company had grown to such an extent that the resources became available as a new service from training and development. From that point forward, I had them design, implement, and manage our awareness survey. Training and development provided me with the data.

The concept of relieving yourself of responsibilities allows you to do more. You cannot be all things to all people, nor will you have the time to manage every aspect of your program if you keep it too close to the vest. My suggestion is to find others in the company who can take on the responsibility of distribution and even implementation of certain aspects of your program. Again, this gives you more time to work on developing the next component of your program versus administrating what is already in place.

There was another side-benefit to adopting this process. When would a new employee be most interested in reviewing material and have the time to do it? Prior to starting the job with a new company! By receiving the QRG in the new hire package, there was not only a better chance of their reading the QRG, but it also told the new employee that the company believed that safeguarding sensitive information properly at the company was very important.

To team or not to team, that is the question

The very first step in creating your information security program is putting a business plan in place. Your manager may want you to team with others in your division to accomplish this task and that can become a challenge. In large companies there are so many opinions on what a program should look like that it can be confusing. Of course, there is safety in numbers, but well-meaning efforts can be wasted in teams. There is a paradox called the Abilene Paradox,[8] which basically states that a group of people will make a decision to do something that no one wants to do. The result is the project goes nowhere. If you are responsible, then you MUST have the authority to make it happen. Again, as an intrapreneur[9] you take permission to do this; don't ask for it. I offer the following suggestions that worked for me:

- Independently design the program without the input of a team.
- Review weekly progress with your manager.
- Create a presentation of the program for your Chief Information Security Officer's approval.
- Once you have the CISO's approval, you are free to move the program forward.

Let's go back to the team concept for a minute. Did I ever use teams? You bet I did! As the program became reality, I would create teams according to what was in my business plan. In many cases I partnered with other departments within the company to get the resources I needed to move the program forward. For example, I partnered with the privacy department to create the platform for our online information security awareness web-based training program. I created a team to design the information security content for that web-based training program.

> **NOTE**
>
> There were many reasons why I partnered with privacy, none less than the Gramm-Leach-Bliley Act (GLBA) that required employee training. If I could partner with privacy to deliver an online information security / privacy awareness training program under the GLBA mandate for privacy, I could add a significant touch point to my program. It did not hurt that employees did not recognize the difference between information security and privacy. Since information security was better known throughout the company because of our marketing efforts, privacy saw the advantage in exposure as well as sharing costs.

Our online information security/privacy web-based training program was created in the early 2000s prior to emerging web-based training and learning management systems emerging technologies. Timing is everything, and embracing new technology to deliver a program was, and is, a smart way to move your program forward. We shared the costs and were able to use many resources of other groups too. Don't underestimate your abilities. Our combined effort to create the first web-based training program at the company was very successful and an important component of the Information Security Awareness Program. I'll talk more about this later on in the chapter.

Creating a business plan for your Information Security Awareness Program

Your objective is to create and implement an Information Security Awareness Program that will cover the next 5-year business period. And it must be created in the next 90 days. That sounds great, but, where do you start? What should it include? I'd suggest everything, including the kitchen sink! Well, that might be going a little too far, but the point is to create a 5-year comprehensive plan. Create a vision of what your program will look like over time. Do not worry that you are including too much. This is your time to be creative. My vision was simple: that every employee clearly understood their responsibility to safeguard sensitive information properly at the company and exhibited the right behaviors. Pretty scary, but by the time I left the company we had statistically achieved the vision with over 230,000 employees worldwide.

Don't second-guess what will work and what will not. Remember, your objective in the first 90 days or less is to put your business plan together. This is the time to be a visionary and be creative. Don't worry about budget and how things will be funded. Too often we constrain our creativity by worrying about things that actually do not exist. Start being creative by putting all your ideas down on paper or note cards so that you can see the components in front of you. This will help you determine the directions you want to take the program and the products, tools, and resources you will need to accomplish this. Do not underestimate your abilities.

The presentation

I titled my presentation, "A Marketing Campaign for Information Security at Bank of America." The presentation had four sections:

- Overview
- Product Fact Sheets
- Product Roll-Out with Audit Compliance
- Budget Projection

> **NOTE**
>
> Audit Compliance was included because the information security awareness program was an audit issue. That would be one of my CISO's biggest questions. So, I actually sat down with audit prior to making the presentation to my CISO to ensure that what I was presenting would meet with their approval. I will elaborate later in this chapter, under "Let's Talk More about Alliances," how important partnering with audit and other departments within the company can help you implement your awareness program.

The Overview section of the presentation was modeled on the best presentation I have ever heard. A salesperson was trying to sell a satellite phone system to an Arab sheik back in the 1980s. Rather than present facts, figures, and technical jargon, the salesperson went out and hired a graphic artist. His presentation would be a one-pager. The picture he had the artist draw was of the sheik in his tent, in the desert, sitting in his comfortable chair, speaking on his satellite phone to someone who was on another continent. The picture also showed the phone communicating with a satellite. On the backside of the presentation sheet was the price tag to make this picture come to life. I think it all came to about $3 million back then. According to the salesman, the presentation lasted less than one minute. The sheik looked at the picture and knew it was clearly what he wanted. When the salesman flipped the presentation page over to reveal the price, the sheik signed his approval on the page. Deal done! This is exactly how I approached presenting my business plan to my CISO. I wanted to show the components of the marketing concept and how they would support a successful information security awareness program. The same principle of the sheik's one-pager applied. Keep your presentation simple. Each component had a title page that included a picture or graphic and a bullet point or two.

The other three segments of the presentation, Product Fact Sheets, Rollout of the Program, and Budget Projection, supported the Overview. For example, Product Fact Sheets indicated:

- The product name
- Description of the product
- Dimensions, if applicable
- Audience
- Distribution
- Criteria, if applicable, such as awards, etc.
- Process, if applicable
- Internal support/vendor
- Unit cost

These segments of the presentation were loaded with detail and indicated the cost of each item to implement. I knew that my CISO was not interested in the cost of each item but rather the bottom line. My challenge was for her to buy into the marketing concept, the products, the vision, and the cost. As you go through the Overview section of your presentation, you will get a sense of your CISO's acceptance of the program. If your CISO is not showing interest, you probably will never get to the fact sheets, roll-out (calendar), or budget sections. Fortunately, my presentation went well. Little time was spent on the fact sheets or product roll-out. Why? She was already sold on the program, and all that really interested her was the cost. It also indicated that the numbers I was coming up with were not just pulled out of a cloud but the result of a lot of research. It said I had done my homework.

Presentation is everything!

When my CISO asked the key question, "How much is this going to cost?," I laid out the final budget this way:

- Product release
  Product by title
- Audit item
  What audit item the product was addressing?
- Release month
  What month it would be released?

- Quantity
  In what quantities would it be released?
- Unit cost
  What was the per item cost?
- Extension
  What would it cost to print and release the product, and then what would be the total cost now and over time to implement the program?

When it came to the budget section of the presentation, it was easy for my CISO to see how I had come to the dollar amounts I was requesting. I painted the picture, showed how it all connected, and indicated what it would cost. It was the plan that would solve her audit issue. Her final question was, "Have you checked with Audit to see if this meets their needs?" If I had not then I would have not gotten her approval to implement the plan.

> **NOTE**
>
> When putting your presentation together, take the time to anticipate questions that you may get. Some will be obvious, but others will randomly pop into your head. Do not ignore these thoughts. Write them down and craft an answer to them. You'll be surprised how better prepared you are when these questions are asked during the presentation.

Components of an awareness program

It's time to take out your creative brush and fill your canvas with ideas. Here are a few of the ideas I came up with:

- Using a slogan.
- Creating a character associated with information security. I have used cartoon characters in the past and think they are a great way to get messages across, but it is a matter of choice and what is acceptable in your corporate culture.
- Creating an all-purpose Quick Reference Guide that would be sent to each employee.
- Producing a video for new hires. This is not as costly as you might think. You can visit my website, www.stealthawareness.com, to view *"The Ten Keys to Safeguarding Sensitive Information Properly"* for an example. If your company has an in-house video production studio, partner with them. That's why they are there. My CISO was convinced that a video would cost $50,000 to produce. I did it for less than $3,000 using the company's in-house resources. What my CISO did not know at the time was that I was a video producer, director, writer, actor, and editor. So, it was easy for me to partner with our in-house resources to produce the video at a reduced cost. This is an example of using your skills. You may have expertise in graphic arts. Use that in your program design of materials to save costs. It's a value added that you can bring to the program. Another key concept.

- Creating a sticker employees can affix to their computer. This will provide them with your division's contact information such as telephone number, email address, and website for information security.
- Writing articles for existing in-house publications. I liked this better than creating my own newsletter. I did not have to feed the beast every month or worry about distribution, printing costs, etc. because I worked with another in-house newsletter.
- Creating an awareness section on your division's intranet website. Don't have a website? What would it take to create one that employees could access? Does someone in your organization have the skills and ability to create one for you? Think of the intrapreneur[9] in you. If this was your own company and you needed this resource to move your business forward, what would you do?

Next steps

Once you are finished getting your ideas down on paper, design what the products would look like.

For example, if your business plan indicated creating a Quick Reference Guide, the key topics might be:

- Information and how to classify it
- Keeping your work area clean of sensitive information
- Creating a good password
- Using password-protected screen savers
- Remote computing
- Safeguarding the transmission of sensitive information
- Destruction of sensitive information
- Social engineering risks
- Insider threats
- Incident response

I would also include information and guidance on the use of smartphones, social media, and the risks of eDiscovery.

The Classification of Data Matrix

The Classification of Data Matrix was a one-pager stitched into the QRG that could be pulled out and posted in an employee's workspace. This matrix outlined how information is classified at the company and included:

- Definition of each classification
- Naming of each classification, such as Confidential or Proprietary. The matrix will explain the difference
- Appropriate marking of each classification on printed or electronic information
- Appropriate transmission of electronic and nonelectronic information

Company Name or Logo	Classification of Data Matrix				Information Security email, website, and/or phone	
	Classification	Example	Marking	Transmission	Storage & Retention	Destruction
LEVEL 1						
LEVEL 2						
LEVEL 3						

FIGURE 8.1

Levels of sensitive information

- Appropriate storage and retention of electronic and nonelectronic information
- Destruction policies for information

The above should be displayed in a one-page printed document that can serve as a deskside resource for employees to follow. Additional clarification should always be available and referenced in a standard or other guidance. As shown in Figure 8.1, each classification your company uses to define a level of sensitivity can be coded to visually indicate importance on the Classification of Data Matrix. You can't see in black and white print, but in this example Red = Confidential (Level 1), or your highest level of sensitivity; Yellow = Proprietary information (Level 2) that is internal to the company and not defined at a higher level of risk; Green = information that is available to the general public (Level 3).

Manager's Quick Reference Guide

Creating an information security Quick Reference Guide for managers is also an important step in your program. You want managers to ensure that employees are safeguarding sensitive information properly. Topics that may be included in this guide are:

- Information security as a team effort
- Application development and working with IT
- Knowing your employees are properly safeguarding sensitive information
- The importance of encryption and properly transmitting electronic and nonelectronic information

- The downloading of unlicensed software
- The importance of being an enabler
- Consultant or vendor guidelines
- Updating or deleting an employee's system access immediately when transferred or terminated
- Social engineering risks
- The risk of insider threats

Finding materials for your program

Where can you find the content for the products and materials you're putting together for an Information Security Awareness Program?

The content of your deliverables, as shown in your awareness program's business plan, will come from:

- The standards and other guidance already in place at the company.
- The subject matter experts you can work with in information security to ensure continuity to published guidance. Realize that, if there is no published guidance, you will in effect be creating it when you release a guide, brochure, video, etc. Thus, there needs to be an approval process that includes your CISO because they are responsible for the implementation of the information security program at the company.
- Your review process. Obviously, your SMEs (Subject Matter Experts) will want their input. Here is where you begin to partner with others within the company.

The importance of a good editor

Always use a good editor. The credibility of your program hinges on this person. A few spelling or grammar errors can hurt the perception of your program. Be professional. I started out with an editor in corporate communications assigned to support our division. She helped us get off the ground. As our needs grew we were able to bring on a full-time editor to support the division. Look around you, and hopefully you can find some resources to help you.

IMPLEMENTING AN INFORMATION SECURITY AWARENESS PROGRAM

Before you implement your program, you may want to send out a survey to a cross-section of employees to determine a uniform level of awareness in the company. This will provide you with a benchmark as the program progresses. This survey will determine your starting point by creating an awareness quotient for each question you ask. Do this each year, and you will see how effective your program becomes over time. Remember, as awareness rises, incidents should fall.

So, now your business plan has been approved. It is time to create the products and the distribution process to your employees. There are three key points that need to be considered:

1. *If the program is going to be successful, you will need the support of the CEO.*
   The one question I hear most often is, "How do you get the CEO to endorse the program?" You could ask your manager to go to the CISO, who in turn, can go to their manager, who in turn, can go to their manager, who ultimately reports to the CEO and ask for their support. If your manager believes this the politically correct path, then you have to follow that process. I found a simpler way of doing this. I found out the name of the CEO's secretary. I called her and told her I was with information security and that we would be releasing a Quick Reference Guide. This guide would include information for associates on how to safeguard sensitive information properly at the company. I told her I wanted to put a picture of our CEO on the inside cover of the QRG along with his personal message to all our associates. We wanted his message to explain the importance of safeguarding sensitive information. He would explain how vital their knowledge is to the security of our company and it was his expectation that all our associates would fully follow the program. I told her I had already written the message and she asked me to send it to her. Within a week, I received approval and had my copy back with a few minor edits. I was also given the CEO's electronic signature. Most CEOs do not write their own messages. Their communications people craft those documents. I simply took the same approach. Craft it and ask for approval.

2. *If the company does not have a corporate information security policy, then you should consider having one drafted.*
   The corporate information security policy, not to be confused with an information security policy, is a document approved by the company's board of directors. This policy states that the company has an information security program in place, who is responsible for implementing it (usually the CISO), and that all employees are required to follow it and what could happen to them if they didn't.

   This policy may be required if your company is in the financial services or other heavily regulated industries. Your regulators can advise you. The policy places the onus on the board to be responsible overseers of the program by having in fact approved the policy, and it defines the person responsible for the development and implementation of the information security program. The policy is very generic, and one that would see little or no change over the years.

   The reference to an information security policy means any standards put in place that states corporate information security's criteria for safeguarding information properly—i.e., information classification, access, etc. Sometimes these are referred to as policies too.

   The information security awareness training program falls under "programs" as noted in the corporate information security policy and thus can be supported with a standard.

Do you need a corporate information security policy? It depends on your industry.

3. *An information security awareness standard.*

   This standard becomes part of the corporate information security program as cited in the corporate information security policy. It gives you the authority to implement the information security awareness program. The standard states the employee responsibilities for safeguarding sensitive information properly as well as who should take training, whether it be new hires, all employees completing an online training program, and so on. And then comes when. What are the expectations to complete specific awareness training? Should it be done prior to system access or within 30 days of hire? This standard is just like any other standard and should be housed where other standards, such as classification of information, access, encryption, roles and responsibilities, etc., are kept.

TIP

Be sensible about the standard you create to ensure the processes can be followed in a timely manner. You don't want to create a mandate that's unreasonable and thereby cause non-compliance. You could create your own nightmare. An example of a bad requirement: *All employees must complete information security awareness training prior to system access.* I know we would all like to see that, but it's not going to happen, especially in a large organization. If you can have all new employees complete information security awareness training prior to system access, terrific!

After your proposed awareness standard has been reviewed with your manager, have audit review. Audit's approval is not necessary, but your CISO is always concerned about audit's approval. If he or she knows your program has already been approved by audit, you're in a much better position to have it approved. Of course, if your CISO makes changes in the standard, take it back to audit. This is more courtesy than asking for approval. The final decision rests with the CISO. You do not want your program to burden the company. You simply want to enhance awareness and validate that all employees are receiving awareness training on a timely basis and that each employee understands and acknowledges the responsibility to safeguard sensitive information properly.

Who writes the awareness standard?

If there isn't an awareness standard in place, don't wait for someone else to write it. You do it. Vet it with your manager and your CISO, and then walk it through your company's internal approval process.

It really doesn't matter if you are part of a large organization or a small one. It is critical to have an awareness standard. Someone is sure to ask, "Why do we have to do this?" It's so easy to answer with the following:

- The CEO mandates it (your message from the CEO).
- The board of directors mandates it (the corporate information security policy approved by the board of directors).
- The awareness standard mandates it (the information security awareness standard).

Finding win-win solutions

Because you have been given approval to implement an information security awareness program, do not let the "power" go to your head. The "Do it my way or else" is an old attitude to getting things done in the corporate environment. You can get more done with a kind word than you can with a gun! Always look for win-win solutions when implementing your program, even though you have the benefit of a mandate. Be an enabler!

NOTE

One of the best illustrations regarding the ability to enable people is called "The String Analogy." Begin by placing a piece of string on a flat surface. The string represents how people are motivated. If you try and push the string, you'll find it will crumble. If you push people, like the string, you will encounter push back or resistance and the string goes nowhere. Let's try pulling the string from one end. The string will stay straight and will follow, no matter where you pull it. People like to be pulled along and not pushed. That is what I hoped to accomplish with my awareness program. The goal was for employees to embrace the principle of safeguarding sensitive information properly, and thereby change the company's culture to one that says: "We value safeguarding sensitive information properly". So, the program was designed to pull people along over time by providing consistent and ongoing messaging and tools. It worked!

Building a perpetual awareness program

What do you do when management in other divisions, departments, etc., is not supportive of the Information Security Awareness Program?

Sometimes management may object to implementing a new training program due to time constraints rather than the necessity of the program. Managers and senior executives recognize that employees are busy people and they do not want to take employees away from servicing customers, meeting deadlines, etc. If your program interferes with their expectations or bottom line, then you will receive push back. So, your program needs to be nonintrusive and at the same time provide awareness training in a concise, understandable format. You need to pull the string and find a way to fit required training into their schedule. A win/win solution.

An awareness program is not a one-time event. It should be a marketing approach with specific touch points and requirements, such as QRG and viewing a video. This softens the process and achieves the outcomes you are looking for. The most important benefit to your program is the acknowledgment that the employee has received awareness training.

Who should take the training?

Everyone! Each employee is an ambassador for the company. Imagine being at a party and someone says to you, "I'm concerned about what your company does with my personal information. "What happens to my social security number or driver's license number after I give them to you"? Well, "I don't know" is not a good answer. The reply must be, "Our company really takes your confidential information seriously. No one has access to your information unless he or she is acting on your behalf or has a valid need to know. Everyone in our company is tested annually on their knowledge of safeguarding sensitive information properly, and they receive safeguarding tips on a regular basis. We are constantly looking for new and better ways to take safeguard all your sensitive information through technology and employee awareness." That type of reply is the result of an employee's familiarity with the information security message you are promoting on a continuing basis. You want the employee to be trained to the extent that safeguarding sensitive information becomes an automatic behavior and a mindset. Over time, safeguarding sensitive information properly will become a universal behavior in your company and the risk to an unintentional incident will be significantly reduced. So, the answer to the question "Who should take the training?" EVERYONE!

WARNING

If your company has the resources to implement an online information security awareness training program you should be aware of a potential risk: That it is treated as a requirement of compliance, such as sexual harassment, code of ethics training, and other topics as defined by regulations. The reason I say this is that most compliance training is a once-a-year program (that's O.K.), but in your case it should only be one component of your program and not the whole program! "Oh yes, I passed the training" should not become the mantra of your program. It is an ongoing process of making employees aware. Remember, repetition is the aide to memory. Creating an Information Security Awareness Program that evolves into a cultural change in your company to safeguard sensitive information properly cannot be achieved in a one-time awareness course. It should be considered as one of many touch points in your program, albeit an important one.

The most important advantage of having an online Information Security Awareness Training Program is the ability to document the acknowledgment by each employee as they successfully complete the program. By employees passing, it validates the other components in your awareness program.

So that you do not blind-side employees to changes in standards or other guidances, it is recommended that you place a preview page of changes at the beginning of the annual training session and prior to the option to test out.

Getting the program off the ground

My first product release was the Information Security Quick Reference Guide. It's nice to think that everyone receiving the QRG will be excited to receive it, read it, believe it, and follow it. However, the reality is that the guide will get thrown on a desk, in a drawer, and not looked at by most employees. That is why management is the key to a successful response to the QRG. With their support and endorsement, the QRG will be received by employees with enthusiasm and utilized often once they understand the content and its importance. This is a good way to engage managers into the process of information security. Practicing good physical security and information security is not an employee option. It is a company imperative.

Making information security accessible

I think the most important thing about an information security awareness program is that people know how to contact information security when they have a question or concern.

I discovered that our division had an 800 number for managers to set up new employee access (add/change/delete) and for employees to have their access reset. There were several extensions on this number. Why not add an information security awareness extension? This idea of utilizing our 800 number transformed into a sticker that simply had our name, Corporate Information Security, the bank's color banner, the 800 number and extension, and our info@ email address on it. I had the sticker stitched into the Quick Reference Guide, with a note to associates to remove the sticker and place it on their monitor. We did not have a website developed at that time, but if we had, it would have been included on the sticker too. Today, affixing a sticker to a flat screen may not be ideal, but the idea is to get your division's contact information in front of your employees. So, do not be afraid to be creative.

TIP

When you plant the seeds for success in your program, one simple product can make a big difference. Associates had a universal way to communicate with us, ask questions and receive guidance. Over time, we created an index of the most frequently asked questions so that the 800 number operators could answer the question or direct the caller to the answer, which most often was answered in the Quick Reference Guide. If the question was not answered in the QRG and the operator could not answer the question, it was sent to me. You might think that you would become overwhelmed with many calls, but we didn't find that to be the case. This simple process opened additional doors to implementing the information security awareness program several years later when privacy became a group within the company. When privacy started their awareness program, guess who started receiving their calls from the employees? You got it, we did. Privacy did not have an 800 number. What we learned was that the employee saw information security and privacy as one. That event opened the door for information security and privacy to partner in developing the first web-based training program at the company. We also provided privacy with an extension on our 800 line.

A lesson learned

You will learn many lessons along the road to designing and implementing your information security awareness program. Sometimes, the lesson comes from a very unexpected source. I, along with my boss and CISO, thought we had a terrific marketing campaign with a slogan that was catchy and would support the program. My boss and I went to corporate marketing to make sure the idea would be acceptable. It simply said: "Just PIP it!" "PIP" stood for "Protect Information Properly." I wanted our slogan to be a key component to the marketing approach. Could you imagine employees saying: "Hey, Just PIP It!" Marketing thought the idea was terrific too. With their approval in place, "Just PIP It!" became a key element in the marketing of our program. We were pretty excited, until we talked to corporate communications. A resounding "No" could be heard across the enterprise. "No acronyms are allowed at the company!" it was exclaimed. "We like the idea, think it is very creative, but NO acronyms are allowed."

"Is that your final answer?" I said.

"If we make an exception for you, we need to make an exception for everyone." So, I was forced to change the slogan to: "Protect Information Properly—it is your responsibility!" Notice that I didn't say: "everyone's responsibility" but "your responsibility!" That is where the emphasis needs to be placed. Each employee needs to value the principle of safeguarding sensitive information properly. The word *everyone* takes employees off the mental hook of responsibility. The lesson learned is to remain flexible when designing your program. There is always someone else, in some position of authority, somewhere, who does not like what you are doing or who wants to exercise their authority over you, right, wrong, or indifferent. Incidentally, the acronym rule was rescinded a year later. Unfortunately, the campaign was in full gear by then.

The dollars and cents of your program

A common reason awareness programs are not supported is because your CISO has decided not to fund it. It's not the CEO's responsibility to fund your program. It is your CISO who holds the purse strings. Here are some ideas on how to fund your program:

1. Earlier, as you'll recall, we discussed the importance of creating a good business plan and to include a budget. At the time of presentation, all you are looking for in your presentation is formal approval of the budget to get the first year of the program off the ground and establish an expectation of what it will cost to move the program forward in subsequent years. You might be surprised to know that I did not have a line item budget.

2. Ask for the money. If you need additional dollars above and beyond what you requested in your presentation or that has been allocated to your program, simply ask for it. Present your ideas and why they are important to the overall program, and ask for the money to fund it. If funds are not available, ask that it be put in the budget process for next year. There may be other sources available to you. Take a look at these ideas:

- If your company acquires another company, normally transition dollars are available. This is good because those dollars do not come out of your budget, but rather a special fund (bucket) set up by the company. Often, you can kill two birds with one stone by using these additional dollars for the transition as well as other items you want to add to your enterprise-wide program.
- Another source is the division's supply budget. If there is going to be money left over at the end of the year, put your request in for it. Don't ask for money out of this fund at the last minute. Let your boss know you are looking for additional money before the end of the year for a specific project. Most of my life I have been fond of saying, when the mind is ready, the money is ready. You experience the truth of that statement when you purchase an item that you are excited about. Like buying a new car. If you can justify it in your mind, you will find a way to afford it. And, if you do not have the money, often others will find the money for you in the manner of creative financing. This is no different. If your boss sees the value in the product or idea that you are selling to them, they will go and find the money for you.
- It's always nice to use other people's money. Go back to your alliances, and see where you can partner to share the expense of your program. Online training is an example where information security and privacy can partner and share expenses. This brings value added to the company.
- What budget dollars are available in other departments within your division? There can be internal products they want to distribute to a specific division(s). This product(s) becomes another touch point for your program and makes sure the image the division is portraying is consistent throughout information security and thereby the company.
- Finding the money can be as simple as asking for it. Budgets do run in cycles, and there are times when nothing can be spent. Most important, if you are budgeted, make sure you spend it. And last, a severe incident almost always raises the need for greater awareness. There is nothing like an emergency to loosen the purse strings. It is why I encourage anticipating issues and how you will handle them. There is no greater advantage than being prepared in advance for the next question or need from your CISO.

Above and beyond

Be creative. You are your own best resource. I never took a concept or idea to my manager for approval other than my business plan. I always took what appeared to be a finished product. Do not be concerned about the perception of "Why did you put this together and waste time?" You are the manager of the awareness program and are presenting the product to your manager to keep your manager advised. Some of these items might be dummy mockups of a brochure, poster, a QRG, a short video. It's one thing for your boss to say: "That's a good idea," and another when they say,

"That's a good idea and the product concept looks great!" A picture is worth a thousand words. Conversely, if your manager is a control freak, then it is better to follow his direction, as much as it hurts me to say that.

NOTE

When I create presentations, I always assume that the person I am presenting it to is not the decision maker. So I create the presentation in a manner that is easy for someone else to present and explain. Remember the sheik? This is why I use pictures and graphics as much as possible in a presentation. The same holds true when presenting a concept. There was a time when the budget was tight and an opportunity showed itself. It would require producing some infomercials. This was a short promotional video that I was able to produce myself that we aired on our in-house video channel and, later, on our in-house website when it was developed. Because I had the skills to produce these infomercials myself, that is what I did. When I suggested the concept to my boss, he told me we did not have the budget but thought it was a good idea. I said, "That is fine, but take a look at this." I showed him the infomercial I'd already created and he approved it immediately. I know this is not the norm, but I was vested in my program and it was a way to keep it going during a time when there were budget restraints. Remember, risk taking and innovation can help you move your program forward. Ah, the intrapreneur.[10]

If you have a company intranet, this is a great place to support information security services. If you are a small company, having your policies, standards, procedures, baselines, and other guidance housed on your information security website makes it easier for those with a need to know to find the information they are looking for. Usually your company will have a standard layout they want website developers to follow. Figure 8.2 provides a general template for what a website could look like.

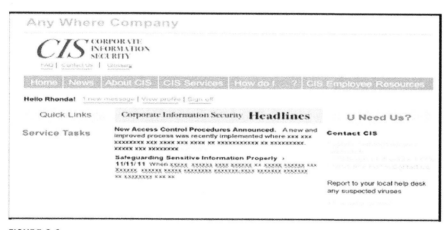

FIGURE 8.2

Example of an information security website

MAKING SECURITY PART OF THE COMPANY MIND-SET

Each department in CIS will probably want to have their own section on the website. If you institute a CIS website at your company, I guarantee that over time it will become the second largest at the company. Usually the company's main employee website is the largest in respect to content. You should have a web master, which is one other opportunity for you, if you are so inclined and skilled. This skill may bring value to you and your job within the company. If your company is large and has these capabilities in place, the group that manages the intranet will provide training and templates for you to follow. This is another touch point and another resource for your program. Do not underestimate your abilities. List the service tasks that information security provides, including your awareness program. This is where you can house and archive articles you have written, as well as other products used in your awareness program. The Employee Quick Reference Guide, the manager's guide, and even an orientation video are some of the materials you want to make easily available on your website. You'll be amazed at how many employees will utilize the materials you've put in place. Some of those materials are:

- CIS policy, standards and guidelines
- Awareness program
- Change access
- Request access
- Transmitting and storing data
- Consulting

You may want to include a "How to …" page on the website:

- How do I check for a virus on my computer?
- What is spyware?
- What is phishing?
- Remote computing and you
- When to use encryption
- Laptop security
- Tips for working remotely

Place your website's link on other division intranet websites. The company's main intranet website for employee information is a key place to have a link to your website.

To make it easier for employee access, materials, such as shown in Figure 8.3, were made available on our website (www.stealthawareness.com) for download.

The importance of communication with other lines-of-businesses

When implementing components of your Information Security Awareness Program, it is important that you have established a good communications matrix.

Though your CISO, and his or her direct reports, will or should be well connected, you need to develop your own contacts. Though your program includes manager

Welcome to the CIS Awareness Program. These products are available to support the Information Security Awareness Program in your area.

The Employee Quick Reference Guide

This 36 page guide should be given to all new hires upon hiring. It includes 10 keys steps to safeguarding sensitive information properly at the company. You can order through (insert your supply source). Reference code: CIS101

The Manager's Quick Reference Guide

Each manager should have a copy of this guide. It provides managers with the ten important management keys to safeguarding sensitive information properly at the company. You can order through (insert your supply source). Reference code: CIS102

New Hire Video

This 13:30 minute video covers the ten key steps to safeguarding sensitive information properly and should be used with the Employee Guide. You can order through (insert your supply source). Reference code: CIS103

FIGURE 8.3

An example of posted security awareness materials

responsibilities, you cannot always guarantee that managers will follow guidance. They are busy people, and busy people often forget to do things, especially when they do not see it related to their job function. Contact those who handle new hire orientation within a division and other contacts who provide services corporatewide or to a specific division or group. Recruit them to help you implement your program within their division. For example, you are about to send a document to every employee in the company. You can send the document out to everyone using employee distribution lists, and assuredly, every employee will receive your document whether it is hard copy or electronic. However, if you notify your contacts and managers that the document is coming, and what your expectations are, you may find that they have a different distribution process that they would prefer to follow. Failing to communicate properly can reduce the trust relationship you want and need to develop with management to effectively implement your awareness program.

Let's talk more about alliances

What are the various departments, divisions, etc., within your company that you can build alliances with?

Audit department

Yes, Audit is your friend! You'll find life easier for you, and any products and programs you create, if you run things by Audit on a continuing basis. Build the relationship and make them part of your team. I know this is not normal for Audit to have a close relationship with those they are auditing, but it made life a lot easier for me and them too once they realized we were all on the same team.

Legal department

Submitting materials to your legal department is the right thing to do. Rarely will you ever get a "you can't do this" statement from your legal counsel. It is managing the perception and protecting your program that counts. So, when implementing portions of your awareness program, such as an online training component, you want your legal department's input for obvious reasons and to make sure you have not overlooked something, such as how contractors are treated in reference to taking online awareness training.

Privacy division

Your company's privacy division can be your best partner. If your company is mandated by a federal regulation such as the Gramm-Leach-Bliley Act to implement an awareness program, then I highly suggest you partner with Privacy. One of the things we found was that employees did not know the difference between Information Security and Privacy. You want to eliminate that confusion. It benefits everyone in the company and also provides an additional shared resource to fund your program. In essence, by partnering with Privacy in implementing a corporatewide awareness online training program, we brought the awareness program to full exposure in the company. All other materials and delivery channels used were reinforced by the corporation's mandate by Compliance to take the information security and privacy training.

Compliance department

When I partnered with Privacy, we actually built the first web-based training platform at the company through the assistance of Training and Development and others. The company was working on a Learning Management System (LMS), but it would not be available for a couple of years. The first year Information Security and Privacy rolled out the online awareness training program, we had pockets of employees throughout the world who did not have system connectivity. Bandwidth, computers in the field for employees to take the training, etc., were not available in some markets. So we instituted a paper-based version at the same time. Our program was so successful in the second year of implementation that Compliance wanted to take over our program and add it to the new LMS platform they were ramping up. When instituting any new program, such as an online awareness training program, you will run into implementation issues. It takes time to make everyone (managers and employees) comfortable with the process.

WARNING

It's very important to understand that when you place the implementation of your program in the hands of another group, such as Compliance or Training and Development, you will lose control of the product, but not the content. You MUST be willing to do that and understand why you should do it. The reasons are simple. Compliance would take over the ongoing development and cost of the course. In other words, you become a subject matter expert. This does not mean you do not have control of content, just the manner in which it is being presented. You also lose control of implementation, which is not a bad thing to lose control of. It is very time consuming and takes you away from other opportunities to explore with the awareness program. So, if you get the chance to build an information security online awareness program, don't allow it to bog you down once it has been implemented and is running effectively. The more responsibility you can give away to others for implementing your program, the less cost and time is required to support it. This allows you to go on to creating other touch points for your program unencumbered. Again, you will always remain the subject matter expert.

Training and communications division

If your company has a training and/or communications division, embrace their services. In some cases, you will have no alternative. For example, if your company has an LMS, it would be counterproductive to not use an established training platform. In addition, you want to make sure your materials are written in "corporate speak." Coordinating your division's internal messages to the enterprise style is important. You are not the only one in your division communicating to the enterprise. You want to ensure that conflicting messages are not being sent out and that what is being communicated is in "people speak," not "technical speak," unless that is your audience.

Additionally, if your company has an employee website, nurture a relationship with the individual who updates the site. When an emergency occurs and you have an alert you need posted, you can save a lot of time getting it posted because a relationship has been created. I even went as far as sending my contact gift certificates for dinner for him and his wife to enjoy. Whenever I needed an alert communication to go out, Communication's review process was waived because we were able to establish a separate process and had developed a good working relationship.

Personnel department

Personnel can help you in many ways. For example, if you have a survey you want to send out to a demographic of the company, Personnel can slice and dice the distribution profile and provide you with lists—i.e., the SVPS, VPS, and the corporate officers, by hierarchy, so you have a good representation across the enterprise.

Personnel is probably the group in your company that sends out postacceptance materials to new hires. This is the team you want to coordinate with to distribute your QRG, manager's guide, or other information. This eliminates distribution costs from your budget. This is an example of getting more done for less.

Information security consultants

If your company is large enough to have internal information security technical consultants working with the various departments, then get to know these people. One of the dangers of implementing an Information Security Awareness Program is releasing a product or requirement that is in conflict with another division's calendar. Your internal information security consultants can help you with this issue. Your division contacts are also helpful.

Here are some final thoughts around alliances. Do not forget the importance of other direct reports in your division. When building your Information Security Awareness Program, ask those who report directly to the CISO to designate someone on their team you can interact with in the development and/or review of the program you are putting together. Everyone in Information Security should be an advocate of the awareness program. Many of your coworkers support other employees in the company. Make sure everyone knows that information security awareness materials are available, where to find standards and other guidance, and how to contact Information Security for clarification of questions, to voice concerns, or to report an incident.

Keeping your program viable

The answer lies in a simple concept to grow is to progress and to progress is to change. If you continue to change the look and feel of your program you keep the interest of employees. As an example, I produced video quick tips that were aired on the company's in-house television network and were also posted to our intranet website. The website provided tracking capabilities, and the number of people who watched those videos was amazing. Those statistics served as one measurement in the program.

The one product that I never used was a poster. Not that I have anything against them, because I don't. But, in my circumstance, we were not allowed to put posters on walls, only corkboards, which meant they had to be reduced in size, which reduced their effectiveness. If you are a small company, posters are a great idea if you are allowed to place them on the walls. For example, having a poster on an easel in the company's entrance foyer or elevator landings is an unobtrusive reminder to employees of right behaviors or an event you want to promote.

Other resources

If you have a university in your area or a school of the arts, you might consider sponsoring a contest for students to create an awareness poster or a short video that supports the information security messages at your company. This is an inexpensive way to get product created for your program and be involved in the community too. If you have an idea but not the creative ability to bring it to life, who inside your company can help you create the product? Never underestimate your own ability to create. Now, let's move on to the final portion of this chapter where I describe the most difficult thing you'll need to do: measure an information security awareness program.

MEASURING YOUR PROGRAM'S SUCCESS

"What gets tracked and measured gets done." This quote appears in many forms throughout the years, and is an adaptation of a longer quote by Lord Kelvin. It is always nice to have statistics in your favor when the viability of your program is questioned. And, be assured, sometime, someplace, somewhere, the need for an information security awareness program will be questioned or challenged by someone outside of your group.

Historically, it is difficult to measure the effectiveness of an information security awareness program. If you can connect your training to specific behaviors and have a way of monitoring those behaviors to see if compliance has improved, then that is what you are looking for. It validates the training. However, I caution that awareness is not training in the sense of learning how to operate a widget or a process. For example, knowing why and when sensitive information should be encrypted is awareness. Knowing how to encrypt sensitive information is training. The difference is in the understanding of and exhibiting the correct safeguarding sensitive information properly behaviors. What can you measure that will justify the effectiveness of your program? Here are a few ideas:

- How many employees have received training in any form (the acknowledgment process)?
- How many employees have received the Quick Reference Guide or other key materials you have distributed?
- How many "awareness" calls have you received and what categories are they in?
- If you do some marketing on creating easy-to-remember yet hard-to-crack passwords and your password resets go down, this is a good indicator that your program is working.

You want to capture before and after information to show improvement. It is not always easy to find applications or programs that can give you timely and accurate information that you can measure against your program. Think about processes in your company that can be tracked. If you can track it, you can measure improvement over time. For example, how many sensitive customer documents that include social security numbers, account numbers, and so on are not truncated as they are emailed outside the company without encryption? If this is tracked, request the data so that you can measure it against your efforts to enhance employee awareness on the importance of encrypting sensitive information when transmitted electronically outside of the company.

In my experience, I relied heavily on subjective measurements that ultimately validated the effectiveness of our program. It showed steady improvement over time. It also provided critical objectives to the program so that we complied with the Six Sigma quality management process already in place at the company.

Here's what I did initially. I created a paper mailer, because we did not have an online survey resource. To maximize the return of the survey, it was sent out with a way for the employee to respond anonymously. I actually had two surveys. One survey was for new hires and the other was for all other employees. The new hire survey was done on a monthly basis, while the employee survey was done once a year. I needed 600 responses on the annual survey to have valid statistical information. The easiest way to figure this out was to go on the Internet and search "sample size calculator." I can tell you that when I went from a paper to an online survey, the number of respondents went up. I can also tell you that offering a trinket or other incentive to respond to the survey did not increase the number of responses. It's important to have a valid cross section of your organization. So distribute the survey to a good cross-section of the company's employees, up to and including the CEO. If you work for a large company, your personnel department should be able to provide a report that provides this information for you. If not, ask your personnel department how you can get the information you need. Obviously, you want the employee's full name, mail code and hierarchy, and position (CEO, SVP VP, officer, or designate by bands). If your survey was delivered via an online channel, then you would want the employee's email address, too. My response ratio was always high.

I asked questions in six basic categories:

- Passwords
- Viruses
- PC security
- Information security standards
- Data classification
- Other threats, such as remote computing, social engineering, and social media

I also asked questions that pertained to the level of service our division was providing. Even though this had nothing to do with the awareness program, it was in support of our division and a way to get that input while minimizing the intrusion of employee time from filling out another survey. I tracked all the questions CTQ (Critical to Quality). I only used ten questions in what I called our "awareness quotient," for lack of a better term. It showed, over time, how the program was working and where there was a need for improvement. According to our regulators, over a 5-year period of time, our awareness quotient was highest in the industry. The chart in Figure 8.4 reflects one question but gives you an idea of what improvement looks like over time.

Identifying key components and cumulative results

Is it possible to define one product or component that made all the improvements? I don't believe so. It was a cumulative effect of the total program over time. As long as the program is constantly updated, it will show improvement and a behavioral difference in your company. When the company came out with an online survey application we could use, the administrative nightmare was over, and surveying became a lot easier. Keeping in line with respecting employee time, I surveyed existing employees once a year. Our response rate was very high and statistically validated the success of the program.

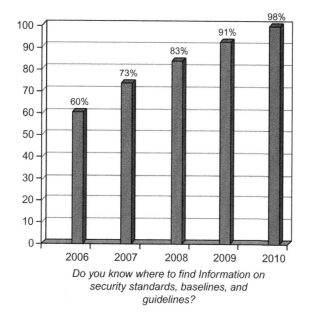

FIGURE 8.4

How awareness has improved over time

The survey gave us some important data. We began to identify who understood the training, what levels of management most often complied, and what areas within the company were being most impacted. This allowed us to understand what areas in the company needed more attention and where opportunities lay.

Depending on the number of data points you measure in your survey, you want to be able to show them and present statistics over time as depicted in Figure 8.5. I had this posted in my workspace so that when anyone walked in they could see how our program was being measured as well as our progress.

SUMMARY

The design and implementation of an effective information security awareness program is far more complicated than what can be included in a single chapter. An additional source of information is the Internet. But be cautious. Not everything you read is good, solid information. There are individuals, associations, and companies available to help you design and implement your program. Fortunately, I had the opportunity to design and implement an Information Security Awareness Program at one of the largest companies in America and, for that matter, the world. So, I bring you real world experience and not theory. Nothing, however, is better than your own

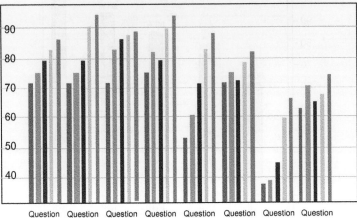

FIGURE 8.5

A graph displaying your program's progress

spirit, enthusiasm, and desire to create a viable awareness program for your company. Again, do not underestimate yourself!

Keep in mind that AWARENESS IS UNDERSTANDING RISK. Awareness is being proactive to those risks with sensible solutions, right behaviors. Each employee can significantly reduce the exposure of sensitive information by following simple behaviors and raising their hand with conviction when they see a potential or real risk. It is the same concept adopted by Homeland Security's "If You See Something, Say Something™" campaign. It's your responsibility to create a program that effectively embraces employee attention with guidance on how to safeguard sensitive information properly. Over time, your program will change the culture to one that not only understands the importance of but also exhibits the right safeguarding sensitive information properly behaviors at your company. Let every employee at your company become a security officer because your employees are your most valuable countermeasure.

If employees are not made aware of their responsibilities, they cannot be held accountable. Each company in America can significantly reduce the loss of sensitive information, and thereby the exposure to the financial risks, through an effective employee awareness program. Make it happen at yours!

And finally, thank you for reading this chapter, as it is one more touch point in my mission to help others become more today than they were yesterday through presentation and awareness.

We fully acknowledge use of Chapter 4, "Developing an Effective Security Awareness Program," from Techno Security's™ Guide to Securing SCADA: A Comprehensive Handbook on Protecting the Critical Infrastructure *(ISBN: 978-1-59749-282-9, Syngress).*

ENDNOTES

1. Brier S, Clark C, Hewitt N, et al. Who Built America? Working People and the Nation's Economy, Politics, Culture, and Society, Vol. 1, 2nd Edition. New York: Bedford/ St. Martin's, 2000.
2. Ibid.
3. Ibid.
4. Ibid.
5. Pinchot G, Pellman R. Intrapreneuring in Action: A Handbook for Business Innovation. San Francisco: Berrett-Koehler Publishers, Inc., 2000.
6. Report – Ponemon Cost of a Data Breach. 2010 http://www.symantec.com/about/news/ resources/press_kits/detail.jsp?pkid=ponemon In Defense of Data, http://www .indefenseofdata.com/data-breach-trends-stats/.
7. Ibid.
8. The Abilene Paradox and Other Meditations on Management © 1988 by Jerry B. Harvey, ISBN 978-0669191790 (paper). Jossey-Bass Publishers, San Francisco.
9. Pinchot G, Pellman R. Intrapreneuring in Action: A Handbook for Business Innovation. San Francisco: Berrett-Koehler Publishers, Inc., 2000.
10. Ibid.
11. Ibid.

Index

Note: Page numbers followed by *b* indicate boxes, *f* indicate figures and *t* indicate tables.

802.1X
  AP connection stages, 89
  crack attack, 114
  default password break-ins, 127
  legacy SSIDs, 123
  rogue-on-rogue attack, 107
802.11
  acronyms, 120
  ad hoc bridged interfaces, 125–126
  basic wireless technology, 102
  Doctor Reflecto, 94
  Farewell Attacks, 106
  IBSS, 119
  WiFi/WLAN EMR spectrum, 89
  wireless hacking, 91
  wireless network characteristics, 89*t*
802.11a, 96
802.11b/g/n
  access point example, 97*f*
  Doctor Reflecto, 96
  11b, Queensland Attack, 103
  illegal channel beaconing, 108
  jammers, 103
802.11w, 106
802.15.1, 89, 89*t*, *see also* Bluetooth
802.15.4, 89, 89*t*
802.16, 89, 89*t*
802.20, 89, 89*t*

A

Abilene Paradox, 200–201
Access control lists (ACLs)
  crack attack, 114
  guest wireless hacking, 116
Access point (AP)
  ad hoc bridged interfaces, 126
  ad hoc networks, 119
  aluminum foil enclosure, 97*f*
  antenna shorting, 100*f*
  basic wireless technology, 102
  Bogus Beacon attack, 108
  crack attacks, 114
  dead-end hijacking, 110–111, 112
  default password break-ins, 127
  Doctor Reflecto, 95, 96
  examples, 92*f*, 97*f*
  Fake AP project, 109

Farewell Attacks, 105
FCC regulations, 101
flooding attacks, 108
Google hacking, 129
layer 1 denial of service attacks, 91, 94
locking ceiling tile enclosure, 95*f*
man-in-the-middle attack, 111*f*
mirror/monitor attack, 115
peer-to-peer-to-hack, 117
rogue, *see* Rogue access points
rogue-on-rogue attacks, 106
rogue SSID additions, 122–123
virtual AP, 119
whack-a-rogue, 107
ACLs, *see* Access control lists (ACLs)
Ad hoc networks
  bridged interface abuse, 125–126
  wireless hacking, 119–120
Adobe, Inc., social engineering attack, 24
Agency phone books, building security, 37–38
Aireplay-ng, Farewell Attacks, 105
AirJack, Farewell Attacks, 105
Airplane safety, expert advice, 185
AirTight Networks, 120
Aluminum foil
  access point enclosure, 96, 97*f*, 98*f*
  access point RF analysis, 99*f*
Antennas, *see* Access point (AP)
Anti-virus software, wrappers, 174
Anxiety, penetration tester approach, 172
Anywho.com, 140
AP, *see* Access point (AP)
Archetypal antennas
  access point examples, 92*f*
  beamwidths samples, 93*t*
  examples, 93*f*
  layer 1 DoS attacks, 91–93
ARP flooding, crack attack, 113
Ask.com, for initial identification, 141
ATM machines
  expert advice, 180
  skimming, 182
Auditors
  Information Security Awareness Program,
    202, 218
  Information Security Awareness
    standard, 209

Auditors (*Continued*)
  internal, physical security, 47–48
Automated attacks
  crack attack, 112
  penetration testing, 173–174
Automated surveillance, 155–156
AV, social engineering considerations, 25
Awareness, *see* Information Security Awareness
      Program
Azimuth
  access point RF radiation pattern, 92
  omnidirectional antenna, 93*f*

B

Backdoors, penetration testing automated attacks, 173
Baker, Greg, expert advice, 187–191
Bank account information, surveillance tactics,
      148–149
Basic Service Set (BSS), definition, 120
Basic Service Set Identifier (BSSID), definition, 120
Beamwidth
  access point RF radiation pattern, 92
  antenna types, 93*t*
Behavior, penetration testing, 166
Bing, for initial identification, 141
Biometrics, building security, 38
Bittings
  definition, 76–77
  depth keys, 78
  key creation, 78–79, 80
  mortise cylinder locks, 81–83
  mortise *vs.* rim cylinder locks, 84
Black hats, social engineering effectiveness, 2
Blippy.com
  false login data, 146
  financial data mining, 148–149
  frequented locations, 149
  targeting prevention, 161
Block, Matt, 74–75
Blogs
  financial data, 148
  initial identification, 141
  online exposure, 151
  signature phrases, 154–155
  social network/media disclosures, 144, 145–146
  third-party disclosures, 152
Blogspot.com, false login data, 146
Bluetooth
  EMR spectrum, 89
  miniature surveillance equipment, 158
  wireless hacking, 91
  wireless network characteristics, 89*t*

Body language, penetration testing approaches, 172
Bogus Beacon attack, 108
Bomb threats, Chicago example, 40–42
Boolean strings, search terms, 146
Booth, Evan, 74–75
Bot herding, spear phishing, 188–189
Bot net, spear phishing, 188–189
Bridged interfaces, ad hoc networks,
      125–126
BSS, *see* Basic Service Set (BSS)
BSSID, *see* Basic Service Set Identifier (BSSID)
Bugmenot.com, false login data, 146
Bug-sweeping, miniature surveillance equipment, 158
Building security, *see also* Physical security
  basic considerations, 35–40
  corporate/agency phone books, 37–38
  employee badges, 36
  key control example, 81*b*
  lock checks, 35–36
  off-shift staff training, 39–40
  shredder technology, 36–37, 37*b*
  tailgating, 38–39, 39*b*
  tailgating countermeasures, 39*b*
Bump keys, 78
Burn bag, expert tip, 37
Business plan, Information Security Awareness
      Program, 196, 200–202, 213

C

Caller ID Spoofing, Paul Henry interview, 23
Car alarm, EMR spectrum, 88
Carrier Sense Multiple Access with Collision
      Avoidance (CSMA/CA)
  basic wireless technology, 102
  Queensland Attack, 103
Cartoon character, Information Security Awareness
      Program, 204
CCA, *see* Clear channel assessment (CCA)
CCTF, *see* Cyber Crime Task Forces (CCTF)
CCTV, *see* Closed-circuit television (CCTV)
CDs, penetration testing
  case study, 176
  overview, 168–169
  technology selection, 173
Cellular technology, wireless network
      characteristics, 89*t*
CEO, *see* Chief Executive Officer (CEO) support
Certified Information Systems Security Professional
      (CISSP), 195
Chabris, Christopher, 164–165
Chicago bomb threat, physical security example,
      40–42

Chief Executive Officer (CEO) support, Information Security Awareness Program, 208, 221–222
Cialdini, Robert, 166
CISO, *see* Corporate Information Security Officer (CISO)
CISSP, *see* Certified Information Systems Security Professional (CISSP)
Classification of Data Matrix
  example, 206f
  Information Security Awareness Program, 205–206
Clear channel assessment (CCA), Queensland Attack, 103
Closed-circuit television (CCTV), EMR spectrum, 89
Combination lock
  bait and switch example, 71–72
  and commercial shim, 72f
  lock access, 68
  as popular lock, 54
Communication methods
  disruption concerns, 193
  expert advice, 181
Communications Act (1934), 103
Communications Division, Information Security Awareness Program, 219
Communications matrix, Information Security Awareness Program, 216–217
Compliance Department, Information Security Awareness Program, 218–219
Computer rooms, high security locks, 42
Computer systems
  crime perpetrator *vs.* victim, 179
  penetration testing case study, 174
  penetration testing permission considerations, 175
Conkel, Hans, 63
Cordless phones, EMR spectrum, 89
Corporate Information Security Officer (CISO)
  auditing issues, 202
  awareness program lessons, 212–213
  communications matrix, 216
  Information Security Awareness Program, 208
  Information Security Awareness Specialist, 195
  Internal Information Security Consultants, 220
  new-hire video, 204
  team benefits/drawbacks, 201
Corporate Information Security Policy, Awareness Standard, 209
Corporate security

expert advice, 189
phone books, 37–38
Cost risk benefit, information security awareness, 197–198
Countermeasures, *see also* Awareness training
  Chicago bomb threat example, 40
  forced entry, 62
  lock vulnerabilities, 58
  padlock shims, 73–74
  physical security risk assessment, 34
  social engineering, 27–29
  tailgating, 39b
  video security log review, 43
Crack attack
  overview, 112–114
  rainbow table, 113
Craig's List, for initial identification, 143
Credit card fraud
  expert advice, 182
  financial checks, 146–147
  home document security, 46
Credit card readers, social engineering, 26–27, 27f
Critical infrastructures, definition, 190
Critical to Quality (CTQ), Information Security Awareness Program effectivness, 222
Cross cut shredders, expert tip, 37b
CSMA/CA, *see* Carrier Sense Multiple Access with Collision Avoidance (CSMA/CA)
CTQ, *see* Critical to Quality (CTQ)
Cuts, *see* Bittings
Cybercrime, law enforcement help, 189–190
Cyber Crime Task Forces (CCTF), FBI-local law enforcement relationship, 190

D

Data leakage prevention (DLP) tools, ad hoc attacks, 119
Data theft, information security awareness, 196–198
DDoS, *see* Distributed denial of service (DDoS) attack
Deadbolt lock, semi-high-secure-room break-in example, 63–64
Deadbolt retraction
  basic tool, 65f, 67f
  semi-high-secure-room break-in, 64–66
Dead-end hijacking, 110–112, *see also* Man-in-the-middle attack
Deauthentication, Farewell Attacks, 105
Decoy SSID, 109–110
Default configuration wireless hacking
  Google hacking, 129–130, 130f
  overview, 126–130
  passwords, 127, 128f

Default configuration wireless hacking (*Continued*)
  WPA keys, 127–129, 128*f*
Defcon Security Jam (2008), 110
Denial of service (DoS) attacks, *see also* Layer 1
    denial of service (DoS) attacks; Layer 2
    denial of service (DoS) attacks
  802.11w standard, 106
  overview, 91–112
  rogue SSID additions, 122
Depth keys
  characteristics, 78
  example, 79*f*
  mortise *vs.* rim cylinder locks, 84
DHCP, *see* Dynamic host configuration protocol
    (DHCP)
Directional antennas, layer 1 DoS, 94
Disassociation
  Farewell Attacks, 105
  rogue-on-rogue attacks, 106–107
Disclosures
  social networks/media, 144–146
  surveillance and targeting, 152–154
Disk drives, disposal, 46*b*
Disk-type pin tumbler lock, example, 57*f*
Distraction, penetration testing, 165
Distributed denial of service (DDoS) attack,
    Queensland Attack, 103–104
DLP, *see* Data leakage prevention (DLP) tools
DNS, *see* Domain Name Server (DNS)
DocStoc.com, 148
Doctor Reflecto
  effectiveness, 96–98
  layer 1 DoS attack, 94–98
Document retention/destruction policy, information
    security awareness, 197
Domain Name Server (DNS), static
    IP hack, 131
Door signs, physical security, 42
DoS, *see* Denial of service (DoS) attacks
Drake, Phil, expert advice, 19–22
Drop ceilings, physical security, 47
DVDs, penetration testing, 168–169
Dynamic host configuration protocol (DHCP)
  dead-end hijacking, 110–111, 112
  MAC address switching, 133
  mirror/monitor attack, 115
  static IP hack, 131

E

Eavesdropping, third-party disclosures, 153–154
Ebay, for initial identification, 143
eDiscovery, 197

Editor, Information Security Awareness Program,
    207
800 number, Information Security Awareness
    Program, 212
Electromagnetic radiation (EMR)
  definition, 87–88
  spectrum chart, 88*f*
Electromagnetic spectrum, 87–90
Electronic Crimes Taskforce, 183
Elevation
  access point RF radiation pattern, 92
  omnidirectional antenna, 93*f*
Email addresses
  awareness program information, 205, 212
  employment information, 143
  for initial identification, 139–140, 143
  penetration testing case study, 174
  PeopleFind sites, 140
  purchase habits, 146–147
  spoofing, 154, 157
  throwaway, 140, 160
Email attachments
  expert advice, 187–188
  spear phishing, 188–189
Employee awareness, information security,
    196–198
Employee badges, building security, 36
Employment information, targeting and
    surveillance, 142–144
EMR, *see* Electromagnetic radiation (EMR)
Energy companies, spear phishing attacks, 24
Equipment "burial ground," physical security, 46
ESS, *see* Extended Service Set (ESS)
Executive protection, basic considerations, 186
Executive Protection Institute, 184
Extended Service Set (ESS), definition, 120

F

Facebook
  automated surveillance, 156
  data mining, 23
  disclosures, 144, 145–146
  false login data, 146
  with financial data, 148–149
  frequented location information, 149
  safety recommendations, 161
  social engineering, 29
  surveillance, 144
  third-party disclosures, 152, 154
Fake AP project, 109, 109*f*
FALE Association of Locksport Enthusiasts,
    74–75, 75*f*

Farewell Attacks
  characteristics, 104–106
  and dead-end hijacking, 110–111
FCC, *see* Federal Communications Commission
      (FCC)
Federal Bureau of Investigation (FBI)
  contact by victim, 189
  Cyber Crime Task Forces, 190
  expert advice, 187
  InfraGard, 190
  spear phishing, 188–189
Federal Communications Commission (FCC)
  wireless hacking, 101
  wireless regulations, 101–102
Federal law enforcement,
      CCTF, 190
Federal Trade Commission (FTC)
  credit card recommendations, 183
  identity theft, 186
File cabinets, lock bypass example, 54–55
Financial data, surveillance and targeting,
      146–149
Firefox, automated surveillance, 155–156
Firewall
  ad hoc attacks, 119
  social engineering considerations, 25–26
Flickr
  disclosures, 144
  surveillance, 144, 145–146
  travel patterns, 150–151
Flooding attack
  characteristics, 108
  crack attack, 113
Forced entry
  locks, 60–63
  method, 61–63
Forced reflection, wireless hacking, 94
Foreign spies, expert advice, 181, 188
4-1-9 advance fee fraud, expert advice,
      181–182
411.com, 140
FourSquare, 149, 150
  false login data, 146
  targeting prevention, 161
  target interaction, 157
Frequency analyzer, WWII device example, 90*f*
Frequented locations
  case example, 150
  place as target, 151–152
  targeting and surveillance, 149–152
  target interaction, 157
FTC, *see* Federal Trade Commission (FTC)

G
Gift cards, as targeting prevention, 160
GLBA, *see* Gramm-Leach-Biley Act (GLBA)
Global Positioning System (GPS)
  with financial data, 148–149
  travel patterns, 150–151
Google, Inc., social engineering attack, 24
Google Advanced, for initial identification, 141
Google Alerts, automated surveillance, 155
Google Analytics, automated surveillance, 156
Google Blog, for initial identification, 141
Google Chrome, automated surveillance, 155–156
Google Groups, for initial identification, 141
Google hacking
  default password break-ins, 127
  wireless device mgmt interface, 129–130, 130*f*
Google Maps
  for initial identification, 142–143
  targeting and surveillance, 142–143
Google search
  businessman surveillance case study, 145
  for initial identification, 141, 143
  surveillance and targeting, 141
Google Street View, surveillance information,
      151–152
GoWalla
  frequented locations, 149
  targeting prevention, 161
  target interaction, 157
  user information posting, 150
GPS, *see* Global Positioning System (GPS)
"Graffiti-man," place targets, 151–152
Gramm-Leach-Biley Act (GLBA), 201
Gucci, social engineering attack, 24
Guest attack, 116–117

H
Half-duplex system, basic wireless technology, 102
Handheld authentication device, building
      security, 38
Hashes, rainbow table, 113
HBGary, social engineering attack, 24
Headless devices, ad hoc bridged interfaces, 126
Henry, Paul, expert advice, 22–26
Hole 196 attack, 114
Homeinfomax.com, 142
Home security
  documents, 46*b*
  physical security tips, 48
  security cameras, 48*b*
Hotel safety, expert advice, 185
HP WESM, legitimate-looking rogue APs, 124

HTML, *see* Hypertext Markup Language (HTML)
Human factor, penetration testing
    basic considerations, 164–166
    magic as distraction, 165
    selective attention, 164–165
    trust and behavior, 166
Hypertext Markup Language (HTML), free Wi-Fi
    hack, 134

I

IBSS, *see* Independent basic service sets (IBSS)
Icerocket.com, 145
ID badges
    building security, 36
    Chicago bomb threat example, 40–41
    penetration testing case study, 176
Identity theft
    expert advice, 186
    home document security, 46
IDS, social engineering considerations, 25
Illegal channel beaconing, *see* Bogus Beacon attack
Impendance mismatch, access point antenna
    shorting, 100, 100*f*
Independent basic service sets (IBSS)
    definition, 120
    wireless hacking, 119–120
Industrial-scientific-medical (ISM) band
    EMR, 87–88
    wireless network uses, 89*t*
Infomercials, Information Security Awareness
    Program, 215
Information Security Awareness Program
    accessibility, 212
    administration component, 200
    alliance building, 217–220
    Audit Department, 218
    Awareness Standard author, 209–210
    Awareness Standard requirements, 209
    business plan, 201–202
    Classification of Data Matrix, 205–206, 206*f*
    communications matrix, 216–217
    Compliance Department, 218–219
    components, 204–205
    creativity in, 214–215
    design, 198–207
    editor's importance, 207
    effectiveness measurement, 221–223
    funding, 213–214
    GLBA, 201
    group support, 199
    implementation, 207–215
    importance of repetition, 199
    improvements over time, 223*f*
    informercials, 215
    Internal Information Security Consultants, 220
    key components/cumulative effect, 222–223
    Legal Department, 218
    lessons from, 212–213
    manager's QRG, 206–207
    on-line program risks, 211
    perpetual program, 210
    Personnel Department, 219
    presentation components, 202–204
    presentation importance, 203–204
    presentation question anticipation, 202–204
    Privacy Division, 218
    product appearance, 205
    product/material content, 207
    program control, 219
    program materials, 217*f*
    program viability, 220
    progress graph, 224*f*
    QRG as initiator, 211–212
    resource alternatives, 220
    security as company mindset, 216–220
    "The String Analogy", 210
    team benefits/drawbacks, 200–201
    touch points, 199–200
    trainees, 211
    Training and Communications Division, 219
    web site example, 215*f*
    win-win solutions, 210
Information Security Awareness Specialist, 195
Information Security Awareness Standard
    author, 209–210
    Corporate Information Security Policy, 209
    requirement examples, 209
Information security awareness training
    business plan, 196
    characteristics, 195
    cost risk benefit, 197–198
    data theft, 196–198
    employee awareness, 196–198
    information security awareness specialist, 195
    intrapreneur, 195–196
    key control, 71
    non-compliance costs, 197
    overview, 194–198
    people involved, 194–196
InfraGard, 187, 189, 190
Initial identification
    PeopleFind sites, 140
    surveillance, 139–142
    targeting example, 141

Injection attacks, cracks, 113
Inside threats, physical security, 34–35
Instant Messaging
    safety recommendations, 161
    target interaction, 157
Intelius.com, 140, 146
Internal auditors
    lock auditing, 68
    physical security, 47–48
Internal Information Security Consultants, 220
Internet
    for initial identification, 139–140
    on-line blackmarketing case, 155
    penetration testing automated attacks, 173
    penetration testing case study, 175–176
    personal information removal, 142
    safety recommendations, 160–161
Internet Explorer, automated surveillance,
        155–156
Internet Service Provider (ISP), default PSK
        lookup, 127, 128f
Intrapreneur
    characteristics, 195–196
    team benefits/drawbacks, 200–201
Investment information, surveillance, 146–149
"The Invisible Gorilla", 164–165
iPad
    information security awareness, 196
    MAC address switching, 133
    as scanning device, 158
    SSID issues, 117
    WiFi scanner app, 159
IPS, social engineering considerations, 25
IPSec tunnel, mirror/monitor attack, 115
Iran's Nuclear Fuel Centrifuges, SCADA system
        attack, 24
isearch.com, 139–140
ISM, see Industrial-scientific-medical (ISM) band
ISP, see Internet Service Provider (ISP)

J

Jammers, layer 1 DoS attacks, 102–103
"John attack," wireless hacking, 98–101
Juniper Networks, social engineering attack, 24

K

Karma tool, dead-end hijacking, 110–111
Key control
    awareness training, 71
    basic considerations, 70–71
    building security example, 81b
    individuals with access, 70–71

    social engineering, 70
    system set-up, 71b
Key covers, example, 84f
Key gauge
    example, 79f, 84f
    key creation, 80
Key Ghost hardware loggers, 13, 15f
Key-in-knob lock
    lock access, 68
    lock removal, 78–79
    secure room break-in example, 63–64
Key micrometers, key creation, 79–80
Key retention
    lock quality/effectiveness, 57
    padlock shims, 74
Keys
    creation, 78–79
    creation without machine, 79–81
    creation tools, 79f
    depth keys, 78
    examples, 77–79, 77f
    overview, 76–79
    pin tumbler/warded, 56f
    rim cylinder lock, 60f
Keystroke logger
    expert tip, 15
    social engineering, 13–16
    USB thumb drives, 167
Kindles, SSID issues, 117
Knowx.com, 140–141

L

LANs, see Local area networks (LANs)
Laptop security, information security
        awareness, 196
Law enforcement
    CCTF, 190
    expert advice, 180–191
    overview, 179
Layer 1 denial of service (DoS) attacks
    access point antenna shorting, 100f
    archetypal antennas, 91–93
    directional antennas, 94
    Doctor Reflecto, 94–98
    electrical tampering, 98–101
    FCC regulations, 101–102
    jammers, 102–103
    overview, 91–104
    Queensland Attack, 103–104
Layer 2 denial of service (DoS) attacks
    Bogus Beacon, 108
    dead-end hijacking, 110–112

Layer 2 denial of service (DoS) attacks (*Continued*)
    decoy SSID, 109–110
    Farewell Attacks, 104–106
    flooding, 108
    man-in-the-middle attack, 110
    overview, 104–112
    rogue-on-rogue attack, 106–107
    whack-a-rogue, 107–108
Learning Management System (LMS), Information
    Security Awareness Program, 218–219
Legal Department, Information Security Awareness
    Program, 218
LinkedIn
    data mining, 23
    false login data, 146
    with financial data, 148–149
    safety recommendations, 161
    surveillance, 144
    third-party disclosures, 152
Listening devices
    example, 17*f*
    social engineering, 16
Litigation, information security awareness, 197
LMS, *see* Learning Management System (LMS)
Local Area Networks (LANs)
    characteristics, 89*t*
    decoy SSID, 109
    default PSK lookup, 127
    virtual, *see* Virtual local area networks (VLANs)
    wireless hacking, 91
Local law enforcement, CCTF, 190
Lock examples
    disk-type pin tumbler lock, 57*f*
    high-quality high-security lock, 64*f*
    mortise cylinder lock, 81–85, 82*f*
    mortise *vs.* rim cylinder locks, 83–85
    pin tumbler padlock, 53*f*, 54–55, 55*f*, 56*f*, 57*f*, 68
    rim cylinder lock, 60*f*
    warded padlock, 54–55, 56*f*
Lock picking
    FALE team example, 75–76
    learning, 74–76
    legal issues, 53*b*
    overview, 51–59
    penetration tester permission, 52*b*
    suggested reading, 62*b*
Lock picking example
    bait and switch, 71–74
    padlock shims, 73–74
    pin tumbler hack, 68
    secured office complex door, 69*f*
    semi-high-secure-room break-in

    bolt hack tool, 65*f*, 67*f*
    bolt retraction, 64–66
    lock access, 66–69
    lock example, 64*f*
    overview, 63–69
Locks
    access point enclosures, 95
    advanced reference materials, 59
    building security, 35–36
    bypassing example, 54–55
    computer rooms/phone closets, 42
    forced entry, 60–63
    forced entry method, 61–63
    overview, 51–59
    popular types, 54–56
    quality *vs.* effectiveness, 57–58
    rack houseing, 96*f*
    suggested reading, 62*b*
    vulnerabilities, 58–59, 59*f*
Login2.me, 146
Long, Johnny, 73, 129
"Looking the part," penetration testing, 170*b*

M
MAC address
    ad hoc bridged interfaces, 126
    Farewell Attacks, 105
    free Wi-Fi hack, 134
    legitimate-looking rogue APs, 125
    peer-to-peer-to-hack, 117
    rogue access points, 122
    security tool bypasses, 130
    spoofing, 132
    static IP hack, 131
    switching for access, 133
Magic tricks, distraction component, 165
MAN, *see* Metro Area Network (MAN)
Manhole covers
    example, 45*f*
    subterranean vulnerabilities, 44
Man-in-the-middle attack, *see also* Dead-end
    hijacking
    example, 110
    peer-to-peer-to-hack, 118
Marino, Tony, expert advice, 180–187
Marlinspike, Moxie, 113–114
Master keys
    key control, 71
    key creation, 79
    mortise *vs.* rim cylinder locks, 83
MD5 hash, rainbow tables, 114
Medeco locks, key control, 71

Metasploit, penetration testing automated attacks, 173
Metro Area Network (MAN)
 characteristics, 89*t*
 EMR spectrum, 89
Micrometer
 example, 79*f*
 key creation, 79–80
 mortise *vs.* rim cylinder locks, 84
MicroSD USB storage device
 penetration testing, 168, 168*f*
 usage, 168
Microsoft, social engineering flaw remediation, 26
Microwave oven, EMR spectrum, 88
Military.com, for initial identification, 141–142
Miniature surveillance equipment, 158–159
Mirror/monitor attack, 115–116
Mobile Broadband Wireless Access (MBWA), EMR spectrum, 89
Mogull, Rich, 110, 118
Morse, Samuel, 193
Mortise cylinder lock
 characteristics, 81–85
 example, 82*f*
 vs. rim cylinder lock, 83–85
Motion-sensing cameras, home security, 48
Motion-sensing lights, as physical security, 43–44
Mounting plate, lock forced entry, 61
Murdoch, Rupert, social engineering attack, 24
Mushroom pins, lock quality/effectiveness, 57
MySpace
 disclosures, 144
 false login data, 146
 safety recommendations, 161
 surveillance, 144
 third-party disclosures, 153
 travel location information, 151

N

NAC, *see* Network access control (NAC)
Neighborhood routes, targeting and surveillance, 142–144
Nemesis, Farewell Attacks, 105
Netronline.com, 142
Network access control (NAC)
 ad hoc bridged interfaces, 126
 MAC address switching, 133
 mirror/monitor attack, 115
 rogue access points, 122
 security tool bypasses, 130
 static IP hack, 131

Network Interface Controller (NIC)
 ad hoc bridged interfaces, 125
 Bogus Beacon attack, 108
 dead-end hijacking, 110–111
 Farewell Attacks, 105
 Queensland Attack, 103
 rogue-on-rogue attacks, 106
 signal extender, 93*f*
New-hire video, Information Security Awareness Program, 204
News Corp., social engineering attack, 24
NIC, *see* Network Interface Controller (NIC)
"Night Dragon" malware, energy company spear phishing, 24
Nine Lives, 184
NMAP
 ad hoc bridged interfaces, 126
 guest wireless hacking, 116

O

OFDM, *see* Orthogonal frequency-division multiplexing (OFDM)
Office complex, secured door example, 69*f*
Off-shift staff, building security training, 39–40
Ollam, Deviant, 59, 62, 73
Omnidirectional antennas
 azimuth and elevation radiation charts, 93*f*
 beamwidth sample, 93*t*
 characteristics, 92
123people.com, 140
Online directories, building security, 38
On-line Information Security Awareness Program
 GLBA, 201
 program control, 219
 risks, 211
 team concept, 201
Operating systems
 CD/DVD-based penetration testing, 168
 malicious attacks, 187–188
Operation Aurora, social engineering attack, 24
Organizational culture, penetration testing, 170
Organizational Unique Identifier (OUI), MAC address switching, 133
Orthogonal frequency-division multiplexing (OFDM), 802.11a/g/n, 104
OUI, *see* Organizational Unique Identifier (OUI)
Outside threats, physical security, 34–35

P

P2P, *see* Peer-to-Peer (P2P) network searches
Padlock shim
 countermeasures, 73–74

Padlock shim (*Continued*)
  example, 72*f*, 76*f*
  key creation, 78–79
  mortise cylinder lock, 81
  mortise *vs.* rim cylinder locks, 83
  types, 76
  usage considerations, 73
PANs, *see* Personal Area Network (PAN)
Parabolic dish antennas, beamwidth sample, 93*t*
Passive intelligence collection, and target
    interaction, 156
Passports, protection, 185–186
Passwords, default configuration wireless hacking,
    127, 128*f*
Patch antennas
  beamwidth sample, 93*t*
  characteristics, 92
  example, 93*f*
PATRIOT Act, 183
Payload introduction, penetration testing, 172*b*
Payment Card Industry Data Security Standard (PCI
    DSS)
  legitimate-looking rogue APs, 125
  rogue access points, 120
PayPal, for safe transactions, 140
PBXs, *see* Public Branch Exchange (PBX)
PCI DSS, *see* Payment Card Industry Data Security
    Standard (PCI DSS)
Peer-to-Peer (P2P) network searches
  dangers, 147
  safety recommendations, 160
  targeting and surveillance, 147–148
Penetration testing
  approach, 172*b*
  automated attacks, 173–174
  case study
    approaching conference staff, 176
    approaching hotel staff, 175
    overview, 174–176
    permission considerations, 175
  CDs/DVDs, 168–169
  compromising locks, 81–83
  drop ceilings, 47
  equipment "burial ground", 46
  human factor
    basic considerations, 164–166
    magic as distraction, 165
    selective attention, 164–165
    trust and behavior influence, 166
  key creation, 79–80
  location decisions, 171
  lock picking legal issues, 53*b*

  lock picking permission, 52*b*
  "looking the part", 170*b*
  MicroSD USB storage device, 168*f*
  motion-sensing light security, 43–44
  non-functioning lock issues, 68
  organizational culture, 170
  overview, 163
  project organization, 170–174
  staging effort, 169–170
  strategy decisions, 171–172
  subterranean vulnerabilities, 44–45
  target location considerations, 169–170
  target organization, 169–170
  technology basics, 166–169
  technology selection, 172–174
  tester body language, 172
  USB device usage, 168
  USB thumb drives, 166–168, 167*f*
Peoplefinders.com, 140
PeopleFind sites
  financial/background checks, 146–147
  free *vs.* fee-based, 140
  initial identification, 139–140
  personal information removal, 142
  safety recommendations, 160
Peoplelookup.com, 140
People.yahoo.com, 140
Permission considerations, penetration testing, 175
Personal Area Network (PAN)
  characteristics, 89*t*
  EMR spectrum, 89
  wireless hacking, 91
Personal identifiable information (PII), targeting
    prevention, 160
Personal information
  Information Security Awareness training, 211
  initial identification, 139–142
  PeopleFind sites, 140
  removal from Internet, 142
  safety recommendations, 160, 185
  shredders, 37
  spear phishing, 188–189
  third-party disclosures, 153
  vehicle registration, 80–81
Personal protection, expert advice, 184
Personal Protection Specialists (PPS), 184
Personnel Department, Information Security
    Awareness Program, 219
Phillips, Bill, 62
Phishing, *vs.* spear phishing, 187–188
Phone books, corporate building security, 37–38
Phone closets

high security locks, 42
physical security, 42
Phonenumber.com, 140
Photobucket
surveillance, 145–146
travel patterns, 150–151
Photograph data, travel patterns, 150–151
Physical security
access point enclosure, 95f
antennas, 95
buildings
basic considerations, 35–40
corporate/agency phone books, 37–38
employee badges, 36
key control example, 81b
lock checks, 35–36
off-shift staff training, 39–40
shredder technology, 36–37, 37b
tailgating, 38–39, 39b
tailgating countermeasures, 39b
Chicago bomb threat example, 40–42
disk drive disposal, 46b
door signs, 42
drop ceilings, 47
equipment "burial ground", 46
expert advice, 185–186
home documents, 46
home security cameras, 48b
home security tips, 48
internal auditors, 47–48
lockable rack housing, 96f
manhole cover, 45f
motion sensing lights, 43–44
outside threats, 34–35
overview, 31
phone closets, 42
risk assessment example
basic considerations, 32–34
basic risks, 32–33
countermeasures, 34
vulnerabilities, 33
subterranean vulnerabilities, 44–45, 45f
video security log review, 43
Piggybacking, see Tailgating
PII, see Personal identifiable information (PII)
Pin tumbler locks
characteristics, 54–55
as common type, 70
disk-type, 57f
example, 53f, 55f
FALE team picking example, 75–76
keys, 56f, 76–77

mortise cylinder lock, 81
pin removal hack, 68
PIP, see Protect Information Properly (PIP)
Pipl.com, 139–140
Pippin file, key creation, 80
Place targeting, basic considerations, 151–152
Plaintext hash, rainbow tables, 114
Pleaserobme.com, 150
PPS, see Personal Protection Specialists (PPS)
Presentations
infomercials, 215
information Security Awareness Program, 202–204
question anticipation, 204
Pre-shared key (PSK)
crack attack, 112
default configuration hacking, 127
legacy SSIDs, 123
rainbow tables, 114
Printers, ad hoc bridged interfaces, 125–126
Prism Test Utility, Queensland Attack, 103
Privacy Division, Information Security Awareness Program, 218
Private Branch Exchange, phone closet security, 42
Project organization, penetration testing
approach considerations, 172b
basic considerations, 170–174
body language, 172
location decisions, 171
strategy decisions, 171–172
technology selection, 172–174
Property records
self-research tips, 143
targeting and surveillance, 142–144
Protect Information Properly (PIP), 212–213
Proxy servers, penetration testing automated attacks, 173
PSK, see Pre-shared key (PSK)
PSPF, see Public Secure Packet Forwarding (PSPF)
Public Branch Exchange (PBX)
phone closet security, 42
physical security outsider/insider threats, 34
social engineering example, 21
Public Secure Packet Forwarding (PSPF), peer-to-peer-to-hack, 118
Pulford, Graham W., 62
Purchase habits, surveillance, 146–149
Putty tool, Google hacking, 129

Q

QRG, see Quick Reference Guide (QRG)
Queensland Attack

Queensland Attack (*Continued*)
    802.11b networks, 104
    characteristics, 103–104
Quick Reference Guide (QRG)
    awareness program effectiveness, 221
    Classification of Data Matrix, 205–206
    Information Security Awareness Program,
        199–200, 204, 208, 211–212
    for managers, 206–207
    Personnel Department coordination, 219
    security as company mindset, 216

R

Rackspace, social engineering attack, 24
Radio control (RC) equipment, EMR spectrum, 89
Radio frequency (RF)
    access point in foiled enclosure, 99*f*
    access point in foil-less enclosure, 99*f*
    access point radiation pattern, 92
    basic wireless technology, 102
    Bogus Beacon attack, 108
    directional antennas, 94
    Doctor Reflecto, 94, 96
    EMR spectrum, 88–89
    forced reflection, 94
    layer 1 denial of service attacks,
        91–92
    Queensland Attack, 103, 104
    rogue access points, 122
    rogue SSID additions, 123
    wave canceling, 102*f*
RADIUS, default password break-ins, 127
Rainbow table, basic concept, 113
RC, *see* Radio control (RC) equipment
Real estate search engines, examples, 142
Realestate.yahoo.com/Homevalues, 142
Rebate check scam, bank account targeting,
    148–149
Reference books, social engineering
    countermeasures, 28–29
RF, *see* Radio frequency (RF)
Rim cylinder lock
    example, 60*f*
    forced entry, 60
    vs. mortise cylinder lock, 81, 83–85
Risk assessment, physical security example
    basic considerations, 32–34
    basic risks, 32–33
    countermeasures, 34
    threats, 33
    vulnerabilities, 33
Risk management

evaluation process, 33*b*
Information Security Awareness Program, 224
Robmenow.com, 150
Rogue access points
    bridged interface abuse, 125–126
    introduction on network, 121–122
    legacy SSIDs, 123
    legitimate-looking APs, 124–125
    overview, 120–126
    SSID additions, 122–123
Rogue detection, definition, 106
Rogue mitigation
    challenges, 122
    definition, 106
Rogue-on-rogue attack
    characteristics, 106–107
    vs. whack-a-rogue, 107
Rootkit, peer-to-peer-to-hack, 118
Routers
    ad hoc attacks, 119
    Google hacking, 129
RSA, social engineering attack, 24
RSS feeds, automated surveillance, 155

S

Safari, automated surveillance, 155–156
SCADA systems
    data mining, 23
    Iran's Nuclear Fuel Centrifuges, 24
Scanners, surveillance, 158–159
SCIF, *see* Sensitive compartmented information
    facility (SCIF)
Screwdriver
    compromising locks, 81–83
    forced entry, 60, 61–62
    lock removal, 78–79
"Script Kiddy", 187–188
Sector antennas, beamwidth sample, 93*t*
Security cameras
    EMR spectrum, 89
    home security, 48*b*
Security tool bypasses
    free Wi-Fi hack, 134
    MAC address switching, 133
    MAC spoofing, 132
    static IP hack, 131–132
    wireless hacking, 130–134
Selective attention, definition, 164–165
Self-disclosures, social networks/media, 144–146
Self-loading Trojan, USB thumb drives, 167
Semi-high-secure-room break-in, lock picking
    example

bolt hack tool, 65*f*, 67*f*
bolt retraction, 64–66
lock access, 66–69
lock example, 64*f*
overview, 63–69
Sensitive compartmented information facility
   (SCIF), scanner/miniature equipment
   checks, 158
September 11 attacks, Electronic Crimes Task
   Force, 183
Service Set Identifier (SSID)
   Bogus Beacon attack, 108
   cloaking, 117
   crack attack, 114
   dead-end hijacking, 110–111, 112
   decoy SSID, 109–110
   default WPA key hacking, 127
   definition, 120
   layer 1 DoS attack, 98
   legacy SSIDs, 123
   legitimate-looking rogue APs, 124
   peer-to-peer-to-hack, 117
   rogue access points, 122–123
Sheesley, Adam, 74–75
Shim, *see* Padlock shim
Shoulder surfing, definition, 183
Shredder technology
   building security, 36–37
   cross cut shredders, 37*b*
Signature phrases, surveillance and targeting,
   154–155
Simons, Daniel, 164–165
Site survey, RF signal documentation, 96
Skimming, expert advice, 182
Slide hammer
   example, 61*f*
   forced lock entry, 61–62
Slideshare.com, 148
Slogans, Information Security Awareness Program,
   204
Smartphone
   automated surveillance, 155
   frequented location tracking, 150–151
   as listening device, 158
   neighborhood route mapping, 143
   WiFi scanner app, 159
   YouTube videos, 151–152
SMEs, *see* Subject Matter Experts (SMEs)
Smishing, target interaction, 156
Sneakers (1992), 44–45
Sniffers, crack attack, 112
SNMP

Google hacking, 129
mirror/monitor attack, 115
rogue-on-rogue attack, 107
rogue SSID additions, 122
Social engineering
   AV, IDS, IPS considerations, 25
   compromising locks, 81–83
   conversation eavesdropping, 16–18
   countermeasures, 27–29
   credit card readers, 26–27, 27*f*
   effectiveness, 2–3
   email attachments, 187–188
   engineer's point of view, 3
   expert advice, 180
   firewall considerations, 25–26
   flaw remediation, 26
   having fun with, 29
   key access, 70
   key creation, 78–80
   keystroke logger, 13–16
   lock bait and switch, 72
   mortise *vs.* rim cylinder locks, 83
   motion-sensing light security, 43–44
   neighborhood scam, 157
   overview, 1
   Paul Henry interview, 22–26
   Phil Drake interview, 19–22
   phone book security, 37–38
   suspicious phone technicians, 19*b*
   target interaction, 156
   victims, 3–4
Social engineering example
   analysis of scam, 9–10
   follow-up questions, 8–9
   initial question, 7–8
   key information, 8
Social Engineering: The Art of Human Hacking
   (Hadnagy), 28
Social engineering tools
   examples, 4–5, 6*f*
   favorite examples, 5–7
   hat, 10*f*
   listening devices, 17*f*
   overview, 10–18
   penetration team bag, 4*f*, 5*f*
   telephone butt-in set, 18, 18*f*, 19
   tool belt, 11*f*, 12
Social media surveillance, 144–146
Social networks
   identity theft, 186–187
   safety recommendations, 160–161
   surveillance, 139, 144–146

SPAM mail approach, spear phishing, 188–189
Spear phishing
    definition, 188–189
    energy company attacks, 24
    expert advice, 187–188
    target interaction, 156
Spokeo.com, 140
Spoofing
    Caller ID, 23
    ease of learning, 157
    Farewell Attacks, 105
    identity theft, 186–187
    MAC addresses, 132
    target interaction, 156–157
Spy gear, surveillance, 158
SSID, *see* Service Set Identifier (SSID)
Staging efforts, penetration testing, 169–170
State law enforcement, CCTF, 190
Static IP address, wireless hacking, 131–132
Stickers, Information Security Awareness
    Program, 205
Strategy decisions, penetration testing, 171–172
"The String Analogy", 210
Subject Matter Experts (SMEs), Information
    Security Awareness Program, 207
Subterranean vulnerabilities
    manhole cover, 45*f*
    physical security, 44–45, 45*f*
Surveillance
    automated, 155–156
    businessman case study, 145
    employment information, 142–144
    financials, investments, purchase habits,
      146–149
    free *vs.* fee-based PeopleFind sites, 140
    frequented locations, 149–152
    historical overview, 137
    initial identification, 139–142
    military personnel addresses example, 159
    miniature equipment examples, 158
    neighborhood routes, 142–144
    on-line blackmarketing case, 155
    P2P dangers, 147
    personal bank accounts, 148–149
    place as target, 151–152
    planning stage, 138
    property records, 142–144
    safety recommendations, 160–161
    scanner and miniature equipment, 158–159
    self-research on property records, 143
    signature phrases, 154–155
    social network/media disclosures, 144–146

    targeting example, 141
    target interaction, 156–157
    third-party disclosures, 152–154
    travel location example, 151
    travel patterns, 149–152
Surveys
    access points and antennas, 94, 101, 124
    Information Security Awareness Program
      administration, 200
      effectiveness, 221–222
      implementation, 207
      Personnel Department participation, 219
      progress measurement, 222, 224*f*
    RF signal site survey, 96
    social network/media disclosures, 144
Suspiciousness, as social engineering
    countermeasure, 28
Swartz, Aaron, 132
Switches
    ad hoc attacks, 119
    ad hoc bridged interfaces, 126
    Google hacking, 129
Symantec, social engineering attack, 24

T

Tailgating
    building security, 38–39
    countermeasures, 39*b*
    definition, 39*b*
"Take Charge" publication (FTC), credit card
    recommendations, 183
Tamper test, access point enclosures, 96, 97*f*, 98*f*
Targeting
    automated surveillance, 155–156
    businessman case study, 145
    employment information, 142–144
    example case, 141
    financials, investments, purchase habits,
      146–149
    free *vs.* fee-based PeopleFind sites, 140
    frequented locations, 149–152
    historical overview, 137
    initial identification, 139–142
    military personnel addresses example, 159
    miniature equipment examples, 158
    neighborhood routes, 142–144
    neighborhood scam, 157
    on-line blackmarketing case, 155
    P2P dangers, 147
    personal bank accounts, 148–149
    place as target, 151–152
    planning stage, 138

property records, 142–144
safety recommendations, 160–161
scanner and miniature equipment, 158–159
self-research on property records, 143
signature phrases, 154–155
social network/media disclosures, 144–146
targeting example, 141
target interaction, 156–157
third-party disclosures, 152–154
travel location example, 151
travel patterns, 149–152
Target organization
location considerations, 169–170
location decisions, 171
organizational culture, 170
penetration testing, 169–170
Task Force Officer (TFO), 191
TaskForces, USSS, 184
Team concept
Information Security Program, 200–201
manager's QRG, 206
Technology basics, penetration testing
automated attacks, 173–174
CDs/DVDs, 168–169
MicroSD USB storage device, 168f
overview, 166–169
selection, 172–174
USB devices, 168
USB thumb drives, 166–168, 167f
Teflon plumbers tape, compromising locks, 81–83
Telephone butt-in set
expert opinion, 19
social engineering, 18, 18f
Terrorism, expert advice, 181, 188
Texting, third-party disclosures, 154
TFO, see Task Force Officer (TFO)
Third-party disclosures
example, 153
surveillance and targeting, 152–154
Tobias, Mark Weber, 62–63
Tools, see also Security tool bypasses; Social
engineering tools
data leakage prevention, 119
dead-end hijacking, 110–111
Google hacking, 129
Touch point, Information Security Awareness
Program, 199–200
Training, see also Information security awareness
training
key control awareness, 71
lock picking, 74–76
off-shift staff for security, 39–40

Training and Communications Division,
Information Security Awareness
Program, 219
Travel patterns
example case, 151
targeting and surveillance, 149–152
Trojan Horse
man-in-the-middle attack, 110–111
penetration testing
automated attacks, 173
case study, 175–176
permission considerations, 175
self-loading, USB thumb drives, 167
physical security outsider/insider threats, 34–35
target interaction, 156–157
Trust, penetration testing, 166
Tweeting, third-party disclosures, 152
Tweetscan.com, 145
Twitter
automated surveillance, 155
businessman surveillance case study, 145
disclosures, 144, 145–146
false login data, 146
with financial data, 148–149
frequented location information, 149, 150
surveillance, 144
target interaction, 157
third-party disclosures, 154
Two-part authentication, building security, 38

U

USB thumb drives
penetration testing, 166–168
penetration testing case study, 175
penetration testing technology selection, 173
standard size, 167f
usage, 168
U.S. Secret Service (USSS)
Electronic Crimes Taskforce, 183
expert advice, 180–187
TaskForces, 184
USSS, see U.S. Secret Service (USSS)
U.S. State Department, stolen passports, 185–186

V

Victims
computers as, 179
law enforcement help, 189
social engineering, 3–4
Videoronk, automated surveillance, 155–156
Video security logs, review, 43
Virtual access point (AP), 119

Virtual local area networks (VLANs)
    crack attack, 114
    Google hacking, 129
    guest wireless hacking, 116
    legitimate-looking rogue APs, 124
    mirror/monitor attack, 115
    peer-to-peer-to-hack, 117
    rogue access points, 121
    rogue SSID additions, 123
    SSID cloaking, 117
    static IP hack, 131
Virtual machine (VM) software
    automated surveillance, 156
    targeting prevention, 161
Virtual Private Network (VPN), InfraGard, 189, 190
Viruses, peer-to-peer-to-hack, 118
Vishing, target interaction, 156
Visual survey, access points and antennas, 94,
        101, 124
VLAN 2100, legitimate-looking rogue APs, 124
VLANs, see Virtual local area networks
        (VLANs)
VM, see Virtual machine (VM) software
Voice over IP (VoIP), social engineering
        example, 21
Voice over Wireless (VoWiFi)
    peer-to-peer-to-hack, 118
    wireless hacking, 98
VPN, see Virtual Private Network (VPN)
Vulnerabilities
    Chicago bomb threat example, 40
    expert advice, 181
    forced entry, 60
    locks, 58–59, 59f
    mortise vs. rim cylinder locks, 83
    padlock shims, 73–74
    physical security risk assessment, 33
    subterranean, 44–45, 45f

W
Warded padlock
    characteristics, 54–55
    example, 56f
    keys, 56f
Web browser add-ons, automated surveillance,
        155–156
Welborn, Jon, 74–75
WEP
    crack attack, 112
    default configuration hacking, 127
    legacy SSIDs, 123
Whack-a-rogue attacks, 107–108

Whaling, see also Spear phishing
    target interaction, 156
Whitepages.com, 140
Whostalkin.com, 144–145
WiFi scanners, surveillance, 159
Winsock Packet Editor, Farewell Attacks, 105
WIPS, see Wireless IPS (WIPS)
Wireless hacking
    802.11 acronyms, 120
    802.11 and Bluetooth, 91
    802.11w standard, 106
    access point examples, 92f
    ad hoc networks, 119–120
    antenna beamwidths, 93t
    antenna types, 93f
    basic wireless technology, 102
    bypassing security tools, 130–134
    crack attack, 112–114
    default configurations
        Google hacking, 129–130, 130f
        overview, 126–130
        passwords, 127, 128f
        WPA keys, 127–129, 128f
    DoS overview, 91–112
    electromagnetic spectrum, 87–90
    EMR spectrum chart, 88f
    Fake AP project, 109f
    FCC, 101
    forced reflection, 94
    free Wi-Fi, 134
    guest attack, 116–117
    IBSS, 119–120
    layer 1 DoS
        access point antenna shorting, 100f
        archetypal antennas, 91–93
        directional antennas, 94
        Doctor Reflecto, 94–98
        electrical tampering, 98–101
        FCC regulations, 101–102
        jammers, 102–103
        overview, 91–104
        Queensland Attack, 103–104
        RF wave canceling, 102f
    layer 2 DoS
        Bogus Beacon, 108
        dead-end hijacking, 110–112
        decoy SSID, 109–110
        Farewell Attacks, 104–106
        flooding, 108
        man-in-the-middle attack, 110
        overview, 104–112
        rogue-on-rogue attack, 106–107

whack-a-rogue, 107–108
lockable rack housing, 96f
MAC address switching, 133
MAC spoofing, 132
mirror/monitor attack, 115–116
network uses and ISM band, 89t
omnidirectional antenna characteristics, 93f
peer-to-peer-to-hack, 117–119
rainbow table, 113
rogue access points
    bridged interface abuse, 125–126
    introduction on network, 121–122
    legacy SSIDs, 123
    legitimate-looking APs, 124–125
    overview, 120–126
    SSID additions, 122–123
safety recommendations, 160
security challenges, 90
SSID cloaking, 117
static IP, 131–132
virtual AP, 119
WWII frequency analyzer, 90f
Wireless IPS (WIPS)
    default password break-ins, 127
    directional antennas, 94
    Farewell Attacks, 106
    IBSS traffic, 120
    Queensland Attack, 104
    rogue access points, 122
    rogue-on-rogue attacks, 106
    whack-a-rogue, 107
Wireless Local Area Network (WLAN)
    characteristics, 89t
    decoy SSID, 109
    default PSK lookup, 127
    wireless hacking, 91
Wireless Metro Area Network (WMAN)
    characteristics, 89t
    EMR spectrum, 89
Wireless Personal Area Network (WPAN)
    characteristics, 89t
    EMR spectrum, 89
    wireless hacking, 91
Wireless Sensor Networks, EMR spectrum, 89
Wireless Wide Area Network (WWAN), 89t
Withers, Don, 184
WLAN, see Wireless Local Area
    Network (WLAN)

WMAN, see Wireless Metro Area Network
    (WMAN)
WPA2
    crack attack, 114
    default configuration hacking, 127
    legacy SSIDs, 123
WPA Cracker, 113–114
WPA keys, default configuration hacking, 127–129,
    128f
WPAN, see Wireless Personal Area Network
    (WPAN)
Wrappers
    characteristics, 174
    penetration testing automated attacks, 173–174
WWAN, see Wireless Wide Area Network
    (WWAN)

X

Xanga.com, false login data, 146

Y

Yagi antennas
    beamwidth sample, 93t
    characteristics, 92
    example, 93f
Yahoo!
    for initial identification, 141
    social engineering attack, 24
YahooFinance, financial checks, 148
Yale, Linus, 70
Yelp, frequented location information, 150
Yoname.com, 144
Youropenbook.com, 145
YouTube
    forced entry example, 61–62
    key creation, 79
    padlock shims, 73
    place as target, 151–152
    public discussions, 52
    spoofing tutorials, 157
    surveillance information, 145–146, 151–152

Z

Zabasearch.com, 140
ZigBee, 89, 89t
Zillow.com, 142–143
ZoomInfo.com, 140
Zuula.com, 144

 **Techno Security & Digital Investigations Conference**

 **Mobile Forensics Conference**

Here's How to Register For a Free VIP Pass to BOTH Conferences!

Over 1,000+ attendees each year make the pilgrimage to one of the most beautiful locations in the world for three and one half days of non-stop education, networking and just as important, fun for you and your family. As my personal 'Thank You' for purchasing *Low Tech Hacking*, you're invited to attend our next annual training conference as my personal VIP guest.

Attendees will also earn up to *32* Continuing Professional Education (CPE) credits towards your certification renewals.

To take advantage of your Free VIP pass to BOTH Conferences, you must register online using the following instructions:

Go to http://www.TheTrainingCo.com. The registration page link is the fourth drop-down under the Techno Security Conference option at the top of the page. Once on the Registration Page, do the following: Select the Sponsor/VIP Pass Payment Type (No iPad), enter "Special Low Tech Hacking VIP " as the Promo Code, and enter "0" in the Amount Paid box. A confirmation e-mail will be sent to you following your registration.

I look forward to seeing you there.

Low Tech Jack

Printed and bound by CPI Group (UK) Ltd, Croydon, CR0 4YY

08/06/2025

01896868-0010